HEALING CARE

HEALING PRAYER

Also by Terry Wardle:

Whispers of Love in Seasons of Fear
Draw Close to the Fire: Finding God in the Darkness
Wounded: How to Find Wholeness and Inner Healing through Him
The Soul's Journey into God's Embrace

HEALING CARE

HEALING PRAYER

helping the broken find wholeness in Christ

Terry Wardle

NEW LEAF BOOKS / ORANGE, CA

HEALING CARE, HEALING PRAYER
published by New Leaf Books

Copyright © 2001 by Terry Wardle

ISBN 0-9700836-8-8
Printed in the United States of America

For information:
New Leaf Books, 12542 S. Fairmont, Orange, CA 92869
1-877-634-6004 (toll free)

02 03 04 05 06 07   9 8 7 6 5 4 3 2 1

To my daughter Emily

Your love brings
healing to my life

Contents

Foreword

"Freedom is what we have—Christ has set us free," writes the Apostle Paul (Gal. 5:1, GNB). But many, perhaps most, of God's people are not really free. They have salvation, and that is good. But it is as if, once they have come to Christ, the enemy has been able to lock them up in prisoner-of-war camps, away from any effectiveness in the wrestling match or warfare against the Enemy that Jesus has called us to (Eph. 6:10-13). Saved, yes; free, no. On the Lord's side in His battle with Satan, yes; able to participate in the warfare Jesus has called us into, no. But Jesus said He came to release those who are imprisoned from their prisons and, surprisingly, defined these imprisoned ones as "His people," us (Lk. 4:18-19).

Unfortunately, such "unfreedom" is so common in evangelical circles that it is considered the norm. And books like this one have to be written to Christians who haven't learned and, often, can't even imagine that there is more to the Christian life than they are experiencing. They have been taught that salvation is freedom. But they continue to live with deep wounds and bondages that never get healed—unfree and wondering if there isn't sup-posed to be more to life in Christ.

Sometimes such unfree Christians go to secular psychologists for help. And sometimes they do get some help. But professional counseling, as help-ful as it often is in analyzing our problems, seldom includes the power to solve them. And even in the hands of Christians, secular psychology and counseling tends to be strong on analysis but weak on actually healing the problems they are able to identify.

Terry Wardle has been on all sides of the issues he treats. Today God is using him to work in the power of the Holy Spirit to bring freedom to those in spiritual and/or emotional bondage. There was a time, though, when he was in bondage and in need of release. Even as an effective pastor and teacher, he was not free down deep. He got some help from professionals and learned to value their insights. But it was faithful caregivers working in the love and power of a living Jesus in an inner healing way that God was able to use most effectively to free him and to set him on the road to freeing others.

It is to inner healing caregivers, then, that Terry addresses this excellent book. He is concerned that we learn both that many are not free and that there is Holy Spirit power in which caregivers can participate to bring the freedom that Jesus promised. He is not negative toward professionals. As he points out, some of his best friends are professional counselors. But they are learning what Terry has been learning—how to partner with Jesus, working in His power and authority, to go beyond the mere understanding of our problems to healing, to freedom.

Secular counseling has helped us. But it has let us as Christians down at one crucial point. It does not embody the power of the Holy Spirit that alone can set captives free. Inner healing, on the other hand, though usually engaged in by non-professionals, seeks to learn whatever it can from secular psychology and to combine that with the healing power of Jesus. And though we must admit that some have "gone off the tracks" in their practice of inner healing, it is possible to work in this area in a balanced way, listening both to Scripture and to the Holy Spirit while employing the insights God has led professional psychologists to discover, all empowered by Jesus Himself to set captives free.

This book is a welcome addition to a growing list of balanced guides addressed to evangelicals who have the basics of salvation down but have not learned to work in God's power to set captives free. The book will be especially valuable in helping caregivers to prepare themselves for ministering inner healing. It comes out of the now-free-but-once-captive heart of a person who has experienced the freeing power of Christ both within himself and through himself to others. This is a great combination, especially when the author is able to articulate so well both his own struggles and victory and the insights this ministry affords to other caregivers.

But please don't just read this book. Read this book and experiment with ministering inner healing to others. Read other books that Wardle recommends as well and continue to grow in your ability to work with Jesus in this ministry. Please join us in enabling God's people to experience their birthright—freedom. And I can guarantee you, you will never be the same. For you will experience with Terry and me the continual blessing and constant renewal that comes from working with Jesus to do what we cannot do alone but that He loves to do with and through us.

Charles H. Kraft
Fuller Theological Seminary
Pasadena, California

Introduction

One afternoon, soon after I joined the faculty of Ashland Theological Seminary, Judy Allison arrived at my office and asked if I had time to talk. Dr. Allison teaches in the clinical pastoral counseling department at Ashland Theological Seminary and is respected as a gifted psychologist and professor. She had learned of my interest in helping the emotionally broken through inner healing prayer and came to share both questions and concerns. At one point in the conversation Judy spoke openly of her frustrations with traditional counseling practices.

I have been doing therapy for over 12 years now and am thankful for all the opportunities I have had to empower people to make positive changes in their lives. I see that as an important ministry. And I know that it has helped many men and women experience a better life. But frankly that has not completely satisfied me. I want something more for them than a "better" life. There has to be something beyond helping people make changes in the way they think or act. I want them to experience a change that goes deeper, a change that can only come by the hand of God.

Lately, as I've been wrestling with this, I've come to realize that there have been moments in my counseling practice where I have seen this happen. God has broken into the session and done a work of healing and integration that went far beyond what I was able to do. When this happened, I felt as though I was a part of the Holy Spirit's ministry, being used as an instrument of transformation in a hurting person's life. The impact this has had on people has been immeasurable, let alone the impact it has had on me. I wasn't intentionally positioning myself, or my client, for this kind of transformational moment. It just happened, yet I remember these times as some of the most exciting and fulfilling of my practice.

Terry, I know that God wants more for people than just a higher level of functioning. He wants to transform them and I want to be a part of that. I want to open the door for God to come and work every time I sit across from a hurting person. I want to be available for God to use me as an instrument of deep and lasting change instead of pulling Him out like some kind of therapeutic tool whenever it seems appropriate. I want to position myself, and my clients, to experience the trans-forming power of God. I want more for myself and I want more for them.

Dr. Allison's concerns are shared by many Christians who serve the emotionally wounded. On one hand, Christian caregivers are grateful for the insights and techniques available to them through the behavioral and social sciences.[1] But on the other hand, like Judy, they want more than "better" for hurting people. They want to regularly position the broken for the transforming touch of Jesus Christ. I am convinced that one way to do that is through the ministry of inner healing prayer. That ministry is the focus of this book.

I first wrote of inner healing prayer in *Wounded: How You Can Find Inner Wholeness and Healing in Him* (Christian Publications, 1994). Deeply impacted by this form of care, I wanted to encourage hurting people to consider inner healing prayer as a pathway to per-sonal healing. This book, however, is written as a guide for those caregivers who want to include inner healing prayer as part of their ministry. Whether professionals or concerned laypeople, Christians can be used consistently of the Lord to facilitate deep change and healing in wounded people. The material covered in this volume is dedicated to helping the caregiver become just such an instrument of hope and healing.

Inner healing prayer can be defined as a ministry of the Holy Spirit, moving through a Christian caregiver, bringing the Healing Presence of Jesus Christ into the place of pain and brokenness within a wounded person. Each component of this description is foundational to what is covered in this book. I believe it would be helpful to identify and describe briefly each aspect of this definition.

A ministry of the Holy Spirit: Inner healing prayer is thoroughly dependent upon the presence and power of the Holy Spirit. He initiates, directs and empowers the entire process. Thus the caregiver must not only understand the work of the Holy Spirit, but be surrendered to His infilling and empowerment each step along the way.

Moving through the Christian caregiver: Inner healing prayer is not a technique controlled by the caregiver. It is a transformational ministry of the Holy Spirit, with the caregiver serving as an instrument of His activity. The spiritual vitality and emotional maturity of the caregiver are important and integrated aspects of this healing process, and must be prioritized.

Bringing the Healing Presence of Jesus Christ: People need more than solutions to their problems. They need to experience the love and acceptance of Jesus Christ in every aspect of their lives. His Transforming Presence strengthens and satisfies as nothing else, the one true Source of healing for broken people everywhere. Through inner healing prayer, the Holy Spirit uses a caregiver to position hurting people for what Jesus alone can give.

Into the place of pain and brokenness: Life experiences often leave deep wounds that compromise personal well-being. Left unaddressed, these hurts give birth to false beliefs, emotional upheaval, and behaviors that are ultimately destructive. During the process of inner healing prayer, both the source and symptoms of core woundings are brought into the light of Jesus Christ, where He alone can set people free.

I begin this book with a lengthy discussion of the spiritual and emotional life of the Christian caregiver. Chapter one focuses upon the caregiver's commitment to pursue intimacy with the Lord above all else. Chapter two centers upon the importance of emotional healing in the caregiver's personal life. Chapter three encourages the caregiver to prioritize spiritual community as a place of personal growth and empowerment. Chapter four discusses how the Holy Spirit ministers to and through the caregiver in order to develop spiritual health and effectiveness. Some readers may grow restless with the first four chapters, wanting to move more quickly to the specific steps of inner healing prayer. I encourage patience, for the ministry of inner healing prayer must rest securely on a foundation of personal well-being and spiritual maturity.

Chapter five suggests ways the Holy Spirit speaks to caregivers in the inner healing prayer session. Chapter six sets forth the structure of inner healing, and chapter seven focuses on the relationship between dysfunctional behaviors and the cross of Jesus Christ. Chapter eight treats emotional upheaval and the lies that drive it. Chapter nine presents the steps the caregiver should take when praying for deep wounds. Finally, chapter ten deals with spiritual warfare and demonization. In each of these chapters I provide specific suggestions on how to minister inner healing prayer at each level of pain and wounding.

I want to thank my wife Cheryl, and daughters, Cara and Emily, for their love and encouragement. I can get very consumed when writing, and their gentle love reminds me of what is truly important in life. I also want to thank my son Aaron and his dear wife Destry for loving and affirming me in countless ways. Special words of gratitude go to Dr. John Shultz, Dr. Judy Allison, Anne Halley, and Cheryl Schmiedt, for their support and help in developing this material. They are dear friends who have touched my life in incredibly healing ways. Each of the people I have mentioned are part of my spiritual community. They believe in what God is doing in the lives of broken people, such as myself. Finally, thanks to Leonard Allen and New Leaf Books for publishing this material.

Inner healing prayer is far more than a technique to me. It has been a ministry of the Holy Spirit that has changed my life in profound ways, personally and professionally. I encourage caregivers to observe what God is doing through this type of ministry, and consider embracing inner healing prayer as a channel of His transforming touch. I have changed the names of several people in the stories that follow as a way of protecting some very special people.

Terry Wardle
Ashland Theological Seminary
February 2001

1. Inner healing prayer is a ministry that can be effectively embraced by pastors, counselors, therapists, psychologists and mature laypeople. For the remainder of this book the term caregiver will be used as a general reference for all who engage in this form of healing prayer.

One

The Upward Journey

I received an invitation to speak on inner healing prayer at a two-day training seminar for Cornerstone Psychological Affiliates. The organization, located in Ohio, is well respected in the Midwest and has a reputation for solid Christian counseling. It would be a privilege to have the opportunity to share insights about this form of therapeutic prayer. And I saw it as an opportunity to introduce 22 professionals to aspects of healing that I believed critical to true change.

Dr. John Shultz, owner and director of CPA, met with me the week before the seminar to discuss details of the upcoming event. I wanted to get an idea about the attitudes of his people toward the topic. John and I had previously shared several conversations about inner healing prayer and the difference it was making in people's lives. He himself had begun to pray regularly with clients, and his enthusiasm for the work God was doing had piqued the interest of his staff. The seminar was intended to provide introductory training to counselors interested in this approach to care. I was pleased when he told me that most of the people from his four different offices had registered.

As John and I enjoyed Chinese food at a local restaurant, he shared openly what he thought people were feeling about the seminar. He told me that there was significant interest, evidenced by the registration, as well as comments and questions voiced during staff meetings. The psychologists, therapists and counselors wanted to know more about inner healing prayer. But the topic was new for them, and there was some anxiety and concern. The concept certainly had significant theological, as well as therapeutic, ramifications that were not without emotional investments. Inner healing prayer is based on a paradigm of spirituality not shared by all Christians, and it makes some people uncomfortable. That was certainly the case here.

The seminar began on Friday evening and after the normal introduction I passed out the schedule for the weekend. While commenting on various incidentals I noticed some uneasiness with several participants. They were surprised by what seemed to be an inordinate amount of time given to the spiritual life of the caregiver. Five of the twelve hours together were focused upon the spiritual and emotional well-being of the seminar participants. At the end of the first evening there was even time to receive prayer for the Spirit's empowerment. Frankly, whatever level of discomfort there had been in anticipation of the seminar, it had just increased dramatically for several people.

Certain concepts and processes need to be understood by those who embrace inner healing prayer as a pathway to helping others find freedom. And, as I will repeatedly emphasize throughout this book, education in the social and behavioral sciences is a tremendous asset to this ministry, as is a solid theological and biblical grounding. However, the power and effectiveness of inner healing does not depend solely on what the caregiver has learned from these disciplines. Inner healing prayer is dependent upon the Holy Spirit moving through the caregiver to the precious person who is locked in darkness. This demands personal maturity and spirituality, which is far more critical to the broken than all the degrees, licensing and titles people might hold.

Any discussion of inner healing prayer must prioritize the spiritual journey of the counselor, therapist, pastor and psychologist. This and the next three chapters are dedicated to spiritual formation, emotional well-being, accountability and the empowerment of the Holy Spirit, as each relates to a caregiver becoming an instrument of the Lord's healing power.

Let there be no question about the source of healing for the emotionally broken of our world. Jesus Christ is the healer, and through Calvary He has made a way for prisoners to be set free, for the lost to find their way home, and for those who are in bondage from deep wounds to find healing and deliverance. The skills and tools learned as a caregiver are invaluable but powerless on their own to bring about lasting change. The work of Christ must flow into the life of the persons who come for help. And whether they accept this truth or not they are part of that mysterious event. The caregiver's spiritual maturity greatly impacts the process of inner healing. Cooperating with the Holy Spirit in the moment is essential.

Inner healing prayer is a work of the Holy Spirit moving through caregivers to the broken and battered. The Holy Spirit uses them to identify root wounds and to set people free from dysfunctional behaviors. He also exposes lies that bring emotional turmoil and releases the broken from demonic bondage. The Holy Spirit inspires caregivers to use scripture, confession, visualization, repentance and healing prayer to minister grace and hope where darkness once reigned. All of this "inner healing" is possible because Jesus Christ has won the victory over all forms of brokenness and is available to all who turn to Him. Caregivers are not separated from the process. They are always integrated participants in the healing encounter with Christ.

Spirituality matters. This must be the beginning place of any discussion about inner healing prayer. I recognize that many people react negatively to this suggestion. Recently, while interviewing an applicant for a seminary post, the search committee asked the person to talk about his spiritual journey. The gentleman became uncomfortable, and only hesitantly opened the window to his devotional life. Following the interview he complained that he found the question intrusive, that he regarded the subject as a private matter. In truth, effective Christian ministry, regardless of the form it takes, is related to spiritual maturity. And, given the fact that Christian service is to be rooted in community and accountability, sharing the ups and downs of the pilgrimage of faith is essential.

More than ever Christians are asking questions about personal devotion and spiritual formation. People are finding it more difficult to respond to an informational approach to the Christian experience. They are hungry for a personal transformation that flows from an actual experience of the Heavenly Father's presence. Nowhere is this more true than in the counseling context. People are weary of trying to find healing and deliverance through behavioral and cognitive approaches to therapy. Granted, such approaches often help people do more than limp along in life. But where is the healing, the deliverance or the transformation? It is in Christ and in Him alone. Hurting, desperate people want to feel His touch, experience the power of His love and find lasting freedom. We might as well accept this fact: caregivers cannot lead others where they themselves have not gone.

Centuries ago the prophet Zechariah spoke of a future time when people would be seeking those who experience fellowship with the Lord: "This is what the Lord Almighty says: In those days ten men from all languages and nations will take firm hold of one Jew by the hem of his robe and say, 'Let us go with you, because we have heard that God is with you'" (Zech. 8:23).

That day is undoubtedly here for the Christian community. People do not want to hear what we know about God. They want to walk with those who have encountered him, who fellowship with Him, who clearly minister at a transformational level. Many Christian leaders are writing and speaking about this issue today, not the least of which are Larry Crabb, Gary Moon and Gary Collins, each a renowned psychologist. They are, in different ways, calling Christian caregivers to be attentive to the spiritual dynamics of leading others to freedom in Christ, convinced that God's transforming power is central to helping broken men and women.[1]

Eugene Peterson, Professor Emeritus of Spiritual Formation at Regent College and Seminary, wrote:

> The volume of business in religion far outweighs the spiritual capital of its leaders. The initial consequence is that leaders substitute image for substance, satisfying the customer temporarily but only temporarily, on good days denying that there is any problem (easy to do, since business is so good), on bad days hoping that someone will show up with the infusion of capital. No one is going to show up. The final consequence is bankruptcy. The bankruptcies are dismayingly frequent.[2]

The focal point of Peterson's concern is pastoral ministry, but his conclusions fit the counseling profession perfectly. In recent years business has been very good. Desperate Christians have finally been encouraged to seek help for the emotional turmoil that has threatened the stability of their lives. The ministry of the Christian psychologist, counselor and therapist has been legitimized for many evangelical Christians. Countless churches have embraced recovery as part of the overall service offered to the broken and lost. Scan the bookshelves in Christian bookstores and one finds that the literature of Christian self-help and counseling has increased dramatically. Christian colleges, universities and seminaries have seen enrollment increase dramatically in pastoral and clinical counseling programs. Christian counselors have experienced growth in their practices as well.

Even so, the level of frustration is heightening among the broken and lost. Despite all the training, degrees and newfound openness toward counseling professions, do we really have anything of transforming substance to offer? Or has the spiritual capital of our lives been depleted, as many are beginning to suspect? As uncomfortable as these questions are, they must be considered. I am asking them as a person who has sought counsel, given counsel and helped equip others for counseling ministries. I have been helped by caring counselors, and believe that education in the social and behavior sciences is very important. But in reality transformation comes from an encounter with the Living Christ, ministered through the power of His Holy Spirit. The spiritual life of the caregiver is decidedly important to that process.

Thomas Kelly was a Quaker educator, missionary and scholar who died in 1941. His small book, *A Testament of Devotion*, is a classic of Christian devotional literature. He said that "The deepest human need is not food and clothing and shelter, as important as they are. It is God."[3] I believe that. When a person is seeking help, whether he consciously recognizes it or not, he is looking for God, longing for His love and needing His healing. He is often so distant from that inner need that he does not turn to God for help. He is also in distress because of the wounds and bondage that have resulted from that deep emptiness. Whether it is depression, anxiety disorder, sexual addiction or marital turmoil, beneath it all is a desperate cry for God and a hunger to be transformed in His presence.

Cognitive and behavioral insights into people's problems can and do help. Medication and psychiatric care do stabilize those who are unable to function in life. But healing and well-being ultimately result from a connection with God, the Father of love. It is critical that the caregiver recognize that there is something far more important than helping people solve problems and cope with the trials of life. She must encourage people to open up to God in ways they never before considered, leading them into the Embrace that satisfies as nothing else can. This ministry is far more than one of correct information, good advice and a listening ear. It rests upon the caregiver's personal experience of intimacy with God, through Christ. This gives the Spirit freedom to move through the caregiver to the broken and lost seeking her help. Again, the spiritual life matters—to God, to others and to the personal life of the caregiver.

The Soul's Journey into God

Does the Bible support the notion that intimacy with God is the central pursuit of the Christian life? If it does, then many caregivers will need to reconsider how to invest their time, how to set priorities in their profession, and how to serve the broken who come to them for help.

Scriptural Metaphors
Many scriptures, by implication and admonition, call people to draw near to the presence of the Lord and into His intimate embrace. Consider the following texts, with the metaphors they employ, and determine if they suggest that intimacy with the Lord is to be a reality in the Christian life.

> I am the vine; you are the branches. If a man remains in me and I in him, he will bear much fruit; apart from me you can do nothing. (John 15:5)
> Now you are the body of Christ, and each if you is a part of it. (1 Cor. 12:27)
> Do you not know that your body is a temple of the Holy Spirit, who is in you, whom you have received from God? (1 Cor. 6:19)
> Do not be afraid, little flock, for your Father has been pleased to give you the kingdom. (Luke 12:32)
> You are all sons of God through faith in Christ Jesus, for all of you who were baptized into Christ have clothed your self with Christ. (Gal. 3:26)

Vines that must remain attached to the branch. The body of Christ. The dwelling place of the Holy Spirit. God's little flock. Sons and daughters who are clothed in Christ. These are just a few of the many scriptural references which point to a unique and intimate bond between believers and the Lord. Even a casual consideration of these verses reveals that being a Christian involves a deeply attached, submissive, empowered and transforming relationship with the Living Lord.

Each scripture suggests the type of dependence God has called Christians to through the work of Christ. Should the caregiver feel attached to the Lord? Does he experience the presence of the Holy Spirit in his life? Does the Lord intend that His relationship with the caregiver be dynamic, close and experienced? These questions are far from rhetorical. They beg to be answered, and the response given to each says something about the caregiver's understanding of the Christian life. It also reveals what is foundational to his ministry of care and support to the broken.

The Explicit Teachings of Jesus Regarding Intimacy with Him
The Lord did not leave much room for question about the topic of intimacy when teaching His followers kingdom truths. He repeatedly called men and women to enter into a deep and transforming relationship with Him and with the Father. The objective of faith was not simply a set of principles to live by, nor was salvation meant simply to set people free from the sentence of death that sin imposes. While both of these concepts are important, the central treasure of Christian experience is an ever-growing union with God. Jesus came to reunite people with their heavenly Father and help them find rest in His loving embrace. Caregiver's would do well to meditate upon the following words of Christ:

> Now this is eternal life: that they may know you, the only true God, and Jesus Christ, whom you have sent. (John 17:3)
> I am the Good Shepherd. I know My sheep and My sheep know me, just as the Father knows Me and I know the Father, and I lay down My life for the sheep. (John 10:14, 15)
> Not everyone who says to me, 'Lord, Lord', will enter the kingdom of heaven, but only he who does the will of the Father who is in heaven. Many will say to me on that day, 'Lord, Lord, did we not prophesy in your name, and in your name drive out demons and perform many miracles?' Then I

will tell them plainly, I never knew you. (Matt. 7:21-23)

You diligently search the scriptures because you think that by them you have eternal life. These are the Scriptures that testify about me, yet you refuse to come to me and have life. (John 5:39, 40)

Once again the caregiver is confronted with the priority of having a dynamic relationship with the Lord. Knowing Jesus, not just knowing about Him, is central to kingdom life and is in fact the single characteristic that identifies people as His followers. Service is important, as are the doctrines, principles and practices of Christian living that have been taught over the years. But the heart of the Christian experience is the journey toward His intimate embrace. Is that a pilgrimage that a caregiver should invest in, give time to, and commit to with all her heart? Should she long to experience daily the wonder of His presence? These scriptures certainly encourage the caregiver to seek that level of relationship with Him. Scripture promises that it is not only possible, but a reality the Lord brings to her life.

The Story of Mary and Martha

Luke narrates a special visit by Jesus to the home of Mary, Martha and Lazarus. The story focuses upon two sisters who chose very different responses to the Lord's presence. When Jesus arrived in Bethany with his disciples, Martha busied herself with preparations, working hard in the kitchen to feed her guests. But Mary sat at the Lord's feet, listening to every word that he said and enjoying His presence. Martha, distracted with all that had to be done, came to Jesus and said, "Lord, don't you care that my sister has left me to do all the work by myself? Tell her to help me!" (Luke 11:40)

Before focusing upon what the Lord said to Martha, I want to consider what often happens to those who serve in caregiving ministries. People are in desperate need of help, and demand more time than most caregiver's can afford to give. Yet the Christian caregiver is probably trying to serve the Lord faithfully, attempting to be responsible and obedient. He may even be sacrificing his own well being in an attempt to serve others. But is that what the Lord requires of His servants? I believe this story points to a higher and preceding commitment for the caregiver. When Martha asked the Lord to rebuke Mary for irresponsible behavior, Jesus challenged Martha to reconsider her priorities. He told her that while she was worried about many things, Mary had chosen the better part, a treasure that could never be taken from her.

Jesus is not suggesting that service is unimportant. Instead He is calling His servants to be faithful with first things. And when it comes to the Christian walk, time in His presence is the highest priority of life. Mary and Martha represent the two stances that balanced Christians must take to be personally healthy and effective in ministry. Devotion and ministry are essential to spiritual health and maturity, with intimacy preceding and empowering service. If a caregiver seriously desires an effective ministry of inner healing prayer, he or she must first and foremost seek time in the presence of the Lord.

The Writings of Paul

A person cannot spend time reading any of Paul's epistles without recognizing that Jesus Christ was the passion of his life. It is equally clear that Paul believed that every believer should follow his example and seek the Lord above all else. The following scriptures illustrate this central theme in Paul's letters:

> What is more, I consider everything a loss compared to the surpassing greatness of knowing Jesus Christ my Lord, for whose sake I have lost all things. I consider them rubbish, that I may gain Christ and be found in Him. (Phil. 3:8, 9)

> I have been crucified with Christ and I no longer live, but Christ lives in me. The life I live in the body, I live by faith in the Son of God, who loved me and gave himself for me. (Gal. 2:20)

> I keep asking that the God of our Lord Jesus Christ, the glorious Father, may give you the spirit of wisdom and revelation, so that you may know Him better. I pray also that the eyes of your heart may be enlightened in order that you may know the hope to which he has called you, the riches of his glorious inheritance in the saints, and his glorious great power for us who believe. (Eph. 1:17, 18)

These are a fraction of the passages in the New Testament about knowing Christ and the corresponding blessings and benefits that come from a personal relationship with Him. Over and again God's word calls people into the most exciting journey imaginable: a pilgrimage into His embrace. It is real, transforming and most certainly part of the glorious inheritance God gives to His children. Nothing is more central to life. All else is secondary, no matter how important it may be, including helping the lost and broken of the world.

Intimacy Impacts Ministry

Ultimately, the caregiver's relationship with the Lord impacts her ministry. In John 15:1-5, Jesus said that the key to bearing fruit is abiding in Him. Attached to Jesus, the caregiver, like all Christians, will be productive. It will be as natural as it is for a branch of an apple tree to produces apples. But if the caregiver is detached from His intimate embrace, she will find ministry draining and ineffective. And she will discover that it is difficult to bring lasting change to hurting people. Thus we return once again to the premise set forth earlier: the spiritual life of the caregiver matters.

Peter and Paul were not guilty of hyperbole when writing bold statements to early Christians. They each knew that Christ was the author of life, the Lord of the universe, and the sustainer of all that was real. They wanted believers to grow closer to Jesus in order to experience all that was possible for them through Him.

Praise be to the God and Father of our Lord Jesus Christ, who has blessed us in the heavenly realms with every spiritual blessing in Christ. (Eph. 1:3)

His divine power has given us everything that we need for life and godliness through our knowledge of him who called us by his own glory and goodness. (2 Pet. 1:3)

According to these verses, the Christian caregiver is supernaturally equipped to live and minister in His name. She has all that she needs "for life and godliness," and is blessed with "every spiritual blessings in Christ." In order to live and minister in that divine empowerment, she must continually pursue intimacy with the Lord. While many things in life are important and worthy of attention, nothing is more important for her or the people she serves.

I write this to encourage the caregiver to keep Christ as the ruling passion and priority of her life. The journey to His embrace should be the deepest investment she makes. By doing this, the caregiver will experience the transforming touch of Jesus, which will grow more powerful as she daily meets with Him. New life will flow into her personal life and into her ministry. And when it comes to inner healing prayer, the possibilities will be exciting. Jesus will work through the caregiver to free the broken who are desperate for help and healing. Without Christ the caregiver can, at best, relieve some of the pain people experience and to some degree help them function better. But with Christ there is the potential for a transforming encounter with God every time she connects a hurting person with Him. And it all begins when the caregiver accepts the principle that her spirituality matters.

A New Paradigm of Faith

If intimacy with the Lord is as important to the Christian experience as I am suggesting, why do many seem to have missed it? Why has there not been more attention given to this topic in educating and training the Christian caregiver? I believe there is one factor related to these questions that is worth special consideration. Many Christians have been educated and trained within a modern paradigm of education that prioritizes reason above relationship. The central premise of this approach is that "if you think correctly you will then behave and act correctly." And "thinking correctly" demands that people have a firm grasp on all the necessary information. The more relevant information one has at his disposal, the better opportunity he has to live appropriately. And so, upon beginning the Christian life, the believer is encouraged to learn about Jesus, proper behavior, correct doctrine and a host of biblical concepts. By doing this, it is assumed, he will be equipped to live and serve as a healthy and productive Christian.

The current educational process is much like this. A caregiver goes to classes in order to gain knowledge, takes tests to see if he has retained what he learned and, when appropriate, serves an internship to refine the skills he learned in class. The caregiver is graded and advanced according to aptitude and ability relevant to the information at his disposal. Christian caregivers who have been educated within this paradigm often try to impact the people they serve from the same informational approach.

I suggest that there is a much healthier framework for following Christ, which I call the transformational paradigm.[4] In this model the goal of faith is neither right thinking nor right behavior. The central focus of the Christian life is growing closer to Jesus Christ and being transformed into His likeness. This is a life-long pilgrimage, measured not by how much knowledge a person has or how well he behaves. It prioritizes knowing and reflecting Jesus. Information serves to help a person progress toward His embrace, and as such is useful and important. But information is never the goal. Jesus is the goal, and movement toward Him is the standard of personal health and growth. Thus the word transformation: ever changing and moving.

The shift to a transformational paradigm is a step toward greater intimacy with the Lord. Some people will be frightened, thinking this approach does not emphasize right belief, right behavior or right service. I believe these are important and the by-product of knowing Jesus Christ at a personal and experiential level. When an individual concentrates on knowing Him, his life will change and come into alignment with what the Lord desires. But if a person focuses singularly upon right thinking and proper behavior, he may become outwardly religious, but not inwardly transformed by the living Lord of Love. That is a prescription for a passionless and powerless life and ministry.

Beyond an Informational to a Transformational Paradigm

Beyond Learning To Knowing

Beyond Knowledge To Change

Beyond Principles To Presence

Beyond Periods of Time To Moments in Time

Beyond Reading Scripture To Experiencing Scripture

Beyond Prayer To Communion

Beyond Working To Waiting

Beyond Learning to Knowing
Carl Jung, the Swiss psychologist, was once asked if he believed in God. His initial answer shocked some of his listeners. He said, "No." But after a short pause he continued by saying, "I don't believe in God, I know Him." That simple phrase profoundly identifies the first

shift the caregiver must make when moving from an informational to a transformational paradigm of discipleship. He should move beyond believing in Jesus to seeking a dynamic relationship with Him. Christ came into this world for that very purpose. Yes, forgiveness of sin and freedom from the darkness of eternal night are important, as are many other biblical truths and principles. But ultimately Jesus entered the world to embrace people, bringing peace and strength for living. And whether they know it or not, every person who turns to a caregiver for help is looking for what Jesus alone can offer. It is not what the caregiver knows, but whom he knows that satisfies, fulfills and frees the human heart.

Belief is important to spiritual growth and dependent upon learning the content of the gospel message, understanding it and ultimately giving ascent to its claims. But the Christian life is a journey that moves beyond information to the experience of Christ present in daily life and ministry. As the caregiver turns to scripture, sermons, music, art, literature and life, he should remember that there is not only something to learn but Someone to know. He must not be so preoccupied with taking notes that he fails to take note of the One who is there in the moment with him. The world is bathed in God's presence and when the caregiver prioritizes knowing Him, he will bow and worship where others only sit and stare. In that mysterious en-counter, he will be increasingly transformed, a spiritual transaction that will position him to offer hope and healing to people. The broken will experience Jesus in and through the caregiver, led to an entirely new place of wholeness and inner healing.

Beyond Knowledge to Change

For fifteen years I have been involved in seminary education. Each spring I participate in graduation exercises, watching deeply committed men and women walk across the platform to receive their well-deserved degrees. It is always a highlight of my year. Those who have earned academic degrees recognize that a great deal of sacrifice and hard work have preceded the moment of graduation. The celebration, with its caps and gowns, addresses and receptions, is much anticipated and appreciated.

But what does it mean when a person receives a masters degree in a ministry-related field? Does it signify that the individual is now

qualified to serve others effectively? Many who operate from an informational paradigm would probably say yes. But as a seminary
educator, I would not necessarily agree. Most graduate education in
caring professions measures knowledge and skill, evaluating a person's
competency according to standards of performance. A grade is affixed
to the quality of work, and if a person has done well on the prescribed
courses or projects, he or she can graduate. In some cases a degree simply means that the person has a competency in the knowledge and skill
necessary to minister. As important as that is, it does not in itself qualify someone to be a pastor or caregiver.

Ministry from a transformational paradigm moves beyond knowledge to change. Skill and understanding are important, but a deeper,
ongoing transformation must be taking place in the caregiver's life.
This is a work of the Holy Spirit that happens when the caregiver asks
God to take the information of faith beyond the mind and into the
heart. Change is not a matter of behavior modification, but instead
character transformation. That is a work of the Holy Spirit, who empowers the caregiver to live a new and holy life.

A significant part of what qualifies and enables a person to minister
is that she is being changed by Christ. That process of change may be
apparent or somewhat undefined. It may sometimes happen in a dramatic encounter with the Lord, while at other times result from a long
obedience in the same direction. Regardless of the pathway, change is
a qualifying mark of the Lord's servants. The caregiver is invited to journey toward God's embrace, and be continually transformed by His
Spirit along the way. And her willingness, openness and yieldedness
to that process are essential for maturation and effectiveness as an
instrument of the Lord's healing flow.

Beyond Principles to His Presence

What are people looking for when they attend a worship service at a
local church? They are hungry for the presence of the Lord and want
to experience His touch. The symbols, sermons and songs are meaningful but not enough. People are desperate to experience the One
who spoke them into existence. But for many people, attending
church is about information, not an encounter with the living God.
Sermons are the focal point of the hour, with practical principles presented as sure keys to a better life. The pastor often preaches about

"four truths" or "three practical principles" or "five biblical points" related to some important topic. He admonishes the listener to then go and do what is prescribed, promising that life will improve for the diligent. He hands them a recipe for discipleship that they take home and try to prepare. The sermon often ends with a word of encouragement, and then the closing hymn.

But a transformational paradigm of discipleship moves beyond principles to Presence. I contend that men and women are not coming to church for another recipe but for a meal. They want to experience the Lord, feel His love and allow the Holy Spirit to fill their lives. They come to church hungry and want to encounter God far more than receive information about Him. More to the point of inner healing, the broken are in need of a similar experience when they turn to a caregiver. Many have read self-help books that offer good advice on how to handle their problems. Like a recipe, these books show the broken how to do what is necessary to live better lives. Unfortunately, they are starving and too weak alone to do what is required. They turn to the caregiver for help, believing that he can somehow connect them with the Presence that satisfies as nothing else can.

Beyond Periods of Time to Moments in Time

In his book, *A Long Obedience in the Same Direction*, Eugene Peterson writes that Christianity is a life-long pilgrimage that demands faithfulness and obedience all along the way. There are no short cuts, no formulas for instant discipleship, no ATM for easy access "change." Following Christ happens one step at a time. I agree with Dr. Peterson, and know that there is no fast route to mature discipleship. However, a transformational paradigm moves beyond faithfulness over long periods of time to yieldedness in moments of time. Madeline L'Engle once commented that there are two words for time in the Greek language: *chronos,* which refers to segments or periods of time, and *kairos,* which refers to moments in time. In *kairos* moments, God positions a person for a transforming encounter with Himself.

There will be moments during inner healing prayer when a person suddenly senses that God is asking him to open up to His touch. The individual feels the presence of the Lord and knows that God wants him to respond. The caregiver must realize that if he does not help the person surrender into the moment, the potential for a life-changing encounter with the Lord might pass, at least temporarily. That is the nature of a kairotic moment. God invites a person to yield to His presence, allowing Him to bring change deep within.

These moments come as special invitations from the Father. The caregiver must learn to recognize them and by faith submit to the Spirit's work. That will include laying down the predetermined agenda and moving according to the Holy Spirit's direction. By doing this the caregiver will help the broken and hurting experience special divine encounters, and be forever transformed.

Beyond Reading Scripture to Experiencing Scripture
While in seminary I took a number of courses in biblical studies. I learned how to approach God's word objectively, and analyze a text for its historical and theological significance. I was taught to apply proper hermeneutical principles, to accurately parse verbs from the original languages, and to mine the one true meaning intended for the reader. It was also necessary to learn how to make personal application of the text. The process was valuable and to this day I use many of the skills I acquired those many years ago.

Approaching scripture in this way is informationally sound, but is not necessarily faithful to a transformational paradigm. When reading God's word, a caregiver must move beyond analyzing scripture to experiencing God, who is present through the text. Instead of treating God's word as an object to be properly handled, it is far more important to allow God's word to handle him. God is alive in the pages of scripture and is seeking to transform His child. While appreciating what was said centuries ago, we should read the text sensitive to how God desires to meet us today.

Robert Mulholland, professor of New Testament at Asbury Theological Seminary, encourages people to open more than the mind when reading God's word. In his book, *Shaped by the Word*, Mulholland instructs believers to imaginatively open all their senses in order to experience the power of God present in the Word.

> You imagine the things you would be seeing...the things you would be hearing...smelling...feeling...You use all your senses. You let your imagination loose to recreate the setting of the passage of scripture. Once you have created the scene,

then begin to examine your thoughts and feelings about the situation. You may experience harmony/dissonance. This can become a focus for your prayerful response to God.[5]

Recently I was reading the words of Jesus in John 20:21. Jesus said, "Peace I leave with you! As the Father has sent me, I am sending you." And with that, he breathed on them and said, "Receive the Holy Spirit." (John 20:21) While understanding context and intent was certainly important, the transforming moment came when I asked the Lord to reveal Himself in the Word. As Mulholland suggests, I opened my imagination and sought to enter the text. This took me beyond reading scripture to an experience of the peace that Jesus had promised. It also opened the way for me to have a transforming encounter with the Lord. All Christians are invited to meet the Lord in His living Word in the same way. When they do, the Lord will be present to touch, empower and transform them in the most miraculous way.

Beyond Prayer to Communion
Most Christians know that prayer is important. It is one of the first disciplines they are taught upon confessing faith in Christ. Prayer is an invitation to talk with God, to enter His presence and to lay personal concerns before Him. Mother Teresa once said, "The most important thing that a human being can do is pray, because we've been made for God and our hearts are restless until we rest with Him. And it's in prayer that we come into contact with God."[6] Scriptures about prayer abound, including the following invitation of Jesus: "And I will do whatever you ask in my name, so that the Son may bring glory to the Father. You may ask me for anything in my name, and I will do it" (John 14:13).

God welcomes the caregiver to talk with Him in prayer. He wants to hear about his needs and move to care and provide for him. But there is more available in prayer than just listing personal concerns. Through the Holy Spirit people are able to move beyond simple prayer to seasons of communion. Such times are characterized by fewer words, yet deeper levels of genuine communication. Dialogue is suspended as the experience of intimacy with God increases. Silence becomes the invitation for God to reveal His presence and speak into the thirsty soul. It is much like a husband and wife who grow to a place where they experience great intimacy with few words being said.

One of the ways a Christian caregiver can grow to connect with God in communing prayer is by entering into periods of longing and adoration. The opened imagination receives the Holy Spirit's touch, which enables the caregiver to visualize the Lord present with him. With his senses quickened and directed to the Lord, he can then inwardly worship and express feelings of deep love and gratitude. This practice will require some effort to develop a more passive yet open stance before the Lord; but it can provide a far richer connection than could ever be accessed through simple prayer. It may take time and effort for him to learn to quietly capture the moment, but that, as Calvin Miller suggests, is part of the price one must be willing to pay.

> ...the believer who wants an in-depth affair with Christ must not allow time clocks and ledger sheets to destroy that wonderful holy leisure by which we make friends with God. To be a godly disciple means that we transcend the clock, because to be with God mandates that we give our life to become one who waits on God for the sheer pleasure of his company.[7]

Beyond Working to Waiting

A caregiver's schedule of clients for the day is full. Every time slot has been filled with a hurting or misdirected person seeking guidance, understanding and hope. In preparation the caregiver has reviewed every file, dialogued with his peers in staffing, and determined a preliminary course of action for each session. The time arrives for him to work. Or has it?

A transformational paradigm of discipleship would influence the caregiver to do one more thing before busying himself in ministry. He must wait. George Pardington, a Christian leader of the past century, believed that waiting was an essential discipline of the Christian life. He encouraged Christian leaders to get alone and wait for God before beginning to minister. He spoke of silently anticipating the "dew" of God's presence before proceeding to serve people. Pardington told those preparing for ministry that, regardless of their insights or skill, any substantive work needing to be accomplished demanded the presence of the Holy Spirit. And until the minister sensed His presence, it was too soon to work. He must wait.

A.W. Tozer authored a small book entitled, *The Counselor*, where he wrote: "The Holy Spirit is a living Person, and we can know Him and fellowship with Him! Walking with Him can become a habit."[8] An aspect of that habit involves waiting for His presence to fall upon the caregiver as she seeks to help the broken. By quieting herself before the Lord, she will be able to hear the whispers of His love and encouragement. She will also be ready to receive His direction for the people who are seeking her help. This positions her for the quickening of the Holy Spirit and empowers her to minister far beyond her own abilities. She should remember that, although the information she has to offer people is important, it is Christ moving through her that brings life-giving change to clients locked in the prisons of emotional pain. Inner healing prayer is an activity of the Holy Spirit, made possible through Jesus Christ. The caregiver must wait for Him. When she does, the caregiver will be prepared to see people change in ways she may have never anticipated.

There Must be More than This!

There comes a moment in all of our lives when we conclude, "There must be more than this!" As the Christian life begins, people anticipate a walk with the Lord that will be real, life-changing and spiritually powerful. But over time, often without noticing the change, expectations shift. The Christian walk becomes more about ministry than intimacy. A caregiver can get more involved with gaining information than experiencing transformation. Soon, time with the Lord gives way to busy schedules. He is consumed with well-intended ministry to the hurting. But the caregiver realizes that life is spiritually dry and ministry is less effective. It is then that a cry rises up from deep within the caregiver's soul.

There is more. God does not stand at a distance and watch. He is ever-present and longs to fill the caregiver with His own love and strength. He positions Himself in the deepest part of the caregiver's being, waiting to meet her there. I believe the Father is pleased with her desire to serve Him, and blesses the knowledge and understanding that she brings to each moment of ministry. But God longs to touch the caregiver at an even deeper level. He waits to be invited to move through the caregiver and help people lost in darkness and crippled by emotional pain.

Inner healing prayer is a ministry of the Lord, administered through a caregiver who humbly positions herself to be an instrument of His powerful touch. Inner healing prayer is not a technique. It is an encounter with the Living Christ, precisely where the broken have been severely wounded and deceived. Inner healing prayer thus flows from God's anointing in the caregiver's life. It is empowered by her personal journey toward His intimate embrace. That transformational pilgrimage is essential to the healing ministry addressed in this book.

Conclusion

The seminar with Cornerstone Psychological Affiliates held several special moments for me. Meeting all the wonderful caregivers was certainly one of the highlights. But the memory that is most meaningful came a few days after the weekend. One of the therapists saw me at a local grocery store. She thanked me for the seminar and the challenge to keep Christ central to the process of inner healing prayer. "But," she said, "of all that we learned, I will never forget the Friday evening prayer time. You invited us to ask the Lord to fill us as never before. I hesitated, but went forward to receive prayer. He touched me in a way I didn't know was possible. I will never be the same again."

Notes

1. These men have authored recent books encouraging people to seek intimacy with God as the central pursuit of life and ministry. Larry Crabb's two books, *Connecting* and *The Safest Place on Earth* (Word) are must reading for anyone in the counseling, care-giving field of ministry. See also Gary Moon's *Homesick for Eden* (Servant), and Gary Collins, *The Soul Search* (Nelson).

2. Eugene Peterson, *Under the Unpredictable Plant: An Exploration of Vocational Holiness* (Grand Rapids, MI: Eerdmans, 1992), 3.

3. Thomas R. Kelly, *A Testament of Devotion* (San Francisco: Harper Collins, 1992), 77.

4. The seven aspects of a transformational paradigm outlined in this chapter are merely an introduction to the concept. I do not unfold each aspect of the transformational paradigm in this volume, but introduce it so that you might be moved by the Lord to develop your own discipleship

accordingly. The reading list at the end of the chapter includes books that will help you implement much of what I suggest under each point.

5. Robert Mulholland, *Shaped By The Word* (Nashville: Upper Room, 1985), 98-103.

6. Mother Teresa, *A Simple Path* (New York: Ballantine Books, 1995), 9.

7. Calvin Miller, *Into the Depths of God* (Minneapolis, MN: Bethany House; 2000), 57.

8. A. W. Tozer, *The Counselor* (Camp Hill, PA: Christian Publications, 1989), 130.

For Further Reading

Shaped By the Word, by Robert Mulholland
Experiencing the Depths of Jesus Christ, by Jeanne Guyon
The Jesus I Never Knew, by Philip Yancy
Spirit of the Disciplines, by Dallas Willard
The Soul's Journey into God's Embrace, by Terry Wardle

Two

The Inward Journey

Can a caregiver effectively help others in pain if he is not facing his own deep wounds? Is the caregiver equipped to lead others through the darkness if he is not moving through personal places of pain? I have serious doubts. To give direction to those who are lost in an emotional maze, the caregiver must have received, and be receiving, direction from someone else. If he intends to be a channel of healing to those who feel trapped in the wounds of the past, the caregiver needs to be experiencing Christ's touch upon his own disturbing memories.

The caregiver's insights into behavior modification or cognitive therapy may help. But when a person honestly desires to lead another on the journey toward emotional well-being, he must be mindful of his own pilgrimage toward wholeness. The individual who is practicing inner healing should be in the process of being inwardly healed. His wounds should be attended by the Great Physician, becoming the context by which the caregiver understands and helps the wounded who sit before him. The caregiver must be a wounded healer.

The Wounded Healer

In 1972 Henri Nouwen published his now classic work, *The Wounded Healer: Ministry in Contemporary Society*. With this book he called Christians to a form of ministry that was radically different from that being taught in seminaries and universities. Nouwen, educated in psychology and pastoral theology, was concerned that people in caring professions had been trained to minister from a stance of distance and objectivity. But to Nouwen, the tendency to remain professionally aloof was a barrier to the transforming connections necessary between those in need and those trying to help. Nouwen challenged Christian pastors, priests, nuns, counselors and caregivers of all types to minister to others while fully in touch with their own wounds. In fact, as the title of Nouwen's book suggests, those wounds are the very place where true healing flows from one life to another. Nouwen writes:

> How can wounds become the source of healing? This is a question which requires careful consideration. For when we want to put our wounded selves in the service of others, we must consider the relationship between our professional and personal selves....no minister can keep his own experience of life hidden from those he wants to help. Nor should he want to keep it hidden....Making one's own wounds a source of healing...does not call for a sharing of superficial personal pain but for a constant willingness to see one's own pain and suffering as rising from the depth of the human condition which all men share.[1]

Henri Nouwen was not suggesting that the caregiver focus on his own needs when serving the broken. Nor was Nouwen advocating that the caregiver expose every struggle or pain he may have faced along the way. He was, rather, calling the caregiver to be in touch with his own wounds so as to identify with the suffering of others, and point them to the Eternal Wounded Healer. The caregiver will only be able to turn and minister to the broken and lost by allowing Christ to touch the place of personal pain and trial. God's healing, comfort and hope flow through the wounds of Christ to heal the surrendered caregiver who, in turn, offers his wounds as a channel of hope and inner healing to other broken men, women and children. Where the caregiver receives, he gives in the power and name of Christ, extending the healing that comes from Christ to the people he serves. Education and training in the behavioral sciences are important. But in a world filled with debilitating pain, the approach of the wounded healer may be the most important qualification of the healing ministry.

The apostle Paul wrote of this divine exchange in his second letter to the church at Corinth:

> Praise be to the God and Father of our Lord Jesus Christ, the
> Father of compassion and the God of all comfort, who com-
> forts us in all our troubles, so that we can comfort those in any
> trouble with the comfort we have received from God. For just
> as the sufferings of Christ flow over into our lives, so also
> through Christ our comfort overflows. (2 Cor. 1:3, 4)

Two concepts stand out in this beautiful text. First, the source of
help is Christ's suffering, moving into the caregiver's place of pain.
Jesus went to the cross, was wounded for sins, and then offered those
very wounds as the channel of God's grace. And second, the comfort
of God that can graciously flow to the caregiver will mysteriously
overflow to others. The source of pain in the caregiver's life can
become, in Christ, the place of deep and transforming healing for
many other people.

The concept of the wounded healer is foreign to much of our world.
Somehow society, often including the church, believes that it is the suc-
cessful, the beautiful, the bright, the powerful and the educated who
are to be applauded and sought after for advice. It is thought that they
and they alone have the answers to life. The hurting and weak are to
be loved, helped, even pitied. But because of their frailties many
believe they have little to offer. If someone wants to serve or be accepted in a world with such a value system, it is important that he or she
at least appear to have it all together. In such an environment people
cope, they hide, and they pretend.

But scripture testifies to a community of God's people who were
far more comfortable with brokenness as a framework for ministry.
Many of the key people of the New Testament are remembered with
specific mention of their brokenness. There was blind Bartimeaus, the
woman caught in adultery, Simon the leper, the Gadarene demoniac,
and many others. Each of these people had been touched by Jesus
and transformed. Why is their story recalled with reference to their
brokenness? Because it was where Christ met them and dramatically
set them free. Weakness and pain became the very place where Jesus
made Himself so powerfully present, and the broken were healed.

Just as Paul said, "when I am weak, then I am strong"(2 Cor. 12:10). Only in weakness can the strength of Christ flow through a caregiver to the people who turn to him for help. The wounded caregiver must be touched by the Wounded to offer healing to the wounded. What an amazing mystery of grace!

Nouwen tells a powerful story illustrating the call to minister as a wounded healer.

> Rabbi Yoshua ben Levi came upon Elijah the prophet while he was standing at the entrance of Rabbi Simeron ben Yohai's cave...He asked Elijah, "When will the Messiah come?" Elijah replied, "Go and ask him yourself." "Where is he?" "He is sitting among the poor covered with wounds....He unbinds one at a time and binds it up again, saying to himself, 'Perhaps I shall be needed; if so, I must always be ready so as not to delay for a moment.'

Nouwen goes on to comment on the story:

> The Messiah, the story tells us, is sitting among the poor, binding his own wounds one at a time, waiting for the moment when he will be needed. So it is too with the minister...He must bind his own wounds carefully in anticipation of the moment when he is needed. He is called to be the wounded healer, the one who must look after his own wounds, but at the same time be prepared to heal the wounds of others.[2]

Is the caregiver being attentive to her own wounds? Is she prepared to be an instrument of inner healing to others? The answer given to the first question automatically applies to the second. When a caregiver decides merely to cope with the pain, choosing to hide and pretend that all is well, she will have little of substance to offer the broken. But if she is willing to sit humbly among the poor, as both wounded and healer, she will experience the power of his grace as never before. The caregiver will be empowered to heal others in Christ's name as she gives attention to her own wounds. She will be prepared to offer a level of strength and freedom that is transforming to the broken men and women who turn to her for help.

The Inward Journey Begins

How does the caregiver move forward to experience inner healing? Saying yes to the inward journey is an important first step. The caregiver should be supported and encouraged to sit before the Lord and expose deep hurts. The chapters that follow will discuss the process, providing basic steps to inner healing. The immediate discussion seeks to help the caregiver plot a course toward personal emotional well-being. The journey begins with a discussion of the relationship between deep wounds and the destructive behaviors she may have embraced. The material that follows applies to all people, but I have written it with special concern for those ministering inner healing prayer. I pray that the caregiver allows the discussion to be personally, rather than professionally, applied. The later chapters are devoted to helping others. Here the caregiver is my primary concern.

Stolen Treasures and Lost Dreams

What does a person need in order to realize his full potential as a human being and walk successfully through life? What special endowments must he have to experience the wholeness and well being that God designed for him? I would propose that several basic needs are present in individuals, core longings that are to be met and developed in the context of caring and faithful adults. Parents and significant others are to be instruments of the Lord, helping the person become all that God intended, teaching him to rest secure in his identity as His child. Parents and significant others are to provide:

A safe and secure environment.
Constant reinforcement of personal worth.
Repeated messages that the person is valued, unique, and special.
Unconditional love and acceptance.
Basic care and nurture.
Encouragement to grow and develop personal gifts and talents.
A pathway to fellowship with God.

A person's parents were meant to love, cherish, nurture and believe in her. Grandparents were to delight in her, thrilled to see the beautiful human being God has created. They were each meant to recognize and rejoice in the person's unique gifts, listen to and value her opinions, and encourage her to fulfill all the special dreams dancing in her heart. When she failed they were to look beneath the mistake and affirm the wonder that she truly is to them. Their arms were to be a safe place for her to grow, a hiding place against the slings and arrows of a hostile world.

But what if some of the endowments were never given to her? What if part of what she needed was stolen by insensitive or uncaring people? What if the father who was called to love her, ignored or abandoned her? What if her mother gave far more criticism than love, shame and blame instead of nurture and encouragement? What if her opinions were ridiculed, dreams ignored or gifts and talents rejected? How would she have felt if she had turned to her grandfather for affirmation and acceptance, but instead was sexually abused? The affect of such things would surely have compromised her ability to function in life appropriately.

Consider the following illustrations. The first circle represents a person who is fully endowed with all the treasure that God intended her to have in order to experience an abundant and healthy life. It is complete. The second circle illustrates a person moving into life having experienced serious trauma that damaged part of what was needed. The circle is broken.

The pain is great when part of the treasure that was meant to empower a person for life is stolen. Rather than moving into life fully equipped to succeed and experience abundance, she feels empty and insecure. She struggles with deep despair and humiliation, and wears the shame of brokenness like a coat made of iron. She feels fear so powerful that she wants to run away as fast as possible. The constant gnawing deep within threatens to undo her, and no matter where she goes or who she is with she feels unsafe. There might be days when dark clouds settle in, bringing a debilitating depression that feels cold and endless. Instead of believing that life makes sense, she feels confused and constantly at risk.

Deep wounds impact what she believes about herself and her world. The experience of insensitivity and abuse at such an early age can lead to seriously distorted thinking. This is particularly true when the adults who are called to care for a person actually injure her. The child is far too young to process all that happens, and there is nowhere to turn for help. Strong emotions lead her to draw conclusions about life based on what she has seen and experienced. Granted, her assumptions may rest more on feeling than rational thinking, but a very strong belief system gets formed just the same. These values and judgments are often shaped subconsciously, empowered by negative feelings that drive a person to act in unhealthy ways. Unchallenged, they will continue to operate into adult life.

A wounded person may intuitively conclude that she is now damaged goods, unattractive and worthy of rejection. She might believe that if people knew what had happened in her life they would make fun of her, or worse, injure her even more. She may easily presume that all people are unsafe and out to get her whenever possible. She may even assume that God is not there for her, allowing bad people to hurt her without care or concern. She might believe that all the loss she has experienced was somehow her fault, that she is bad and out of control. Possibly she would think that she is all alone to provide and care for herself. Or she may conclude that she is a powerless victim, destined to limp through life, able to receive crumbs to exist, but never food enough to truly thrive.

The deep pain and the distorted belief system leads her to react in destructive ways. Consider the former illustration once again. The broken circle represents the individual robbed of necessary life endowments. The loss is painful as well as very embarrassing, causing her to feel inadequate and vulnerable to further harm. And of course she feels anger. In an effort to address each of these emotions, she begins to construct a multi-layered coping system. She may not be consciously aware of the relationship between her reactions and the deep loss. In childhood this unconscious strategy may have helped her survive. But as an adult what once served to enable her only further compromises her emotional and mental health. The unaddressed wound hidden beneath the layers continues to eat away at the core of her inner being. And the older she becomes the more difficult it may be to see the connection between certain unhealthy behaviors and deep loss. Just the same, a cause and effect relationship does exist, and it must be identified and acknowledged on the journey toward personal well being.

The Pain Layer

The first layer of the coping system represents a person's reaction to pain. Stolen treasures and broken dreams do not happen without great physical and emotional agony. Abuse and abandonment, regardless of the form they take, pierce to the most tender and sensitive places in the human soul. Although the initial hurt seems unbearable, the chronic pain threatens to undo her long after the wounding occurred.

Like the unwelcome shriek of a smoke alarm, pain screams out for the person's attention. Not knowing better, she tries to find a way to silence the alarm, without ever putting out the fire that set it off in the first place. How does she do that? Consider the following list of possibilities.

Dissociation	Alcohol
Food	Drugs
Sexual addictions	Religion
Gambling	Television
Work	Exercising
Shopping	Tobacco
Sleeping	Recreation

Any one or combination of these could temporarily anesthetize chronic pain. But they do not address the deep wound that generated the hurt in the first place. The relief seems to be a welcome alternative to the daily agony of deep hurt. In fact a person initially seems to feel and function better. However, years of inattention to the wounds deep within simply intensifies the inner agony. And over time a person develops a tolerance for the "drug" of choice. This usually results in the need for higher doses or a change to more powerful pain killers. The cycle that results is very destructive. Eventually both the original wounding and the painkillers of choice exact a grave toll on the person's emotions, body and relationships.

The Protective Layer

The next layer of defense is a wall of protection. I had a relative who frequently said, "Hurt me once, shame on you. Hurt me twice, shame on me!" The point is quite clear. When a person is significantly hurt, the pain and trauma of that wounding motivates him to be much more cautious. He would do most anything to keep from experiencing the anguish a second time. Only the powerless, which is most often true of helpless children, or the foolish would blindly walk into harms way again. A person would move quickly and assuredly to establish a fortification as strong as steel and as thick as the Great Wall of China.

Self-protection is not an improper reaction to the threat of wounding. It is quite healthy to learn to set appropriate boundaries with people. Individuals have both the right and obligation to set limits on those who consistently hurt them, be it by intention or insensitivity. No one should be permitted to take or destroy any of the treasures that were intended to help a person fulfill life's dreams. However, many methods of self-protection are actually personally destructive and often harm friends and family as well.

Fearful that he might not be capable of discerning who would or would not bring harm, a person constructs shields to keep people at a distance. The underlying wound remains unaddressed, causing the infection to grow and threaten greater pain. People never really have the opportunity to know the person or call forth the wonder that is his in Christ. This self-protection can grow out of embarrassment and shame. The wound not only robbed the person of some life endowment, it left him believing that he was essentially deformed and unattractive. A person can grow fearful that if anyone saw the brokenness and weakness that lies within, they would openly reject and ridicule. And so, the walls go up through such reactions as:

Pretense	Anger
Denial	Aggression
Avoidance	Isolation
Silence	Shyness
Reaction formation	Hiding

The Layer of Provision
How does a person continue to live without nurture? What does he do when acceptance has been denied and rejection is the order of the day? Can he actually move through life with health and maturity apart from love? These questions cut to the core of one of the most important issues a broken person will face. I believe that each and every endowment is important to personal growth and development. When part of that treasure has been compromised, the absence creates a

noticeable emptiness. In a perfect world mature adults would step in to provide what primary caregivers neglected to give. They would, with God's good help, nurture a person where once abused, and call forth all that had been forced into hiding. Love, acceptance and affirmation would flow through them to fill the places that were robbed.

This is not a perfect world, and a wounded person seldom experiences such gracious infillings from others. And so he begins to provide for himself. Unfortunately, what he often turns to gives little more than further pain and heartbreak. Sexual promiscuity might seem to promise acceptance and love, all the while tearing away at the soul and ultimately leaving him more intensely alone in a bed of guilt and shame. A person might turn to people pleasing as a pathway to approval, only to discover that he has lost his own identity in the desperate quest to be found acceptable by others. Hungry to feel that he had worth and value, a person might embrace some performance addiction. But satisfaction lasts only as long as the applause continues, leaving him alone and frightened when memories of his latest performance fade in people's minds. He might find a way to grab what he so desperately needs, only to watch it turn to dust in his hand. Any of the following could become the substitute for genuine love, acceptance, worth and approval:

Sexual promiscuity	Money
Career	Athletics
Academics	People pleasing
Fame	Manipulation
Control	Popularity
Success	An unhealthy relationship

It is obvious that some of these are not in themselves problematic. But whenever a person tries to fill the internal void with any one of them, he will find that they are far from adequate. Most attempts to do this will fail to meet his deepest needs.

The Punishment Layer

Exacting a "pound of flesh" is not a Christian response to deep wounding. No matter how severely a person may have been hurt, eye-for-an-eye retaliation is not the way of Jesus. Christ calls a person to bless and not offend, and to forgive rather than seek revenge. His teaching is certainly contrary to popular cultural values; it is also very difficult to live.

Pain often births an anger that drives a person to strike back at the one who has perpetuated the injury. While she may not actually act upon the demand for repayment, the deep feeling is often there. She may have even gone so far as to extend the words of forgiveness to the offender, yet struggle with the desire to punish someone, anyone, for the robbery that left her in such pain. For some, the desire to punish turns inward, causing a reaction of self-hate and self-abuse. An individual can believe that there must be something personally wrong for such bad things to have happened.

Reactions include:

Blame	Shame
Abusive words	Physical abuse
Criticism	Unforgiveness
Fantasies of harming someone	Bitterness
Aggression	Withholding
Slander	Rejection
Self-contempt	Self abuse

I recently ministered to a woman who was upset with her grown children. She felt that her two adult daughters were disrespectful and holding her at arms length. Quoting scriptures about honoring fathers and mothers, she was seeking advice as to a strategy to bring them in line. I invited her to tell me her own story, which turned out to be one of significant pain and betrayal as a child. Orphaned in infancy, she lived with an abusive aunt who resented her presence and withheld all love and nurture, all the while showering her own children with generous affection.

The loss and withholding created great emotional upheaval deep within her, which was never properly resolved before the Lord. I asked the woman how she dealt with pain, and after a long silence she said, "When I hurt I want to hurt someone else." And for many years her daughters were the recipients of that rage. Harsh words and angry reactions would come without warning, causing her children to feel increasingly unsafe. As children they had to take it. But as adults they simply distanced themselves from her to escape the unpredictable behavior. The mother had never grasped the relationship between her reactive anger and the deep loss she had experienced, but the cause and effect connection had to be addressed if change was to take place. The same is true for each wounded person.

God wants to meet the caregiver at the place of his own deepest pain. Jesus knows the heartache the caregiver experiences and the unhealthy ways in which he may have tried to deal with the lost treasures of life. The Lord is also well aware that any coping system the caregiver may use is ultimately compromising his own well-being. Christ offers a better way. He is willing to help the caregiver systematically identify and set aside any multi-layered reaction to deep wounding. This is the essence of inner healing. The prospect may be frightening and there will be some initial discomfort when painkillers are surrendered to the Lord. Laying aside coping mechanisms may cause the caregiver to feel vulnerable and at risk. But through the tender guidance of the Holy Spirit, God will take him back to the loss, meeting him there with great love and care.

God is willing to touch the places where pain gains its power and to bring His healing to bear upon the caregiver's life. And most important, He stands ready to replace the stolen treasures and lost endowments with something far greater. He will give the caregiver Himself. The fellowship of His presence will far outweigh the pain of past wounding. Empowered by His Holy Spirit, he will be able to move forward in life to realize more and more his full potential as God's miraculously endowed child. Inner healing will free the caregiver to be a wounded healer, to touch lives with the transforming presence of the ultimate Wounded Healer, Jesus Christ.

Take Care to Take Care

A caregiver must take active steps to care for her own personal well-being. The ministry of inner healing is emotionally and spiritually demanding. Unless the caregiver faithfully attends to her own life, involvement in such a ministry could take a significant toll. For a variety of reasons, many caregivers neglect their own emotional and spiritual health. Diligent to reach out and serve others, they frequently compromise their own lives, with devastating results. The person involved in inner healing prayer must resist this disturbing trend, investing deeply in the pilgrimage toward wholeness and balance. Two words come to mind which lay an important foundation for adequate self-care: right and responsibility.

A caregiver has the right to regularly care for herself. Some in the Christian community would take exception to that statement, believing that it is somehow noble to compromise personal health in service to others. They would encourage a boundary-less lifestyle in which people have access to a caregiver day and night. Some believe that such an approach to ministry best serves the broken and models the sacrificial ministry of Jesus Christ.

I heartily disagree. Having experienced the devastation of burnout, I am well aware of the painful consequences of giving beyond one's emotional, physical and spiritual reserves. There is nothing noble, honorable or Christ glorifying about it. It is a royal mess! The pain and loss can be far reaching, and the prescription for recovery can be costly, both to the caregiver and to those who love her most. There is nothing good or godly about regularly working so long and hard that little time or energy remains for self-care. Jesus himself invested in times of solitude and rest, getting apart from the pressing demands of ministry to refuel and renew himself. While it is true that there may be times when the truly urgent demands of ministry press in, the caregiver has every right to regularly and deeply invest in personal health and well being.

Self-care is the caregiver's responsibility. This means that investing in personal health and well being is the most responsible thing that the caregiver can do. To be an effective servant of the Lord, the caregiver must care for himself. The people who need him, need him to be well. It's that simple. But the other dimension of responsibility is that no one can do it for the caregiver. While he should be accountable to others about personal well being, he alone is responsible. It is his job to make time for the Lord, get good counsel, open his spirit to inner healing and take care to exercise and rest. It is his duty to maintain the primary relationships of his life with diligence and love. The caregiver must make personal health a priority. If it does not happen, it is because he failed to exercise care and concern. He alone is responsible.

While in Northern California, my family and I lived on a small ranch. Our property supported chickens and ducks, a horse, fruit trees, two dogs and a fishing pond. Part of the acreage was fenced, and on top of the hill there was a beautiful view of both Mt. Lassen and Mt.

Shasta. There were other ranches adjoining our property, some smaller and others quite large. While neighbors would help one another when invited, each rancher knew that the condition of their property was the owner's responsibility. None of my neighbors felt compelled to care for what was within my property line, nor did I stay up nights thinking about the condition of their ranches. If my ranch was well maintained and productive, it was because I took responsibility to care for and develop the property. If my ranch was over grown and unproductive, it also was my responsibility. None of my neighbors felt it improper that I exercise care for my property, nor noble if I ignored my ranch to take responsibility for theirs.

Ranches and Responsibility

A ranch can serve as a very helpful metaphor for the caregiver's life.[3] It illustrates the need to exercise proper care and concern, as well as the importance of setting boundaries with people. The ranch itself symbolizes the caregiver's life. What is within the ranch represents the various gifts and endowments that are part of what makes the caregiver healthy and unique. The care and development of every part of the "ranch" is the caregiver's responsibility. He may need help along the way, but the condition of the property is determined by the attention he gives to personal growth. No one else has that responsibility but the caregiver, no matter who wants to assume control or how many people expect him to ignore his development to care for their own deep needs.

The following illustration provides a visual representation of the ranch concept. Notice the particular parts of the ranch.

On the caregiver's ranch are several buildings that are essential for his personal health and well being. First, there is a main house, representing the caregiver's identity, which is to be securely founded upon God. Scripture identifies the caregiver as God's gifted heir, endowed with the power of the Holy Spirit, recognized in the heavenlies as light, and salt, and living water. He is loved, cherished, and accepted by Him, fully pleasing and embraced through the righteousness of the Lord Jesus Christ. This rich endowment is given freely by the God of Love. Growing in understanding and confidence in this God-given identity is the way the caregiver maintains the basic structure of his ranch.

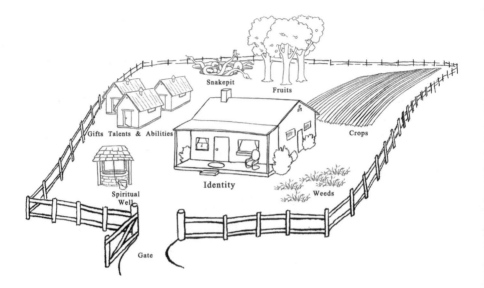

The ranch house serves as a place of personal nurture and protection against the winds of society that seek to blow the caregiver off course in life. The secular culture works hard to convince people that success, money, popularity, and power define who they are in life. But when the main house is built on Christ, the caregiver's identity is securely established in his relationship to Jesus. There is nothing more to earn or prove. The caregiver is established in Him by faith.

Also on this ranch is a well. Like any well, it is the place where Living Water is supplied. The caregiver must keep this well maintained and clear, so that the water always flows, pure and refreshing. Prayer, scripture reading and communion with the Lord are to be a daily part of the caregiver's life, providing regular access to the stream of the Lord. Water is the difference between life and death, so guarding and developing that part of the caregiver's ranch is essential. Spiritual disciplines are like buckets and gutters that enable the caregiver to get regular access to the Living Water in the well and then send it forth throughout the ranch to nourish every part of the landscape.

The caregiver's ranch also has several out buildings. These special shelters represent the unique storehouses for those qualities that make the caregiver special and unique. Like the tractors and machinery that keep a ranch productive and well maintained, these outbuildings house spiritual gifts, special talents, and particular skills. They also store the caregiver's attitudes, appetites, personality traits and preferences. Whenever needed, whether within the boundaries of his own ranch, or out helping a neighbor, or working in the community, the caregiver should choose the appropriate resource and employ it with maturity and satisfaction.

The caregiver's ranch also has designated areas where crops are planted, raised, and harvested. There is an orchard, where the fruits of the Spirit are nurtured and developed. These trees constantly need Living Water and plenty of Light to stay healthy and productive. There are also fields, where a harvest of righteousness is cultivated and, in season, gathered to the glory of the Lord. The produce of these fields sustains the caregiver, as well as providing nourishment and help to others in special need.

And because the caregiver lives in a fallen world and is prone to sin, there are weed beds on the ranch, places that need to be brought under control through the Holy Spirit. Such places are often ignored on personal ranches, growing wildly and eventually getting out of control. The caregiver must not turn a blind eye to such unsightly places, but allow the Lord to help bring that part of the ranch in line with His word. And of course there is the occasional snake pit, where lingering and counter-productive habits dwell, in need of Christ's cleansing touch. Such places are usually well out of sight, hidden in the dark recesses of past woundings. They threaten great harm to the caregiver, so he will want to be diligent in asking the Lord to help remove them from his life.

Finally, there is a gate on this ranch. The caregiver is responsible for determining who is allowed to enter his ranch, and who should be politely yet definitively kept outside. Don't be confused at this point. The ranch concept is not about community or socialization. It is about the caregiver's inner life, representing what is essential to his personal health and identity. A person is invited to enter only to help the caregiver develop or maintain some aspect of his inner life. The visitor/helper would only have access to that part of the ranch that the caregiver felt safe to entrust to their care and instruction. He would stay only as long as the caregiver felt necessary.

For example, if the caregiver is finding it difficult to maintain the well of his spiritual life, he might invite someone onto his ranch who could help. This person might give insights and suggestions about prayer or some other spiritual discipline. He or she would not be able to make the changes or force the caregiver to do anything, for the well is his responsibility. The visitor/helper could give suggestions and direction for equipping the caregiver to find a better flow of living water. Once a person completed the desired task, he or she would leave the ranch, relating with the caregiver only in the normal discourse of community life.

A person known to have done damage on someone else's ranch, such as trying to compromise the main house of identity or putting poison in the well of spirituality or trying to force his or her will upon another, would be judged unsafe and not permitted to enter. That does not mean that the caregiver would be unkind or unfriendly to such a person. He could socialize with him or her in the context of community quite well. But the person would not have access to the precious endowments that bring growth and safety to the caregiver. There is no good or legitimate reason for the caregiver to open himself to just any person's influence. The caregiver's identity belongs to him, not someone else, as do his spirituality, gifts, talents, fruits and so forth.

No one has the right to force his or her way onto the caregiver's ranch and insist that he think, act or behave in a certain way. Nor is anyone free to barge in and redefine who the caregiver is, how he feels, or what he believes. The fence line is the boundary, and only the caregiver is responsible for what happens on the ranch. It is the caregiver's right and responsibility to develop and maintain every aspect of the property. The caregiver may help other ranchers when necessary, even seeing that as part of his life calling. But no one else has the responsibility to make the caregiver's ranch productive, or the right to barge in and do whatever he or she may want. The fence is there to limit access to the caregiver's ranch, to indicate that all must come to the main gate, where the caregiver carefully determines if their intentions are honorable and their help truly needed at the time.

In a perfect world the caregiver would have learned about ranching from parents. At birth, knowing that the caregiver was a helpless child, they would have protected and nurtured his ranch. With God's guidance, they would have set the fence in place to keep the child from harm, begun to lay a foundation for the main house by praying the identity of Christ into his life. They would have started to establish the well of the caregiver's relationship with Christ, and so forth. As the caregiver grew, they would have taught him to develop and maintain his own ranch. First, they would have invited the child/caregiver to watch them care for his ranch. As the caregiver grew, they would ask him to help, as a way of learning. Eventually, they would step back to watch the caregiver care for himself, making sure that he understood the essentials of ranching. When confident that the caregiver had reached an age of accountability, they would lovingly exit the ranch, giving full responsibility to him.

Parents would have taught the caregiver, by word and example, how to identify safe people, when and from whom to seek help, and how to keep hurtful people off the property. Even if they were parents, they would not barge onto the caregiver's ranch and impose their will. They would bring their concerns to the gate like others and ask permission to help. If the caregiver refused, they would honor that response and continue to love him unconditionally. For the caregiver alone is called by God to exercise care and concern for his personal well being. It is his right and responsibility.

Unhealthy Ranches

Unfortunately we do not live in a perfect world. Few people are cared for, trained and equipped in such a way as to develop and appropriately maintain their ranches. As result, countless people are unhealthy, ranches are out of control, and ideas about ranching are often irresponsible. The results are negative, from mildly painful to extremely destructive. More often that not, caregivers need instruction and help as much as those who come to them for help. By pressing the allegory in the following pages, the caregiver will be able to identify unhealthy approaches to ranching.

The Fix Me Ranch

For many people the gate of their ranch is wide open and a sign says, "Fix Me!" Such people have embraced the mistaken notion that other people are responsible for their personal well being. Most likely this notion was caught or taught in childhood. When they hurt or come across an underdeveloped part of their life or believe that some aspect of their ranch is out of control, they say, "Fix Me!" The cry can be as

weak as a nagging whine or as loud and forceful as raging anger. Either way, such people refuse to take responsibility for their own well being and measure love by another's willingness to repair what is broken.

These "ranchers" do not want instruction, they want rescuing. They are often accountable to no one, and believe that everyone is responsible for their lives. Such attitudes, if left unchallenged, drain friendships, ruin marriages, and compromise the health of everyone who plays along with these rules. The first step toward wholeness is to be very clear about one point of ranching: I love you, but you are responsible!

The "I Need You To Love Me" Ranch

A gate controls access to the ranch and it is a person's responsibility to determine who is safe and who is unsafe. For some people the gate has been removed. They have come to believe that to be in relationship with others they must give open and unlimited access to their ranch. They have confused the notion of community and individuality, believing that it is necessary to surrender the latter to have the former. These ranchers are essentially addicted to a people-pleasing formula that says, "I must have your approval to feel good about myself." They surrender their own rights in order to accommodate the desires of other people. They believe what others want them to believe, behave the way others want them to behave, and only expose the feelings they believe others will find acceptable.

One friend told me that in order to maintain a relationship with his father he had to stuff his own feelings and reshape his theological opinions to match his dad's. His father had even said at one point, "No son of mine will ever be a charismatic. I would not have it!" The message was clear. To be in relationship, which my friend honestly wanted, demanded that he compromise his own conviction, and surrender his own right and responsibility. Dad had claimed the right to develop my friend's ranch. My friend felt disconnected from himself and unaware of his true feelings about anything. His father was wrong for linking relationship to the shape of my friend's ranch, and my friend was in error for living without a gate, allowing another to determine how his ranch was maintained and developed. The gate had to be reattached, and my friend needed to learn about his own rights and responsibilities.

The "Stay Out" Ranch

Some ranchers have been so hurt by others that they are now well defended against any and all intruders. They have come to the conclusion that people are unsafe, and that they must protect themselves from anyone and everyone. Not only do they have a fence, they have covered it with barbed wire. Others, having experienced more serious abuse, have built thick walls around the ranch and surrounded it by

a mote filled with alligators. No one will ever enter and hurt them again. These people have determined to mistrust everyone. This "Stay Out" ranch may take one of two forms. Some build a false front, similar to a movie set that is pleasant and well maintained. They give the impression that they are friendly, open to relationships, and willing to be appropriately vulnerable. But no one ever gets beyond the facade to the real ranch, and soon people realize this person is a locked unit. Others have no use for pretense, simply letting people know that they have no interest in help or advice and, if necessary, forcefully communicating that point.

The "You Tell Me" Ranch

The "You Tell Me" Ranch is best described by the following story. Paul Collins had a serious problem with control. He was a large man, with an intense demeanor and aggressive behavior. Paul believed that he had to call the shots in virtually every aspect of life. When he married Sarah, he took charge of essentially every area of her life. He told her what to wear, who to have as friends, what church to attend, and how much she needed to weigh. Paul was kind and generous when Sarah complied, and withholding and mean-spirited when she failed to meet his expectations. Previous wounding had predisposed Sarah to believe

that she did not have the right or ability to determine her own life. Sarah thought she needed someone to tell her who to be.

When Paul and Sarah married, he annexed her ranch onto his own. She expected and experienced no freedom to develop her identity, spirituality or gifts apart from Paul's direction and demands. At one level Sarah believed this type of dominance was necessary for her, but at another she grew increasingly passive and depressed. When Paul and Sarah had children, he annexed their ranches as well, holding the keys to their personal development in his tight-fisted control. Over time Paul's behavior drove the children into various levels of rebellion.

People who are caught in "You Tell Me" relationships are prone to involvement in abusive churches. They are given to legalistic expressions of the Christian faith that bring bondage and brokenness instead of freedom in Christ. Freedom for such people does not lie in simply confronting controlling people who work to dominate others. Individuals like Sarah must be helped in setting proper boundaries and accepting the responsibility to care for themselves and develop as God intends.

The "No One is Home" Ranch

Many people were raised by parents who were, for one reason or another, absent in the child's life. These parents may have been irresponsible, out of control or physically or emotionally ill. The child often

had to take responsibility for the home, caring for both parents as well as other siblings. This parental inversion can carry well over into adulthood, with the now grown child believing that it is her role to care for others. Because her identity is rooted and perpetuated in this role, she ignores her own needs in order to take care of other people's ranches. People like this often choose care-giving professions, including those of counselor and pastor. This way of ranching is unhealthy at two basic points. First, most of these ranchers are grossly neglecting their own well-being. They may appear to have things together, but often that is simply a false front. They never allow people to see the real condition of their ranch, because they are seldom home enough even to give another access. Second, such ranchers can enable others to be irresponsible by taking on the task of fixing them. The "No One is Home Ranch," like each of the other unhealthy styles, must be lovingly challenged and, by the power of Christ, surrendered for the healthy concept of ranching outlined earlier.

Proper and responsible "ranching" is a prerequisite for all effective ministries that serve the broken of this world. I encourage the caregiver to embrace the right to develop and maintain her own emotional and spiritual health. The Lord desires that the caregiver show concern for personal well-being, and through the Holy Spirit He will help her grow and mature as His special servant. The caregiver should remember that self-care is her responsibility. Every person she serves needs her to be faithful to her own inward journey. It is foundational to the caregiver's calling and the only path to an empowered and grace-filled ministry of inner healing prayer.

Notes

1. Henri Nouwen, *The Wounded Healer: Ministry in Contemporary Society* (New York: Doubleday, 1972), 88.

2. Ibid, 81, 82.

3. The idea of using the ranch metaphor was first presented to me by Matt Barnhall when he served as a counselor with Rapha. My own description and detail builds on that initial conversation.

For Further Reading

Draw Close to the Fire, by Terry Wardle
Finding God, by Larry Crabb
The Journey of Desire, by John Eldridge
Boundaries, by Henry Cloud and John Townsend
The Sacred Romance, by Brent Curtis and John Eldridge
Self-Care: A Theology of Personal Empowerment and Spiritual Healing, by
        Ray S. Anderson

Three

The Outward Journey

Serving in a caregiving ministry is demanding. Very demanding. Several times a week the caregiver sits across from hurting, often debilitated people who are looking for help. Their issues are complex and are bringing pain and heartache to more people than themselves. At times primary relationships are at stake for clients, and the trials they are facing impact most every sphere of their lives: marriage, family, work and church. More often than not sessions are intense. Debilitating bondages raise their ugly heads, as well as strong emotions long pent up. Add to that the reality that the forces of evil are seldom dormant in all this.

Caring for the broken and offering helpful counsel to the hurting is far from easy. To be effective the caregiver must be connected to the person, attentive to what is said and careful to properly discern what yet needs to be said. He needs to show compassion, communicate understanding and give corrective direction when appropriate. In short, a great deal is being asked of a caregiver. Ministry like this can be very draining. More than a few caregivers I know find that their spiritual and emotional reserves get used up quickly. If not careful the caregiver is at great risk of entering a season of ill health. Even though efforts are made to maintain objectivity and professional distance while serving the broken, the reality is that care-giving ministries are demanding.

Trends seem to indicate that many people in helping professions are not caring for themselves. As a result gifted men and women are compromising their lives and ministries. As previously stated, embracing the ministry of inner healing demands that the caregiver be attentive to his own spiritual growth and well-being. The first chapter focused upon caring for the soul by prioritizing the upward journey to God's embrace. The second chapter was an invitation to the inward journey toward personal wholeness and responsibility. This chapter discusses the necessity of an outward journey, where the caregiver gathers regularly with a small group of fellow Christians and there experiences the healing power of the Body of Christ. I hope that this discussion does more than convince the caregiver that community is important. I pray that it moves him to seek community and commit to the interpersonal dimension of the Christian life. Any serious consideration of a ministry of inner healing demands nothing less.

The Call to Community

Each year I have the privilege of teaching in the Doctor of Ministry program at Ashland Theological Seminary. The days I spend working with doctoral students are some of my favorite. These people are the salt of the earth, men and women determined to make a difference for Jesus Christ and His kingdom. They come to campus several times a year for intensive courses taught in a one-week format. Arriving fresh from their local place of ministry, they are often in need of care, and are hungry for new ideas and strategies for ministry. Their enthusiasm for learning makes teaching a joy.

It is not unusual for the discussion in class to focus on the trials and heartaches that come with Christian service. Many church leaders have been wounded in ministry and the pain of these hurts often lies close to the surface. Being away from their local context seems to provide an opportunity to talk more openly about their pain. So I sometimes ask the students to gather in groups and answer these two questions: "When hurting, what would you like to receive from a small group of men and women who are committed to your well-being? What would you not want to receive from such a group?" It takes little prodding to get the discussion going, and invariably emotions begin to run high. I make a list of their answers, which typically includes most or all of the following comments:

"I want people to listen, really listen to me."

"I want to know it is a safe place and that my comments will be held in confidence."

"I need to sense that they care, that what I'm feeling matters to them."

"It is important that people respect my boundaries."

"I want to experience healthy touch when I am hurting."

"I need them to point me to the faithfulness of Christ."

"Healing prayer is essential."

"I want to be loved."

"I need to feel their acceptance."

"I don't want to hear spiritual clichés."

"If they try to fix me before loving me I will shut down."

"I don't need condemnation. I am probably doing that to myself already."

"I won't be able to handle a judgmental attitude."

"It is important that they do not minimize or discount what I am going through."

"I don't want people to allow me to take on a victim mentality."

"I need a group of people who will challenge me to forgive as Christ forgives."

As this list takes shape there is a growing recognition among the students that community is actually important to well-being. Students begin to sense that maybe their own hurts and heartaches could find healing in community. They consider the possibility that the pain they are fighting to hide or suppress could find expression in a safe gathering of fellow pilgrims, or that the feeling of isolation they experience could be touched and reduced. They wonder if their spiritual reserves could be replenished by joining with others around the presence of Christ. It is as if a voice begins to be heard from the deepest recesses of the soul, crying out for a place to share life.

As this happens I ask a third question: "Where are you experiencing this type of community?" The classroom grows suddenly quiet. Silent stares speak eloquently. The majority of students are not experiencing this kind of Christian community. Even as the conviction grows that a small group experience would be transformational, the sad reality sets in that they are living in a very demanding context without it. I seldom need to work at convincing them that such a condition is dangerous and only adds to the difficulty of an already challenging vocation. They soon see that involvement in community is a commitment they cannot afford not to make.

Larry Crabb, a respected leader in the field of Christian counseling, has written about the critical role spiritual community plays in the healing and maturing of God's people. *Connecting: A Radical New Vision* and *The Safest Place on Earth*, call Christians in caregiving professions to recognize and embrace the transforming power of Christian community. He writes:

> The greatest need in modern civilization is the development of communities—true communities where the heart of God is home, where the humble and wise learn to shepherd those on the path behind them, where trusting strugglers lock arms with others as together they journey on.[1]

I want to be part of such a community. I desperately need to be part of such a community. I do have such a community, and my life is being transformed as a result. For nearly a decade I have been on a daily pilgrimage toward well-being, initiated by a dark and debilitating time that led to hospitalization and therapeutic care. I am grateful for all the help that professional caregivers provided along the way to my recovery and personal growth. There were old patterns of behavior that had to go and more than a few new habits to embrace. But nothing has brought healing to my life like my small group of friends who have gathered weekly in the name of Christ.

The love, care and encouragement of my spiritual community have seen me through difficult days and the unexpected dark nights. My friends have wept with me, laughed with me and incarnated the love of Jesus in tangible and powerful ways. These fellow travelers have helped me release feelings long hidden away, and then prayed for every empty place to be filled with the incomparable love of Christ. They sat in loving silence when I needed it most, and knew when to speak the words of truth that have brought freedom and new life.

These special friends believe in what the Lord is doing in me and continually call forth the grace-given gifts that lie within my being. They provide a safe place to be honest and open about my struggles, all the while pointing me to the matchless love of the Lord Jesus Christ. Their connection positively impacts everything I do and I am a healthier servant with them as part of my life. Because of these wounded healers the outward journey to spiritual community has become a pleasurable necessity for me.

Several years ago I wrote *Draw Close to the Fire: Finding God in the Darkness*. It chronicles my journey through depression and a lingering anxiety disorder. But the book is primarily about twelve biblical principles that help hurting people find God in tough times. One chapter is titled "Healthy Relationships Move You Toward Spiritual Maturity," and was written to encourage the broken to find a spiritual community as a context for healing and recovery. Here I am writing to the caregiver to be equally committed to community, not only as a therapeutic tool for healing others, but for the well being of his own soul. In that chapter I wrote:

> If you desire support, encouragement, counsel and accountability, become part of a truly spiritual community. By *spiritual* I mean a place where God is welcomed and His Spirit is free to move, actively changing people into the likeness of Jesus Christ. By *community* I mean a gathering of people biblically interdependent and committed to one another as they journey through life…Whatever it is, a spiritual community is a place where the Lord is at work in people's lives, and people are truly there for one another along the way.[2]

Larry Crabb has also defined spiritual community in his book, *The Safest Place on Earth*. He wrote:

> I speak of spiritual community as a gathering of people who experience a kind of togetherness that only the Holy Spirit makes possible, who move together in good directions—and want to—because the Holy Spirit is at work….In spiritual community, people reach deep places in each other's hearts that are not often or easily reached. They discover places beneath the awkwardness of wanting to embrace and cry and share opinions. They openly express love and reveal fear, even though they feel so unaccustomed to that level of intimacy.[3]

I include both descriptions so there will be little question about what the outward journey entails. Christians, including caregivers, were made to grow healthy in spiritual community. The Christian life is a shared life, empowered by the Holy Spirit and experienced most dramatically when the caregiver chooses to gather with two or more people in the name of Jesus Christ. There is an incredible force for healing and strength available when meeting with intimate sojourners. Everything the caregiver does in Christian ministry, including inner healing, depends upon that power flowing to the broken that come his way. If he tries to help while consistently ignoring this reality, disaster certainly awaits.

I have never met James Evans face-to-face, but I will not forget my first telephone conversation with him. He left a message on my voice mail identifying himself as a denominational executive. Thinking that he was interested in one of the programs I direct at the seminary, I returned his call. His first words were both pleasant and professional. He told me that he directed the church renewal ministry for a major denomination, with responsibility for the United States, Canada and Mexico. Anticipating questions about our own church planting program, I was prepared to "sell" him on what we had to offer denominational leaders. But the conversation went in an entirely different direction when he asked, "May I speak confidentially with you?" Though it caught me by surprise I responded positively. He then asked me to stay on the line while he closed his office door.

James then told me that he had read my book, *Whispers of Love in Seasons of Fear*. He had been struggling for months with panic attacks and was fearful that he was losing his mind. James asked if he could cry. When I assured him that it would be perfectly acceptable, he began to weep uncontrollably. For several minutes I prayed and quietly assured him that I was listening and "with" him. It was a deeply painful cry from a tired and frightened man. He was worn out from pretending that all was well with him, when in fact he believed that his entire world was falling apart.

When James was able to talk, I asked about his support system. He told me that he had no one to talk with about his pain. He feared mentioning anything to his superiors because he anticipated rejection and loss of his job. He said little to his wife because he felt she would not understand. As for colleagues, he told me that all his relationships were centered on the task of ministry and held no promise for openness or vulnerability. James did not even want to consider professional care, fearing total disqualification if discovered. He was full of shame, believing that a man of faith would never even consider such a course. He felt absolutely alone and was living in constant terror. Every impulse within him was to run, but he didn't know where to go.

My heart broke for James, not only because I knew the pain of an anxiety disorder, but also because he was fighting the battle by himself. Alone in anxiety is a living hell, and James Evans was caught in that dark and frightening place. He did not know of one safe relationship in his life where he could be honest about his struggle. His only recourse was to call an author he did not know personally, and over the telephone reach for some level of connection that would possibly relieve at least a little of the pain. I can hardly describe my own sorrow as he told me this story, and I did what I could to lead him to safe and effective care. James was experiencing one of the worst conditions possible for a person in Christian ministry: disconnection.

The Problem of Disconnection

James Evans was suffering from a common problem. He was so busy doing the work of ministry that he failed to be attentive to his own spiritual and emotional well being. While seeking to save the world he was losing himself. For a long time he was not even aware of the danger. He was accomplishing much for his denomination, impacting churches in three different countries, gaining responsibility and status. In fact, his superiors were applauding him for his hard work and diligence. The applause felt good, so he picked up the pace. Only after James compromised his health and set off the deafening alarm of panic and anxiety did he even consider that something might be wrong. What made this particularly bad was that he was not part of a spiritual community where he could be lovingly helped and challenged to change his paradigm of ministry.

Larry Crabb calls this condition "disconnection" and defines it as "a condition of existence where the deepest part of who we are is vibrantly attached to no one, where we are profoundly unknown and therefore experience neither the thrill of being believed in nor the joy of loving or being loved."[4] Tragically the church is full of such disconnected Christians, including leaders and caregivers who are busy directing others toward wholeness.

Some would argue that they are in community because they go to church or participate in some group study or fellowship. However, by the definition given, most are experiencing only the "illusion of connection." Though meeting with other Christians, many seldom if ever truly connect at the deepest level of being known, accepted, believed in and loved. The commitments of openness and vulnerability are missing and time together focuses upon some topic or cause rather than truly touching one another at the deepest level of being. Such times touch only the surface of relational intimacy and leave participants essentially disconnected and alone.

Recently I was sharing this concept with an acquaintance who serves as a therapist in a local Christian counseling group. She agreed that spiritual community was important and assured me that it was happening in her life through her work. She said that each week all the members of the group meet to discuss and pray over case loads. Granted that is an important activity, but it hardly qualifies as the kind of connection that genuinely helps a person grow at the levels I am discussing here. Caring, love, encouragement, empathetic listening and healing prayer were not happening as the counselors and therapists met each week. While the Holy Spirit is welcomed to provide insight and wisdom regarding client care, there is little or no expectation that He will move upon the counselors themselves to heal, set free or empower. The meetings are task driven, and necessarily so. But she, as a caregiver, needs to be part of a small, intimate community of Christians who are experiencing intimate togetherness. Without that she runs the risk of moving away from well-being in the very process of pointing others toward wholeness and maturity. In the end, the failure to commit to the outward journey will compromise her and the people she feels called to serve.

Is the caregiver involved in a spiritual community? Is she vibrantly attached to a small group of fellow travelers? Is she experiencing the thrill of being known, believed in, and unconditionally loved? Does she have a place to turn to when the pains of life and burdens of ministry weigh heavily upon her? These questions are important, for the caregiver should be part of such a group. Inner healing happens best through servants who are growing, experiencing the empowerment of

God's Holy Spirit, and addressing their own wounds within a caring Christ-centered community. This is not simply a "pet principle" that I am choosing to set before caregivers. It is a biblical mandate that Christ extends to every believer.

Jesus Calls His Followers into Community

Read the gospels and it soon becomes clear that Jesus believed in the power of community. From the earliest days of his ministry He called people to follow him as He fulfilled the Father's redemptive mission among the lost and broken of the world. He gathered a very diverse group of people, varying in personality, vocation, religious fervor and political philosophy. At first His entourage was little more than a crowd of individuals moving with Jesus as He taught, proclaimed the Kingdom of God, and worked signs and wonders by the power of the Holy Spirit. But not long into His active ministry Jesus called twelve of His followers into a very special relationship with himself and with one another.

In the Gospel of Luke we read that Jesus went up on a mountainside to be alone and, staying there the entire night, he prayed to God (Luke 6:12-16). The Scripture then says, "When morning came, he called his disciples to him and chose twelve of them, whom he designated apostles" (Luke 6:13). Two things stand out to me about this passage. First, while Jesus had many disciples, he called only twelve into a close relationship with him. These individuals would spend the next three years in a deeply connected community of followers. They would experience time growing close, learning from Christ, talking and traveling the countryside, being equipped for ministry, enjoying success, facing controversy and encountering the supernatural presence of the Almighty God. These called-out and called-together men experienced an intimate connection, held together by the common desire to be close to Jesus. In the end, they were ordinary people who were radically transformed in the context of spiritual community, except for the one who chose to step away from community and move out unto his own destruction.

Second, I am struck by the importance Jesus placed upon prayer when making His decision about the apostles. I assume that Jesus prayed about many things that night on the mountainside. And He probably spent some time in worship and communion with His

Father. But it seems clear that He was seeking direction regarding the choice of people who would become His close community of followers. This decision was not made out of impulse, but came as the result of heartfelt prayer before the throne of God.

The gospel narratives indicate that Jesus then went on to choose a community within the community of disciples. You will notice that the Lord seemed to have a unique relationship with three of the twelve: Peter, James, and John. We know that on several important occasions they were invited to be with Christ, most notably at the transfiguration and in the garden of Gethsemane on the night of His betrayal (Mark 9:2-13, and Matt. 26:36-45). They were invited to be with Jesus when He was revealed in heavenly glory, and in the moment when He was most troubled and heartbroken. The Lord had invited them closer than others and thus they knew Him at an even deeper level, which seems to have meant a great deal to the Lord, and assuredly changed Peter, James and John forever.

I am convinced that our Lord's commitment to community was birthed in His experience of the Trinity. Early in my Christian experience I was taught that God created humans because He longed for fellowship. Only by studying God's word and theology did I come to realize how misguided that notion was. God was not, prior to our creation, bored, unhappy, lonely or unloved. Life for God before creation was full of excitement, joy, love and every other quality of delight and happiness, all contained within the community of the Trinity. God did not create people to fill a lonely gap in Himself, but that they might participate in the communion already taking place within the Godhead.

Clark Pinnock writes:

> The social Trinity depicts God as beautiful and supremely lovable. God is not a featureless monad, isolated and motionless, but a dynamic event of loving actions and personal relationality...each person of the Trinity exists eternally with the others, each has its gaze fixed on the others, each casts its glance away from itself in love to the others, the eye of each love ever fixed on the beloved other. God is wonderfully different from what our natural thinking tells us, for this God delights in social existence, ecstatic dance, creativity and spontaneity.[5]

This description opens a beautiful window into the existence Jesus shared before coming to earth. And undoubtedly His call to community for the church was a reflection of His experience in heaven. He was, by modeling and initiating spiritual community, welcoming people into the "dance" that had its origins before the foundation of the earth. The thought of such an encounter with the divine should send people running to community with anticipation and hope.

The words and works of Jesus Christ call Christians to form communities of love and support where the Holy Spirit is free to bring Kingdom realities into their lives. He told followers to gather in groups of two or more, promising to meet them in power and delight (Matt. 18:20). His upper room "new" commandment was to love one another, assuring His followers that nothing would identify them as His more than that level of commitment and relationship (John 13:34, 35). The New Testament authors certainly picked up that theme, sharing over fifty "one another" admonitions in their writings, each admonishing believers to come together in intimate support and embrace.

Paul went so far as to teach that the church, the gathering of the called, was the body of Christ present in the world today (1 Cor. 12:27). And like a body, unity is foundational to health and effectiveness (Eph. 4:3-6). The book of Acts gives us a clear picture of that shared life and unity in the second chapter, where Luke writes:

> They devoted themselves to the apostles' teaching, and to the fellowship, to the breaking of bread and prayer. Everyone was filled with awe, and many wonders and miraculous signs were done by the apostles. All believers were together and had everything in common. Selling their possessions and goods, they gave to anyone as he had need. Every day they continued to meet together in the temple courts. They broke bread in their homes and ate together with glad and sincere hearts, praising God and enjoying the favor of all the people. And the Lord added to their number daily those who were being saved. (Acts 2:42-47)

This passage provides more than a picture of Christian life two thousand years ago. It is a doorway thrown open to the caregiver, an invitation to experience spiritual community. It is not a casual word spoken to the mildly interested, but a clarion call to all who want to live as Jesus lived, and who desire to serve the broken as Jesus served.

The Characteristics of Healthy Community

Earlier I mentioned that being part of a group of Christians does not necessarily qualify as being part of a spiritual community. I am not saying that such gatherings, be they Bible studies, fellowship groups or even small churches, are unimportant. The Christian experience is multi-dimensional in size, makeup and function, with every experience of togetherness holding incredible potential for personal growth. But the focus here is upon the critical importance of having a small group of fellow pilgrims who are committed to connecting with a caregiver at ever deepening levels of relationship, where she can be known, believed in, called forth and enjoyed.

There are several essential elements of such a shared experience that serve as the blueprint for time spent together. The first of these characteristics is an uncompromising commitment to the centrality of Jesus Christ. It is His presence as Lord and Lover that marks a group as Christian and intimate. This means that time spent in worship and adoration is critical to spiritual community, as well as consistent contemplation and reflection upon His teachings and admonitions contained in scripture. The Holy Spirit must be a welcomed part of each meeting, where He is free to draw the participants into the presence of Christ, strengthening them to live as He lived. Group members are encouraged to seek Jesus with all their hearts and allow a spark of love for the Lord to grow into a mighty flame.

Jesus is the treasure that people should encourage one another to sell all to receive, the pearl of great price to be sought at any cost (Matt. 13:44-46). Seeking to integrate a relationship with Jesus into all of life, participants in spiritual community should encourage an openness to share how personal stories interact with Christ's story. Christ-centeredness also means that participants humbly point to Jesus as the object of faith, the subject of personal passions, and the model by which they step out into life and ministry. The continual prayer of the people gathered would be, " Jesus, consume us in you." This characteristic is faithful to the intent of the upward journey. Jesus is to be the center toward which all move for intimacy, transformation and the Spirit's empowerment to serve others as a wounded healer. The spiritual community that transforms is the spiritual community that looks to Christ with longing love and positions itself for His presence above all else.

Second, a spiritual community is full of grace. The gospel of Jesus Christ is about good news and God's wonderful grace. The redeeming message of Jesus Christ is one of acceptance, forgiveness, and lavish love, all made possible through faith in Him. By accepting Christ, people are welcomed into God's family as His children, full heirs of incredible blessings that one could never earn or deserve. The nature of that experience of gracious love births a response of humble submission and consecrated obedience, both of which are empowered by the Holy Spirit. Grace transforms and nurtures spiritual growth and emotional well being.

Some Christian communities seem to be driven by rules and to focus more on sin than redemption. People are often presented with a list of behaviors that are essential to acceptance. They are measured by their performance, and fear disqualification if it is discovered that they do not measure up. Such an atmosphere leads to hiding and pretense and seldom, if ever, invites the true joy that is to be evident in God's eternal family. People will eventually move away from such a community, fearing rejection and condemnation.

Phillip Yancey recounted the following story in his book, *What's So Amazing About Grace?*: "A prostitute came to me in desperate straits, homeless and unable to buy food for her two-year-old daughter...I asked if she ever thought of going to church for help. 'Church' she cried. 'Why would I ever go there? I was already feeling terrible about myself. They'd make me feel worse.'"[6]

The spiritual community that transforms is characterized by grace, not law. Practically this means that there is a non-judgmental spirit in the group, accepting, affirming, and loving. The group seeks to delight in one another as an incarnational experience of God's unconditional love. Grace means being patient as a person struggles to let go of what is bad in his life and seeks to embrace the good. It involves seeing beneath the way a person behaves to the wonderful gift of God she is deep inside. Grace consistently calls forth the potential that lies within another, all the while accepting the person where he is. The spiritual community committed to grace becomes a place of incredible nurture, which encourages growth more than rules ever could.

Third, a spiritual community should be a place of open love and caring. When a caregiver is hurting, what would she like to receive from a small group of men and women committed to her well being? I believe she wants to be heard, understood and supported. She would need to experience acceptance, healthy touch and verbal reminders of being loved. The caregiver would most likely be thankful to receive deep prayer, as well as practical help in day-to-day tasks that may be too much for her at the time. These responses from a spiritual community are critically important to the caregiver's journey, allowing her to feel safe in a demanding and often pain-filled world. And given the nature of counseling and caregiving, a community of people who express love and care is a gift that will bless the caregiver in exciting and rewarding ways.

I am part of a community that works to show love, especially in times that are trying and difficult. On one occasion I was particularly drained from several weeks of heavy work. Not only was I tired, I was battling a feeling of being overwhelmed. Sensing that, the members of my group went out of their way to offer encouragement, words of affirmation, and love. One member made some of my favorite cookies, another bought me a special CD, and a third treated me to an afternoon of golf. While the issues I was facing did not demand great sacrifice on their part, their love and care assured me that if the future held the painfully unknown, they would be there. That is a great comfort and hope, enabling me to step into tomorrow with a confidence that I will be loved, not matter what.

Finally, a spiritual community looks outside of itself to the needs of others. This week I had a conversation with my colleague, Dr. Bill Myers. He is a New Testament scholar as well as a respected pastor in the African-American community. We were talking about the importance of balance in the Christian life. The needs of the world are great, and people who are effective at serving the broken could stay busy day and night. In the African-American community that is often the case. Pastors who work among the poor find themselves under-resourced and overworked. It is critical that God's servants take time for spiritual and emotional self-care, the very theme of these first three chapters.

At the same time, it is important that the spiritual community not be so internally focused that it fails to reach out and help others. A small group of people easily becomes ingrown, so concerned to care for one another that it loses a sense of the broader mission. When this happens it becomes far too easy to lose perspective and begin to think that the mission of life is simply a self-centered pleasure seeking, rather than moving out to change the world from a place of internal well being. Being careful to serve beyond the spiritual community is an antidote for that tendency. The spiritual community must look for opportunities to help others, be that financial support for global concerns, regular intercession for people and ministries in the area, or practical service for local needs. I am convinced such actions fulfill the "Blessed to be a blessing" covenant of scripture, unleashing the power of the Spirit to and through the group (Gen. 12:3, 4).

Invariably, when talking about spiritual community, people tell me that they want to be part of such a group, but do not know how to make it happen. Three simple suggestions provide a starting point. First, if a caregiver is already in a group, but it does not have the vision for the type of experience described here, she should prayerfully look for the opportunity to talk to the group members about the possibility of shifting the focus. In most cases, when people understand the concept, they want to move forward to see it happen in their own group. Prayer and patience will be foundational to that shift.

If that is not possible, the caregiver should prayerfully look for a group to join that already has such a vision for shared life. It may well be beyond her present church experience. She should ask the Lord to guide her to the place where the disciplines of spiritual community are practiced and valued. Or finally, the caregiver can determine to start such a group herself. I have done this at the last two places we have lived. The strategy is really quite simple: do what Jesus did. Go to prayer, possibly for a long season, asking the Lord to bring the people your way who would be part of a spiritual community. The caregiver would do well to allow His leading to direct her movements, timing, and approach. When she thinks she knows whom to contact, she should share her vision and then ask people to pray about participating. She may find that some people will serve the broken like she does, while others come from a different vocational background. Again, clarity of vision and time will be essential to the growth of the community. The journey will be exciting and become a place of incredible nurture and spiritual life.

Spiritual Direction

Before concluding this discussion of the outward journey, I want to share a few thoughts about spiritual direction. The term should not be intimidating, for it points to a wonderful experience of accountability and growth within the Christian community. The practice is centuries old in Roman Catholicism, and has been finding its way to the Protestant tradition in more recent years. Interest in this spiritual discipline has grown to the point that many seminaries, including the one where I teach, have entire departments and programs dedicated to this practice.

Spiritual direction is simply the process of helping another person recognize the activity of God in his or her life and respond appropriately. Much emphasis is traditionally given to what one must "do" to grow in Christ. However, scripture teaches that God is even more at work in a person's spiritual development than he or she is, committed to completing an individual's transformation through Jesus Christ (Phil. 1:6, and 1 Thess. 5:23, 24). Every day, through every moment and circumstance, God is present to shape and nurture the caregiver in Jesus.

Spiritual direction involves entering a special relationship with a mature believer who will help the caregiver discern and respond to what God is doing. Many Christians are so busy that they do not see the movement of God in the events of their own lives. They have lost attentiveness to and awareness of His presence and work, and as a result fail to cooperate with what the Lord is doing. That is tragic, for the wonder of the Kingdom is the commitment God has made to invest in a person's spiritual growth every day. God uses the people who come the caregiver's way, the circumstances he faces, and the deep desires God has placed within his life. The moments that come, be they good or bad, happy or sad, are pregnant with God's presence. A spiritual director serves as a kind of midwife, helping the caregiver say yes to spiritual growth through the circumstances and situations of life.

Imagine that a caregiver is facing a difficult time with a person who has come for help. The person is seldom on time, often fails to do the work assigned between sessions and generally responds to insight with resistant arrogance. If the caregiver were to talk about this matter with co-workers, they would advise him to identify a pathway of care that will break down her defenses, allowing the caregiver to move into the wounded areas of her life. Professionally, that is sound advice.

However, meeting with a spiritual director would define a much different approach. Following a season of prayer, the spiritual director would ask the caregiver a series of questions about this situation. The questions would vary, but may include any of the following. "Where do you sense God at work through this relationship? What is He doing in you? How are you responding to what He is doing and why? How should you be responding? When you wait before the Lord about this relationship, what do you hear Him saying to you? Is He silent when you pray about this? If so, what might that mean?

The role of a spiritual director is not problem solver, but rather a voice calling the caregiver to find God in everything that comes his way. Both what the caregiver does in spiritual disciplines, and what God does through the events of daily life are the substance of spiritual growth. The spiritual director helps the caregiver recognize and respond to God in the present moment, encourages him in the contemplative disciplines and serves as an accountability partner. The spiritual director helps the caregiver keep Christ central and prays for the caregiver's continued empowerment in the Holy Spirit. The spiritual director will encourage the caregiver to be faithful to his own journey toward spiritual and emotional well-being. A spiritual director essentially ministers as a wounded healer to the wounded healer.

Several formats for spiritual direction are available to the caregiver. More and more people today are being trained and certified to function as spiritual directors as a formalized ministry. A relationship with someone like that would be more structured, with an appointed time, possible financial responsibility and for a specified period. I have experienced such spiritual direction and it was a key tool in my own spiritual development. However, this is not the only way to receive direction. It can be of great help simply to find a mature believer whom the caregiver admires and respects and ask him or her to function in essentially the same way. The sessions will probably be less formal and the relationship far more mutual than authoritative. But, if the person understands the concept of direction, the experience can be life transforming. I have that type of relationship with a person now, and appreciate the Lord's movement through her life to mine.

A spiritual director needs to be a believer who is faithfully on the journey to spiritual and emotional well-being. He should be discerning, personally attentive and aware of God's movement in and through the circumstances of daily life. The effective director is humbly aware of his own frailty, as well as the empowering grace of the Lord Jesus. It is best if a spiritual director has a healthy understanding of the contemplative lifestyle, able to model a prayerful response to the activity of God. He should move forward with patience and gentleness, yet be secure enough in Christ to confront unhealthy behavior when necessary. Most of all, a spiritual director is a person clearly committed to the presence of Christ as both Lord and Lover, and able to point the caregiver to that same priority and passion.

The caregiver's interest in inner healing prayer ministries is reason enough to seriously consider spiritual direction as a personal discipline. Broken people need to be served by men and women who know more than the most recently developed techniques. They need to receive help from people who are experiencing the Lord Jesus in their own daily lives, and who are being attentive to their own spiritual and emotional needs. The centerpiece of inner healing prayer is the ability to help people invite Christ into the pain-filled past. The caregiver's ability to know and recognize Jesus in the sacrament of the present moment is prerequisite to that ministry. A spiritual director will help the caregiver grow in discernment and awareness by pointing him to God's activity in the circumstances of daily life. Spiritual direction is a special ministry among God's people, a part of the unique relationship the caregiver is able to have with brothers and sisters who also call themselves Christian.

John Donne long ago said that "no man is an island." This is especially true of the called-out and called-together community known as the people of Jesus Christ. As a Christian the caregiver is to be a connected part of an integrated gathering of believers who are committed to Christ, devoted to one another and committed to reconciling the broken to their Heavenly Father. The caregiver's outward journey is, in truth, a non-negotiable responsibility that must be taken seriously. It is a commitment the caregiver cannot afford not to make, for his own well-being and that of the broken people he intends to serve. The caregiver should evaluate his commitment to and experience of spiritual community, and position himself for this incredible privilege of "one another" life.

Notes

1. Larry Crabb, *Connecting: A Radical New Vision* (Nashville, TN: Word, 1997), xvii.

2. Terry Wardle, *Draw Close to the Fire: Finding God in the Darkness* (Grand Rapids, MI: Chosen, 1998), 158.

3. Larry Crabb, *The Safest Place on Earth* (Nashville, TN: Word, 1999), 22.

4. Crabb, *Connecting: A Radical New Vision* (Nashville, TN: Word, 1997), 44.

5. Clark Pinnock, *Flame of Love: A Theology of the Holy Spirit* (Downers Grove, IL: InterVarsity, 1996), 42, 43.

6. Phillip Yancey, *What's So Amazing About Grace* (Grand Rapids, MI: Zondervan, 1997), 11.

For Further Reading

The Safest Place on Earth, by Larry Crabb
Connecting: A Radical New Vision, by Larry Crabb
Community 101, by Gilbert Bilezikian
Spiritual Mentoring, by Keith Anderson and Randy Reese
The Sacrament of the Present Moment, by Jean-Pierre de Caussade

Four

The Ministry of the Holy Spirit

I have met a host of Christian leaders who are desperate for more of God's transforming presence in their ministries. I have also spoken to many laypeople who are tired of all the talk, hungry for an experience of Christ that satisfies the deepest hunger within their lives. These good people are not saying that they do not appreciate the regular diet of sermons and Bible studies set before them. They are simply saying that it is not enough. They want to be brought into the presence of the One who loves them as they have never been loved and who can change them beyond any changes they can make on their own.

I am not suggesting that talking with hurting people or teaching about Christian living is unimportant. Understanding the foundational practices and principles of the faith is critical to the Christian life. But we must move beyond mere human words to the experienced presence of the Living Christ. Paul spoke to this in his second letter to the church at Corinth:

> When I came to you, brothers, I did not come with eloquence or superior wisdom as I proclaimed to you the testimony about God. For I resolved to know nothing while I was with you except Jesus Christ and him crucified. I came to you in

weakness and fear, and with much trembling. My message and
my preaching were not with persuasive words, but with a
demonstration of the Spirit's power, so that your faith might
not rest on men's wisdom, but on God's power. (2 Cor. 2:1-5)

Here is a clear word from Paul that words are not enough. He was
not saying that they were unimportant. But he was teaching the
Corinthians that people are not persuaded to follow Christ because of
eloquence or superior wisdom, but by the demonstration of God's
power through the Holy Spirit. Men and women believed the gospel
because they experienced it as powerful, as well as true. When a person saw that the Holy Spirit could turn hating people into lovers,
angry men and women into tender servants of God, weak people into
courageous followers of Christ, they were compelled to believe. When
the sick were comforted and cured, and the emotionally broken freed
from bondage, men and women were convinced that the message of
Christ was real. The Spirit's power, not mere words, changed lives and
attracted the broken. Paul reemphasized this point when he wrote,
"The kingdom of God is not a matter of talk, but of power" (1 Cor.
4:20). He believed that the Holy Spirit was to be "an experienced and
living reality" in the lives and ministries of Christian people, not just a
doctrine to be taught but marginalized in the community of believers.[1]

I often meet people frustrated by the absence of *mysterium
tremendum*, the sense of God's dynamic presence among His people. I am convinced that this "soul hunger" is legitimate and placed
within us by the Lord himself. People want more and the Lord Jesus
wants them to experience more. After all, He promised that His followers would have "streams of living water " flowing from within
(John 7:38), signifying the presence and power of the Holy Spirit.

The desire to experience His presence and power should be
accepted as a foundational element of the Christian life. For centuries,
the mystical component of faith was valued, seen as part of the balance necessary to loving God with all one's heart, mind, soul and
strength. It is essential that we stop marginalizing the Holy Spirit in our
lives and ministries, opening up to the only power that can truly
changes lives.

My seminary education was heavily influenced by the Enlightenment. The basis of the educational philosophy was the belief that

right thinking would lead to right faith. It was highly cognitive, emphasizing eloquence and superior wisdom, equipping pastors to rightly divide the truth. It was assumed that the more information and techniques I had, the greater effectiveness I would experience in ministry. Emphasis upon the person and work of the Holy Spirit, beyond a doctrinal position, was missing. No one seemed concerned to help me experience more of the Holy Spirit or grow to recognize His leading. As a result, I was sent forth into the local church to do sound biblical teaching and preaching without an experienced understanding of the true power behind the gospel of Christ.

I learned very quickly that information alone could not satisfy the deepest hunger of the human soul, nor could it bring about the kind of personal renewal needed in my life and in the lives of the people I was called to serve. There just had to be more than principles and doctrines, rules and laws for living. I needed to experience the power that raised Christ from the dead or my ministry would amount to little more than eloquent yet powerless talk. By God's good grace, I came to experience the ministry of the Holy Spirit on a level that was far beyond a textbook discussion. God's Spirit came in, bringing a flood of living water that totally changed my paradigm of ministry. He taught me that the ministry that revolutionizes lives flows from Him. I continue to learn that it is not mere words, but the presence of the Spirit that transforms. Any hope I have for effectively serving the Lord, whether teaching or counseling, must be securely rooted in the living reality of the Holy Spirit who is active in my life. And I believe that what is true of me is equally true of every person.

The ministry of inner healing depends upon the Holy Spirit freely moving into and through the caregiver's life. The caregiver will sit across from people who are hurting in ways words cannot describe. They will feel loneliness that suffocates, fear that drives them into hiding and deep emotional pain from wounds that they do not speak of to anyone. Precious souls will be locked in destructive bondages, enslaved by powers far too strong for them to break. Many will be on the verge of losing hope, if not over that chasm already. Some will be so angry with God that they want to lash out, while others have gone beyond that to believing that He is just not there. Are words and techniques really enough to significantly help them? Or could it be that these dear people need to encounter the power of God in a

way that renews, cleanses and heals their lives? Inner healing is
founded on the belief that the Holy Spirit can and will move through
the caregiver to affect profound change in people.

The Holy Spirit and Jesus

Each time I read the gospel accounts of Jesus and his ministry I am
overwhelmed. Consider the profound impact of Jesus upon broken
people. In story after story deeply hurting people, often shunned and
rejected by others, turn to Him and experience acceptance, healing,
and new life. The honor role of these precious saints includes people
like the Samaritan woman, who tried to kill her pain by moving in and
out of destructive relationships; the Gaderene demoniac, who was
trapped in self abuse and deep-seated personal contempt; Zaccheus,
who had traded away membership in the Jewish community for
money and power; the woman caught in adultery, who tried to find
acceptance by giving away her very soul; and Mary Magdalene, who
lived in bondage to evil powers that she could not defeat alone. Jesus
entered and not one person was ever again the same. They were not
just helped; they were transformed. Jesus touched them with divine,
miraculous power, leaving them all with a deep sense of gratitude,
spiritual hunger, and willingness to follow Him the rest of their lives.

These people are but a few of those recounted in Scripture who
encountered Christ and found their worlds turned upside down. Jesus
brought transformation and healing to all who would receive him, all
the while announcing that the kingdom of God had broken into a
dark and dying world. The signs and wonders he performed pointed
to this kingdom, proof positive that God was full of love and compassion for the lost and hurting.

How was Jesus able to work such transformation in the lives of so
many broken people? One might be tempted to answer that He did
all this because He was God. Certainly Jesus is God, a full member of
the divine Trinity. But according to Paul, Jesus set aside the glory and
power He knew before the incarnation in order to walk this world as
we walk (Phil. 2). Therefore, what He accomplished here in His ministry was not based on His divinity, but instead on the power of the
Holy Spirit moving though Him. He had an intimate relationship with
the Holy Spirit and was empowered to minister life and healing to the
broken and sick.

Consider what scripture teaches about Jesus and the Holy Spirit. Jesus was conceived of the Holy Spirit (Luke 1:35), credentialed by the Holy Spirit at His baptism (Luke 3:21,22), full of the Holy Spirit as He left the Jordan River (Luke 4:1), led by the Holy Spirit into the wilderness (Luke 4:1), and returned to Galilee in the power of the Holy Spirit (Luke 4:14). Scripture tells "how God anointed Jesus of Nazareth with the Holy Spirit and power, and how he went around doing good and healing all who were under the power of the devil, because God was with him" (Acts 10:38).

Jesus regularly pointed to the ministry of the Holy Spirit, admonishing His followers to be filled as He was filled. Jesus said that believers were to have streams of living water flowing within, which John identified as a reference to the Holy Spirit (John 7). Jesus encouraged His followers to pray for an infilling of the Holy Spirit (Luke 11:13), promising that the Spirit would come to them as the Spirit of Truth (John 16:13) and as an abiding Counselor (John 14:26). At one of His first appearances after the resurrection Jesus breathed on the disciples, saying, "Receive the Holy Spirit" (John 20:22). And at the ascension Jesus promised the disciples that they would be baptized with the Holy Spirit, and told them to do nothing until that outpouring occurred (Acts 1:1-8).

Jesus not only moved in the presence and power of the Holy Spirit Himself, but He intended His followers to do the same. He once commented that "The Spirit gives life: the flesh counts for nothing" (John 6:63). Jesus was clear that any ministry focusing on giving life to the dying would be a ministry where the Holy Spirit was free to work. And even a cursory reading of Acts would verify that claim. The disciples did wait, prayerfully. And on Pentecost, the Holy Spirit fell upon them in power, transforming a small band of frightened followers into a mighty force for the Kingdom. The Holy Spirit empowered them to preach the gospel with conviction, release those who were captives to evil, bring healing to the sick and work amazing signs and wonders. Through the Holy Spirit, their ministries saw dead people raised to life and pretentious people fall dead in their tracks. They received incredible spiritual gifts, which became channels of the Holy Spirit's presence and power.

One thing is certain, the first-century church was an exciting place. Average, everyday men and women were filled with the Holy Spirit, and were turning the world upside down. What began as a small sect in Jerusalem grew in just a few years to a mighty movement impacting the very center of the world's greatest empire, Rome. This band of misfits ministered as the very body of Christ, bringing a no-nonsense ministry that left transformed people in its wake. Their lives were filled with a power that threatened every social structure, resulting in systematic persecution and martyrdom. Yet they kept going forward, preaching, teaching and healing in the name of Jesus, all by the power of the Holy Spirit.

The words boring or irrelevant or ineffective were never used to describe life and ministry in the first century church. And neither should those descriptions fit any church or ministry today. The Spirit that raised Jesus from the dead dwells in each believer and is working across the world to transform people, setting them free to experience Kingdom righteousness, peace and joy. He is moving through everyday men and women who have opened to His presence and power and offered their lives as channels of Kingdom power. Anyone who has experienced the movement of the Holy Spirit knows that He brings a quality of ministry that is "naturally supernatural," leaving them praying for even more of His presence and power. Calvin Miller said it best: "Heady inebriation this: Spirit intoxication. It is a glorious addiction. If we but take one sip, we pneumaholics must have more of the Pneuma!"[2]

Keeping Balance

Whenever I share thoughts on the ministry of the Holy Spirit I see a wide range of reactions. At one end of the spectrum are people who are recklessly enthusiastic, ready to move forward without caution or good judgment. They seem so hungry for an experience of the supernatural that they suspend both discernment and common sense. They seem to see an invitation to life in the Spirit as some sort of "spiritual high," and can hardly wait for their own personal "fix." This attitude is dangerous, to say the least.

At the other end of the spectrum are people who are quite fearful, resistant to taking even the slightest step forward for fear of wild excess and extremes. It seems that somewhere they were exposed either to great warnings regarding the work of the Spirit or past experiences that left them terribly charisphobic. The very mention of an "experiential" component of Christian life raises red flags, and the impulse to run becomes strong. This desire to control the Christian experience can box out the Holy Spirit, leaving a person with a form of godliness that is absent of power.

The key to a healthy spiritual life is balance, and I want to share four admonitions that will help the caregiver stay centered in the Christian life. First, the caregiver should always remember that the ministry of the Holy Spirit lifts up Jesus Christ. John's gospel records Jesus' own words on the matter. When teaching His disciples about the Holy Spirit, he said, "But when he, the Spirit of truth, comes, he will speak only what he hears, and he will tell you what is yet to come. He will bring glory to me, by taking from what is mine, and making it known to you" (John 16:13, 14). Here are two key aspects of the Holy Spirit's ministry: He will bring glory to Jesus, and what He teaches will be consistent with the words of Christ. Practically this means that a person can recognize the true work of the Spirit in a caregiver's life or ministry by the degree to which Jesus Christ becomes central.

People who move in the Spirit grow to love Jesus more and more, with Christ becoming the ruling principle and passion of their lives. Any other focus or emphasis, regardless of how supernatural it may be, is not consistent with the ministry of the Holy Spirit. If people begin to point to anything as more important than Jesus, be it spiritual gifts or manifestations or experiences, they are out of balance and out of line with the true work of the Holy Spirit. When the Holy Spirit is allowed to move freely, Jesus is lifted higher and higher.

Second, the caregiver's spirituality must be tethered to the word of God. I have met more than a few people who have set aside God's word to allow spiritual experiences to become their rule of faith and practice. That is dangerous and can lead to disastrous extremes. The Holy Spirit will always move in ways consistent with scripture. God's word has a great deal to say about the person and work of the Holy Spirit. Careful study of God's word regarding the Holy Spirit will reap a tremendous harvest, and will serve as both an invitation to new life and as guardrails along the path. Stray from scripture in matters of faith and practice, and heartache awaits.

The ministry of the Holy Spirit might take the caregiver far outside his or her own comfort zone. I have often commented to people that He can at times be a most uncomfortable Comforter. Any notion that the Holy Spirit will always move in safe, predictable patterns is ill-founded. He is the Fire of God and there can be times when He will burn quite hot. Remember the tongues of fire in Acts 2? The word tame is certainly not a synonym for the Holy Spirit. But regardless of the intensity of His presence or the mysteriousness of His ways, the Holy Spirit will move consistently with God's Holy Word. Therefore, a caregiver should be encouraged to keep that word before him at all times on the journey to spiritual health and well being.

Third, the caregiver must stay connected to other Christians who are committed to the ministry of the Holy Spirit. As we saw in the previous chapter, connection to community in all matters of Christian experience is an essential. Isolation can easily lead to imbalance and eccentricity. The life of faith is designed to be a shared experience, and this is especially exciting when the Holy Spirit is free to work in the spiritual community. Spiritual community enables the caregiver to discern the Spirit's leading, exercise spiritual gifts, hold people accountable and maintain biblical integrity and balance. Furthermore, the tendencies to excess and extremes will be held in check when the caregiver is joined in community. The caregiver can experience the glory, exuberance, passion and love of the pneumatic element of faith in community. When he does, he will find that the presence of the Holy Spirit will only increase in his own life and ministry.

Finally, the caregiver should maintain a balance between technical insights and abilities from the behavioral sciences and the work of the Holy Spirit in care-giving ministries. More than once I have encountered people who believe that one must abandon academic disciplines in order to move more freely in the power of the Holy Spirit. In some circles education is even suspect as a barrier to spiritually sensitive ministries. I would agree that the behavioral sciences must never become the master of the counseling moment. However, they can be wonderful tools that the Holy Spirit can and does use when the caregiver is helping a hurting person. Some of the most gifted and powerful servants of the Lord I know are sound academicians who, filled with the Holy Spirit, minister in a naturally supernatural way.

It is neither necessary nor biblically proper for a caregiver to set aside her mind to be a better channel of the Spirit's presence and power. The Lord created the caregiver with a capacity to learn and grow in sensitivities and understandings germane to her ministry. When she offers those to the Holy Spirit, He will guide the caregiver to use those skills and abilities effectively. She will discover a wonderful symbiotic relationship with the Holy Spirit, where the caregiver's abilities and His power cooperate to set people free in the strong name of Jesus Christ. By daily recognizing and surrendering to His presence, the caregiver will be enabled to move beyond her own limitations to minister in ways that are clearly touched by Kingdom power. Holding to this, as well as the three other admonitions for balance, will position the caregiver for life-giving encounters with God's good, Holy Spirit.

The Holy Spirit and the Caregiver

Wonderful and exciting things are taking place because of the ministry of the Holy Spirit. Knowing and understanding basic scriptural truths about the Spirit's ministry can position a caregiver to recognize the Spirit's work and cooperate with Him in a way that will transform her and her caregiving. And the first of several such realities is the fact that the Spirit that raised Jesus Christ from the dead lives inside the Christian caregiver.

The Indwelling Holy Spirit

One night a well known religious leader secretly came to Jesus (John 3:1-21). His name was Nicodemus, and he held an important position on the Jewish ruling council. He was a Pharisee, influential, wealthy, and devout in his obedience to the law. To have been seen talking with Jesus was unacceptable, so Nicodemus came to Jesus during the night.

He called Jesus Rabbi, which showed his respect, and then confessed that the miracles Christ had done convinced him that Jesus was sent from God. Jesus said, "I tell you the truth, no one can see the kingdom of God unless he is born again" (John 3:3). Nicodemus was puzzled by this remark, thinking that Jesus meant that a person had to somehow re-enter the womb to be born a second time (John 3:4). Jesus replied:

> I tell you the truth, no one can enter the kingdom of God unless he is born of water and the Spirit. Flesh gives birth to flesh, but the Spirit gives birth to spirit. You should not be surprised at my saying, 'You must be born again.' The wind blows wherever it pleases. You hear its sound, but you cannot tell where it comes from or where it is going. So it is with everyone born of the Spirit. (John 3:5-8)

Jesus was telling Nicodemus, and all Christians as well, that being a religious person was not enough to be received into God's Kingdom. Membership would come to those who were born of the Holy Spirit. That rebirth, available to all who believe in Jesus, is a transaction of the Holy Spirit and marks a person as a child of God and heir to all His promises.

Centuries before Jesus met with Nicodemus, the prophet Ezekiel spoke of a day when God would put a new heart and a new spirit within his people. Ezekiel then promised a time when God would place the Holy Spirit within people in order to help them walk in faithfulness and holiness before God (Ezek. 36:24-30). When Jesus spoke to Nicodemus about being born again, He was referring to that promise and telling him that it was now being fulfilled through His ministry. To be a part of God's kingdom, people need to experience a spiritual birth, which can be accomplished through the ministry of the Holy Spirit. An important part of that new birth is the promised indwelling of the Holy Spirit in the lives of all who believe.

What does all this mean for the Christian caregiver? Simply stated, it means that the Spirit that raised Jesus Christ from the dead dwells within her. The Holy Spirit, who is a full member of the Trinity, who hovered over the waters at creation, who empowered Moses and David and Isaiah and Peter and Paul and Jesus, who descended at the Lord's baptism, fell with power at Pentecost and transformed the first-century church into world changers, is present in the Christian caregiver. The "Flame of Love," as Saint John of the Cross called Him, is living inside her body. He is within her spirit, working moment by moment to accomplish God's purposes for her life, anxious for her to cooperate with all He is wanting to do in and through her.

The Holy Spirit is not with the caregiver merely in principle. He is present as an experienced reality. He is not an unidentifiable entity that is elusively attached to the caregiver. The Holy Spirit is God, present within her from the very moment she accepted Jesus Christ.

When the heart is fully surrendered to Him, He becomes its personal, permanent, indwelling Guest....Our whole spiritual life is nourished and cherished by His love and care: all we are, and have, and may become in our Christian life, is due to His personal indwelling and His faithful love and infinite grace.[3]

"Personal, permanent, indwelling guest!" These words are trans-formational in their implication for the caregiver's life and ministry. The Holy Spirit's presence is so much more than functional. He is there to be in relationship with the caregiver, wanting to have her turn to Him as she would her closest friend. The Holy Spirit is the living person of God, abiding within the caregiver's spirit to love, nourish, and care for her as no one else could.

For many Christians the magnificent reality of the Holy Spirit's presence is little more than a doctrinal principle. Whether that is a result of ignorance or fear, there is a continued neglect of the Holy Spirit, who is "too evident to deny and impossible to justify."[4] It is as if the Lord of the universe were living right within their own house, yet they never take time to talk with Him, seek His advice, receive His help, or commune with Him as an intimate friend. It is not that they do not know that He is present. But they are not sure why He is there or how to properly relate to Him. This loss leaves a person living the Christian life by his or her own power rather than by the power of the Holy Spirit.

When teaching about the indwelling presence of the Holy Spirit I encourage people to do a simple little exercise. First, I ask them to look at their own abdomen and say, "Holy Spirit, You are in there." I realize that He indwells far more than our stomachs, but by doing this people are able to connect with the reality of the Holy Spirit's presence within their own bodies. For many this little exercise helps them move from seeing the Spirit as "out there" to being an ever-present reality right inside their own lives. Second, I encourage them to pray a simple prayer, asking the Holy Spirit to help them to recognize His presence throughout their day and surrender to His leading and guidance. Through this prayer they are asking for help in developing eyes to see and ears to hear.

Third, I lead them in a prayer of repentance, asking forgiveness for living much of the Christian life in their own strength and not according to His power and authority. Most people are thrilled to pray this, for to them the Christian life seems like a lot of personal effort, empowered more by will than by living water flowing from deep within their lives. Though a simple step, the caregiver may find these prayers as a starting place for her own deepening relationship with the Holy Spirit. From here, she can move to understand and experience more of what the Holy Spirit does related to personal growth and development into a mature Christian servant.

The Holy Spirit Works to Help the Caregiver Grow

Jesus could not have been more clear about the role of the Holy Spirit in our lives. He referred to the Holy Spirit as the Paraclete, which has various meanings, including comforter, counselor and helper. And when speaking to His followers, Jesus told them that, ultimately, it was good for Him to go away, because only in His leaving would the Helper come to be with them (John 16:5-11). Jesus went on to tell the disciples that the Holy Spirit would lead them into all truth and speak to them of all that the Father wanted them to know (John 16:12-15). Jesus was so emphatic about the importance of the Holy Spirit's arrival, that He told the apostles to wait in Jerusalem for the Spirit to come, not beginning public ministries until they experienced His mighty outpouring (Acts 1:4, 5).

These early followers of Christ soon experienced the coming of the Helper and knew that His presence was the key to personal growth and effectiveness in ministry. More precisely, they grew to understand that it was the presence of the Holy Spirit that helped them resist temptation, respond to people in ways consistent with the character of Jesus, discern the will of God, and face dark powers with confidence and supernatural strength. The thought of marginalizing the Holy Spirit or moving out in ministry without His direction and power was ludicrous to them. They knew that His help was a joyful necessity, always to be recognized and appreciated, never to be assumed or taken for granted.

A.W. Tozer has been called the prophet of the twentieth century. He was an eloquent writer, powerful preacher and a man passionate for God. He knew the importance of personal sensitivity to the presence and ministry of the Holy Spirit, and repeatedly called Christian leaders to greater dependence upon the Flame of Love. On one occasion, when speaking on the Holy Spirit, he commented that if the Holy Spirit were to withdraw from the local church, 95 percent of what was happening there would not change. I believe he said this to emphasize the point that far too much Christian living and ministry is done by human will power and not by the Spirit's leading and empowerment. I often consider this warning from Tozer, and repeatedly repent from a tendency to move out on my own, assuming that the Holy Spirit will willingly be a part of all my plans and actions. Instead, He desires that I surrender, every moment of every day, to His activity in and through my life. This seems to be a far more effective and efficient way to progress, as well as an invitation to an ever-growing relationship with Him.

Maturing in faith and growing in effectiveness are not activities the caregiver can do alone. To try is both exhausting and frustrating. It is also unnecessary, because the Lord Jesus has given the Holy Spirit. Scripture not only calls Him the Paraclete (helper, counselor, comforter), but also points to Him as the Spirit of Truth (John 16:13), the One who will teach the caregiver (John 14:26), and the One who will fill the caregiver with joy, peace and hope (Rom. 15:13). Paul said that the Holy Spirit was given to help the person in weakness, search his heart, and intercede for him in accordance with the will of God (Rom. 8:26, 27). He also wrote that the Holy Spirit was present to transform believers into the likeness of Jesus Christ with ever increasing glory (2 Cor. 3:17).

These promises should stir excitement in us. The caregiver is indwelt by the same Spirit that moved so mightily through Jesus and the apostles. The caregiver is not alone in the Christian life, nor is he obliged to help broken people out of his own strength or cleverness. This unbelievable truth should make the caregiver hungry for a deeper relationship with the Holy Spirit, knowing that He is, every moment of every day, present within to help. Is it any wonder that scripture teaches Christians not to resist (Acts 7:51) or grieve (Eph. 4:30) or quench the fire of the Holy Spirit (1 Thess. 5:19)? He is the promised first fruit of all that is ours in Christ Jesus (Eph. 1:13); we need never walk in barrenness again.

Spiritual Gifts

One of the most exciting and freeing teachings of scripture centers around the subject of spiritual gifts. The Apostle Paul wrote about spiritual gifts in three different letters: Romans 12, 1 Corinthians 12 and Ephesians 4. He introduced this theme in his letter to Corinth by calling the church, "the body of Christ." Using the human body as a metaphorical image, he said that each Christian serves as a part of that body, united with other believers, submitting to the head, Jesus Christ.

Paul said that the Holy Spirit determines the part a person plays in the body of Christ, and He does this by distributing spiritual gifts to people.

> Now to each one the manifestation of the Spirit is given for the common good. To one there is given through the Spirit the message of wisdom, to another the message of knowledge by means of the same Spirit, to another faith by the same Spirit, to another the gifts of healing by that one Spirit, to another miraculous powers, to another prophecy, to another distinguishing between spirits, to another tongues, and to still another the interpretation of tongues. All these are the work of one and the same Spirit, and he gives them to each one, just as he determines. (1 Cor. 12:7-11)

A simple summary of this passage indicates that the Holy Spirit gives spiritual gifts to people, to be used for the benefit and good of the body of Christ, and that the gifts are diverse and distributed according to the will of God, through the Holy Spirit.

Paul's list is not exhaustive but representative of the many gifts the Holy Spirit gives to people. Romans 12 lists additional gifts, such as service, teaching, exhortation, giving, leadership and mercy. In Ephesians 4, Paul identifies evangelist, apostle and pastor as spiritual gifts. It can also be argued that references to hospitality and intercessory prayer are also legitimate examples of spiritual gifts. I am convinced that there may be spiritual gifts not even identified in scripture.

The simple fact is that all Christians are gifted by the Holy Spirit. It benefits people to find out which gift or gifts they may have and then grow to use them in ministry. After all, a spiritual gift is a channel through which the grace of God flows in a special way, producing Kingdom growth and change in people's lives. It is a wonderful endowment of supernatural power that enables people to help others find freedom and joy in Jesus Christ.

Practically speaking, the caregiver would do well to consider the many gifts listed in scripture and ask the Holy Spirit to help identify her particular gift or gifts. This search is helped when the caregiver considers her passions, where she is already experiencing fruitfulness in ministry, and what other people see as gifted areas in her life. This may take some time in prayer and examination, but what an exciting treasure hunt it will be!

The caregiver is a special servant of the Lord, with a critically important ministry to broken people, who has the Holy Spirit of the living God dwelling deep within her life. He is there to help her, moment by moment, draw close to Himself for intimacy and empowerment. In addition to that marvelous reality, He has placed spiritual gifts within the caregiver as special channels of Kingdom power, graced abilities to move in a naturally supernatural ministry in this world. As a Christian this reality is the caregiver's privileged inheritance. But there is still more. There is the invitation to be filled with Him as the caregiver has never been filled before.

Be Filled with the Spirit

In some ways all that I have said thus far is an introduction to the main point of this section. The caregiver cannot expect to experience regularly the transforming ministry of the Holy Spirit moving through him to the broken unless and until he is filled with the Holy Spirit. This is not merely my opinion, nor is it simply another way to say what is already true of all people who are indwelt by the Holy Spirit upon their conversion. Being filled with the Holy is an express command of God's word and a level of spiritual experience that is both identifiable and transforming. While it certainly builds upon the abiding presence of the Spirit in a person's life, it moves beyond, bringing a new level of power, intimacy and effectiveness following the experience of infilling. Countless Christians have testified to the reality of this experience and the radical difference it makes in a person's life and ministry.

Dwight L. Moody was a powerful Christian statesman of the nineteenth century, who preached the gospel of Christ to hundreds of thousands of people. He is regarded as a leading evangelistic figure in the history of the church. Many factors contributed to Moody's amazing rise from shoe salesman to a world impacting Christian leader. Not the least of these was the power of the Holy Spirit present in His life and ministry.

R.A. Torrey, a contemporary of Moody, said that in the early days of his ministry Moody had great zeal but little power.[5] However, two Free Methodist women, Auntie Cook and Mrs. Snow, began to pray regularly for D. L. Moody. Once, upon asking about the content of their prayers, Moody discovered that they were asking God to fill him with spiritual power. He was so moved by their response that he joined them in prayer right then and there, asking the Lord for the very power they had been requesting.

Soon after, Moody was in New York preparing to leave for England. While walking on Wall Street, the power of the Holy Spirit ambushed him. Moody was so overwhelmed by the Spirit that he hurried to a friend's home and stayed alone for hours in the presence of the Lord. He later reported that the Spirit so filled his soul that he had to ask God to withhold His hand or else He would die on the spot. His subsequent ministry in England was marked by God's power, and the church there experienced an incredible visitation of the Lord.

What happened to Moody has also transformed people throughout the history of the church. The Holy Spirit has moved upon untold lives, changing ordinary people into effective servants of the Lord. If the caregiver desires, the command to be filled with the Spirit can and will become a reality. The caregiver may not travel to foreign lands, lead great revivals or win thousands to Christ. But the presence of the Holy Spirit moving in and through him will dramatically change people's lives, not the least of which will be his own.

Paul makes four key statements about the Holy Spirit in his letter to the church at Ephesus. First, he assures believers that they have received the Holy Spirit as God's seal upon their lives and as a deposit of the future inheritance that awaits them (Eph. 1:13, 14). Second, Paul urges every possible effort toward keeping unity in the church body, reminding the Ephesians that there is one and the same Spirit at work in all Christians (Eph. 4:4-6). Third, Paul commands the reader not to grieve the Holy Spirit, pointing to relational sins such as anger, bitterness, rage and slander as sinful behaviors that sadden the Holy Spirit. He admonishes the Ephesians to be kind, compassionate and forgiving, attitudes that enhance the flow of the Spirit in the Christian community (Eph. 4:9-32).

Finally, Paul gives a straightforward statement regarding the ministry of the Holy Spirit. Writing about general principles of Christian living, he says: "Therefore do not be foolish, but understand what the Lord's will is. Do not get drunk with wine, which leads to debauchery. Instead be filled with the Spirit. Speak to one another with psalms, hymns and spiritual songs. Sing and make music in your heart to the Lord" (Eph.5:17-20).

John Stott believes that understanding the above passage rests upon an adequate definition of the verb "be filled." Stott lists four points regarding the verb that are most helpful to the discussion here.[6] First, he writes that it is in the imperative mood. "Be filled is not a tentative suggestion, a mild recommendation, a polite piece of advice. It is a command which comes from Christ with all the authority of one of his chosen disciples."[7] God's word is commanding the caregiver to "be filled with the Spirit." As with all the commands of God's Word, the caregiver is not free to respond in a cavalier or apathetic way. It is an imperative that points to the essential relationship the caregiver must have with the Holy Spirit to live and serve as the Lord intended.

Second, the verb "be filled" is in the plural form. Stott correctly emphasizes that all Christians are to be filled with the Holy Spirit. This is not a relationship reserved for the few, but for the whole of Christ's body, the church. This truth should create a sense of joyful, yet humble anticipation in the caregiver who is positioned by the Lord to be a recipient of this great work of the Spirit. God never intended that anyone be left out or relegated to some second-class participation in Kingdom spirituality. This infilling is for the caregiver.

Third, this verb is in the passive voice. To me, this is one of the most freeing aspects of life in the Holy Spirit. Filling is a work that He does, not something that the caregiver needs to earn, figure out or strive to accomplish. Being filled with the Holy Spirit requires that the caregiver surrender to Him and by faith receive the glorious gift being offered. Granted, there are ways that the caregiver can best position himself for that work, which I will suggest before closing this discussion. Still, the work is His, a gift of God's great grace made possible through the Lord Jesus Christ.

Finally, Stott points out that the command to "be filled" is in the present tense. It is at this point that our English language fails to relate the full meaning of this verb in the original Greek. The phrase would be translated more accurately, "Keep on being filled with the Spirit." This is a critical distinction. This work of the Holy Spirit is not something that happens to a Christian once and for all, but rather is a repeated experience. The caregiver is to open up to the fullness of the Holy Spirit over and over again. And, just as the capacity for liquid gets larger as a person grows from an infant to an adult, so the caregiver's capacity for the Spirit increases as he grows in Him. Equally, the caregiver's ability to sense His presence and discern His guidance increases the more he surrenders to Him and invites His fullness.

Some Christians believe that being filled with the Holy Spirit is a work the Lord brings to people from above, as if they were an empty pitcher and He pours the Holy Spirit into them, much as one would pour water into a pitcher. I have a much different image of being filled. When I was a boy I often went to a spring that bubbled up from the earth deep in the forest near our home. We boys would go there each spring as baseball practice began, since it was only a few hundred yards above the field where we practiced. When we would first arrive each spring it would not be running well. The debris and rocks that winter weather deposited upon the opening would keep the spring from flowing freely. But as we removed the barriers, the water would bubble up fresh and clear, flowing strong all throughout the summer heat.

I see being filled with the Holy Spirit in much the same way. The Holy Spirit is present deep within the inner places of the caregiver's soul, much as an artesian well flows deep within the earth. He is there in all His power and truth. Being filled with the Spirit means surrendering to the full flow of His presence already within the caregiver's life. The debris of sin must be cleared. If there is doubt or fear the caregiver needs to move them aside (He will help you). If the caregiver is actively sinning, he will need to repent (Jesus will lovingly forgive). If the caregiver is struggling with doubt and disbelief, he will need to be honest before the Lord (the Spirit will gently lead him to truth). As he does, the flow of the Holy Spirit will begin and the caregiver will experience the living water Jesus promised so long ago.

If the caregiver has not experienced the ongoing fullness of the Holy Spirit in his life and ministry, and if he is both awakened to the possibility and hungry to walk in His presence and power, I have a few suggestions. First, the caregiver should search scripture on the topic of the Holy Spirit. The Bible says much about the Spirit's presence and ministry, and a prayerful study of those passages will open the caregiver to Him in new and exciting ways. Second, the caregiver should read books dedicated to the ministry of the Holy Spirit. I will include several of my favorites at the end of this chapter. Third, the caregiver should find a place to talk about the Holy Spirit and His ministry. That might be a conversation with a pastor, a Bible study group or class on that subject or a spiritual director who can help the caregiver move forward in understanding and experience.

Fourth, the caregiver would do well to seek out places where Christians move in a balanced, yet observable relationship with the Holy Spirit. I find that getting close to those who are close to the Lord genuinely helps my own spiritual growth. Admittedly the caregiver may experience some initial discomfort. If he holds fast to the balancing factors I mentioned previously, he will be able to discern what God is doing in their midst.

Finally, the caregiver should pray. The Lord Jesus has invited the caregiver to ask Him for what she needs and wants. If being filled with the Holy Spirit is a new or renewed hunger in her life, she should tell the Lord in prayer. Jesus will move to answer that request, much as He promised when He told His disciples: "If you then, though you are evil, know how to give good gifts to your children, how much more will your Father in heaven give the Holy Spirit to those who ask him!" (Luke 11:13). This promise has been fulfilled in the lives of countless Christians, not only through the past centuries, but right now, in our day. It is a word of hope and promise for the caregiver as well.

Notes

1. Gordon Fee, *God's Empowering Presence: The Holy Spirit in the Letters of Paul* (Peabody, MA: Hendrickson, 1994), 1.

2. Calvin Miller, *Into the Depths of God* (Minneapolis, MN: Bethany House, 2000), 127.

3. A. B. Simpson, *The Gentle Love of the Holy Spirit* (Camp Hill, PA: Christian Publications, 1983), 30, 31.

4. A. W. Tozer, *God Tells the Man Who Cares* (Camp Hill, PA: Christian Publications, 1970), 90.

5. R. A. Torrey, *Why God Used D. L. Moody* (Chicago, IL: Moody Bible Institute, 1923).

6. John R. W. Stott, *Baptism and Fullness: The Work of the Holy Spirit Today* (Downers Grove, IL: InterVarsity, 1964), 60-63.

7. Ibid, 60.

For Further Reading

The Gentle Love of the Holy Spirit, by A. B. Simpson
By the Power of the Holy Spirit, by David Howard
Surprised by the Spirit, by Jack Deere
The Holy Spirit, by Billy Graham
God's Empowering Presence: The Holy Spirit in the Letters of Paul,
　　by Gordon Fee

Five

Listening to the Spirit

I doubt that there is a program in pastoral care or counseling anywhere in the United States that does not teach students the basic principles of listening. If a caregiver doesn't know how to hear what people are saying, she will never be able to help them. An effective caregiver listens to the words being spoken, as well as to the meanings that lie beneath the words. She must even be able to catch the messages being communicated when not even a single word is being spoken. Body language speaks volumes to the caregiver who has learned to listen with her eyes as well as her ears.

Recently I was walking by one of our own classrooms when I heard a colleague teaching on this very topic. I lingered in the hall to eavesdrop, hoping to improve my own skills. He presented several important principles, commonly accepted as foundational to effective counseling, including:

Remember that it is better to be unavailable than to be inattentive.
Adopt an open posture that communicates acceptance,
    appreciation, and interest.
Maintain appropriate eye contact.
Identify and set aside potential distractions in order to concentrate
    on what the person is saying.

Respond in ways that invite a person to further explore his or her situation.

Give the person appropriate feedback that lets him or her know that you have heard what has been said.

Listen to non-verbals, evaluating the degree to which it matches the verbal message being communicated.

Be an empathetic listener, connecting with and responding to the feelings being shared.

While such principles may be thought of as mere basics, listening skills such as these are essential to effective caregiving. A good counselor is first and foremost a good listener, and hurting people are perceptive enough to know the difference. If they know a caregiver is really and truly listening, they will begin to extend a level of trust that is foundational to the healing process.

This brings me to the matter of inner healing and a question that looms in my mind. What voices does the caregiver need to be listening for in the counseling session? The ability to listen well brings more healing than most of what will be said to a hurting person. Certainly the caregiver needs to listen for the voice of the client. The caregiver also needs to recognize her own voice, communicated by her thoughts and feelings throughout the session. She needs to be attentive to the messages the subconscious self is sending, and be able to interpret whether the message is helpful to the moment or a symptom of some unaddressed issue in her own life.

There is also the voice of the evil one speaking in many counseling sessions. That is true, and no amount of pretending otherwise will silence that voice. At one level or another evil is present in the problems people face, whether it is central to the cause of the pain, taking dark advantage of an already difficult situation, or seeking to oppose and harrass the healing process itself. Such a position should not startle a Christian caregiver, for it is entirely consistent with a biblical worldview. The caregiver needs to learn to recognize such messages and be able to respond appropriately. More will be said about that in a later chapter.

But are these all the voices that are present in a counseling session, or could there not be another? I believe there is, and it is the most important—that of the Holy Spirit. We have already established the fact that He is present and active when the caregiver positions herself to help a wounded, hurting person. It is certain that the Holy Spirit is not there as a passive observer, but rather to lead and empower the caregiver to be a channel of hope and healing. Hearing the voice of the Holy Spirit takes skills and sensitivities that are not often taught in traditional pastoral care and counseling programs. The fact that most caregivers are not equipped and apprenticed to hear His voice deafens them to the wonderful insight and direction that He offers each time they sit to help another person.

It is critical that the caregiver learn to recognize and respond to the presence of the Holy Spirit in the counseling setting. This is particularly true in the ministry of inner healing, where the caregiver serves as a bridge between a broken person and the healing power of the Holy Spirit. It is not professional insight or technique that brings change, but His presence and power touching the pain. The caregiver needs to hear the broken person's deepest cry and the direction of the Holy Spirit, often simultaneously. When, by God's grace, the caregiver is able to serve that level of connection, hope and healing will begin to flow.

Foundational to listening to the voice of the Holy Spirit is a set of presuppositions that are important to recognize. While in traditional secular counseling the caregiver is in charge, the Holy Spirit must be in control during inner healing prayer. His direction, not the caregiver's, makes the difference. People may come to a counselor to hear what the professional has to say, but transformation depends upon the voice of the Holy Spirit. The caregiver is there as His servant, wanting to perceive His leading and follow His direction for the hurting person. This is most important because the issues people bring to the inner healing moment are usually dark, crippling and complicated. Touching deep levels of pain and watching people experience healing and hope are works that flow from the presence and power of the Holy Spirit. Listening for His voice is foundational to the entire process.

A Paradigm of Power

Inner healing prayer is not a technique, but instead a partnership with the Holy Spirit. Believing that He speaks to the caregiver in many different, yet perceivable ways is essential to being fruitful in this type of ministry. This understanding is rooted in four very important truths about the work of God in the world today. First, inner healing prayer is founded on the belief that God is present in the world today. Elizabeth Barrett Browning, in a well-known poem, wrote:

> Earth is crammed with heaven
> And every common bush afire with God;
> But only he who sees takes off his shoes,
> The rest sit round it and pluck blackberries.

This simple verse captures a very important theological truth. God, who certainly transcends understanding, experience and definition, is very present in the world. His immanence must not be minimized in Christian thought. Doing that only pushes people toward deism, a belief that recognizes God as creator but sees Him as no longer present or active in the world.

Our world is crammed with His presence. As the psalmist says:

> Where can I go from your Spirit?
>> Where can I flee from your presence?
> If I go up to the heavens you are there;
>> if I make my bed in the depths, you are there.
> If I rise on the wings of the dawn
>> and settle on the far side of the sea,
> even there your hand will guide me,
>> your right hand hold me fast.
> If I say, "Surely the darkness will hide me
>> and the light become night around me,
> even the darkness will not be dark to you;
>> the night will shine like the day,
>> for the darkness is as light to you."
> (Psalm 139:7-12)

Consider the practical implications of this truth. There is not a place anywhere that God is not present. There is no night so dark, no mountain so high, and no planet so far out into space that He is not there. There is not a single moment in time that is not full of His presence. Believing that should impact the way the caregiver lives and change the way he approaches caregiving.

Inner healing prayer begins with the belief that God is present in every moment of the caregiver's ministry. Whether light or dark, joyful or sad, pain-free or pain-filled, each second is full of Him. The effective caregiver is the one who recognizes this truth. She seeks to find God in the moment, daily practicing His presence in order to experience His guidance and His embrace, as expressed above in Psalm 139, and to live in adoration and devotion.

Second, inner healing is grounded in the belief that God still interacts with the world, in both ordinary and extraordinary ways. From Genesis to Revelation, scripture contains story after story of God's supernatural intervention in the daily life of human beings. Dreams, visions, angelic visitations, audible voices, inaudible inspirations, and supernatural encounters with God are recorded as verifiable acts within human history. They are there as testimony to God's redemptive purposes through ancient history, all pointing to and flowing from the full intention of God's heart as revealed in Jesus Christ. These stories are taught and preached across the globe with the purpose of helping people learn important theological principles about the God we serve. Yet, in the first years of my Christian experience, I was taught that all such acts of God ended centuries ago when the last book of the Bible was received from God. As a young Christian, I was lead to believe that God no longer engaged our world as He did in Bible times. Thus I neither considered the possibility of encountering Him in such a way nor learning to have eyes to see or ears to hear.

David Pytches, former Episcopalian Bishop of Chile, Bolivia and Peru, wrote a book entitled *Does God Still Speak Today?* This short book contains numerous true stories of men and women, many of whom are still alive, who encountered God's intervention in their lives in unexpected yet biblically faithful ways. In the introduction Pytches speaks to the issue of encounters with God today and our various responses to the notion.

There seems to be two ways of responding to these issues. The first is to set out to prove that God is not doing this today, and to refute or ignore the evidence of what it is claimed God is doing. This was the tactic of the Jewish critics in the case of the man born blind. He himself believed that Jesus had healed him: the Jews did not. Their major problem proved to be the man's own testimony: "One thing I do know: I was blind but now can see!" (John 9:25)

The other option is to accept that God does communicate directly with people today and to look for ways of being open to it and of evaluating, weighing and testing it. In our rational Protestant tradition (and here we are in no way seeking to undermine the precious intellectual gift that God has given us) there is really very little received wisdom on how to do this....[1]

I find his advice helpful and encouraging. First, as a Christian, I should carefully examine the biblical and the historical data regarding God's intervention into life today. I have wrestled with the implications of this and concluded that yes, He does act. Second, I need to grow in my sensitivity to hearing His voice, be that a gentle whisper within my own mind or a supernatural encounter that sends me to my face before Him. Third, I must learn to be discerning, able to recognize the difference between a genuine encounter with God and a counterfeit. And finally, I should not expect or demand that God come to me in any particular way, but instead recognize and receive His message and help however it comes.

A third foundational consideration directly impacts the ministry of inner healing prayer. God still uses His people as instruments of supernatural power, particularly through, but not limited to, spiritual gifts. He not only directly touches people, but moves through indirect means, using a Christian man or woman as a channel of the Holy Spirit's presence and power. Once again, scripture affirms that God does use ordinary people to do extraordinary things. In the New Testament alone one will find many people empowered by the Holy Spirit to minister in a naturally supernatural way. Individuals like Paul, Peter, John and James were filled with the Holy Spirit, experienced God's intervention into daily life, were used to heal the hurting and set captives free in Jesus' name. Though human, they were touched by the Divine and gifted to reach out to hurting people on His behalf.

What is true of them is equally true of Christians today. God can speak through the caregiver, deliver people through her, heal through her, and direct lost people toward wholeness through her. Such ministries are not reserved for spiritual superstars, but are given by God's grace to everyday people who are filled with the Holy Spirit. There was a day when I myself questioned such a notion. But the experience and encouragement of more experienced friends and colleagues helped open me to the idea. Since then the Lord has ambushed me with His presence and power, and frankly, there is no turning back.

While this issue is certainly controversial in some settings, it is foundational to the ministry of helping a hurting person find healing in Christ. It is impossible to have an effective ministry of inner healing without believing that God will use an ordinary Christian to supernaturally touch a hurting person. He may work through a caregiver to bring a direct word of instruction, direction, or move through her to set a person free from demonic bondage. He may empower the caregiver to speak blessing or physical healing over a broken person sitting before her. Experiencing this begins with believing that it can and does happen. It then moves forward by several simple, yet important practices in the caregiver's Christian life.

The fourth and final foundational consideration is a practical one. Experiencing the power and presence of the Holy Spirit in the counseling/inner healing session requires that the caregiver learns to hear and respond to His voice. I was fearful and intimidated when I first considered opening to the Lord in such a spiritually sensitive way. I felt under-equipped and in some ways wanted to turn back to the practice of just giving out good information and counsel to hurting people. Thankfully, the Lord would not allow me to stay there, encouraging me to trust His teaching and move forward with caution and care.

My friend, Judy Allison, says that moving in the power of the Spirit is similar to learning to drive a car. She told me that when she first got behind the wheel, she was both excited and intimidated. There was a steering wheel, three mirrors, three pedals to work with her feet, a gearshift, road signs, and other cars all to be considered at one time. Judy said that she was hesitant, intense and overly deliberate in everything she did. But with practice and good instruction she quickly grew to handle all those requirements at one time as well as listen to the radio, eat pizza, talk with friends and hang out the window waving to passersby. Her description is accurate and appropriate to this discussion.

Listening to the voice of the Holy Spirit takes time and practice. Initially the caregiver might experience some apprehension and discomfort. But over time he will grow to appreciate the power and effectiveness the Holy Spirit brings to his life and ministry. I want to suggest several things that will help the caregiver hear His voice for the ministry of inner healing prayer. These concepts are a brief beginning, but like the foundation of a house, they serve as a good base for building an effective ministry.

Spend time learning from a gifted mentor. I participate in a ministry that trains people to minister inner healing prayer in the presence and power of the Holy Spirit. Following initial instruction, newcomers are paired with experienced and gifted caregivers who are recognized as moving in the Spirit. They then pray together for people, with the more experienced person leading. Over time, the newcomer is given specific responsibilities in the prayer sessions, followed by debriefing, encouragement and advice from the mentor. Eventually, the newcomer leads most of the session with the mentor supporting. Such an experience serves to guide and encourage people in a healthy approach to praying for the hurting. At first, the people receiving prayer are fellow class members. Later, individuals come to our seminars specifically to receive healing prayer for a stated problem.

Finding a mentor in such matters is important, yet not always easy. It may involve attending special seminar classes on inner healing that include lab time as part of the instruction. The seminars I hold are designed with this need in mind, and I find that the hours in directed prayer experiences integrate the principles of inner healing as little else. If that option is impossible, the caregiver should seek a colleague who has an interest in inner healing, and through reading and experimentation grow together. They can share ideas about what they are learning, and hold each other accountable to move prayerfully and with caution. Finally, an excellent way to learn about inner healing prayer is for the caregiver to receive it. Many of the most effective caregivers I know have been on their own inner healing journeys.

Initially practice hearing from the Lord in a safe and secure environment. As a pastor I would never allow a person to exercise his or her gifts in a large, public gathering before they had done so consistently and maturely in a small group setting. A person had to be part of a spiritual community where they could "experiment" with his or her newfound gifts and graces. There are reasons for this. Initially, there is a certain degree of trial and error in hearing the voice of the Lord. It takes time, and the help of other mature believers, to discern the difference between a prophetic dream and too much pizza before bed.

Learning in a small group setting saves unnecessary embarrassment, as well as the tragedy of immature statements being imposed upon hurting and vulnerable people.

I insist that phrases like, "Thus saith the Lord," be eliminated from a person's approach regardless of how experienced he or she may be. The caregiver may "suggest" that the Lord is inspiring the thoughts or direction being given. This allows for the person receiving prayer personally to confirm or reject the idea. Such safeguards do not restrict the work of the Holy Spirit, but provide guardrails that keep everyone on the direct path toward help and healing. Moving in the power of the Holy Spirit demands a certain level of maturity, confirmed by several responsible people. Before being released in a formalized ministry, the caregiver's gifting and readiness should be recognized and affirmed by those who know him best.

Daily practice the presence of God. This point was mentioned earlier, but demands repeating. Moving effectively in a ministry of inner healing requires sensitivity to the presence and direction of the Holy Spirit in the caregiving session. It is not enough to wait until the caregiver is sitting across from a hurting person before seeking God's direction. Every person that I know who is effective in inner healing prayer spends a great deal of time alone with the Lord. They do this for three reasons. First, they love Him and want to be drawn into His embrace on a regular basis. Second, they do this because it is a great place of refilling. Serving broken people is draining, and time with God becomes an oasis of refreshment and rest. Third, they spend time listening for God in the quiet place, so they will be able to recognize His voice when things are far more active and intense.

I was once speaking at a church close to an air force base. One night I had the opportunity to have dinner with several test pilots. They told me of an experiment that was being considered to help pilots recognize mechanical trouble when in an intense air battle. The pilots commented that one's senses could become so intensely focused in battle that a pilot would often fail to notice the gages registering a problem. It was suggested that a voice be used to identify the problem, as well as a gage. And, according to these pilots, the voice needed to be that of a very familiar person such as the pilot's son or daughter. When in battle and trouble was detected, the voice of the pilot's daughter would say, "Daddy, your engine is on fire." The

theory was that such a familiar and dear voice would be immediately recognized and heeded regardless of the level of battle. So with
ministry. To hear the voice of the Holy Spirit in the time of battle, the
caregiver must spend time listening to that voice in the intimate and
quiet moments of life.

Spend time in concentrated prayer, seeking God's help to recognize the Spirit's voice during the inner healing session. Jesus said,
"And I will do whatever you ask in my name, so that the Son may
bring glory to the Father. You may ask me for anything in my name,
and I will do it" (John 14:13). He invited disciples to trust His willingness to answer prayer, understanding that asking in His name
means seeking those things consistent with His nature and character.
And, given His many teachings on the Holy Spirit, the request to better recognize and respond to the Spirit's voice will be granted, in the
Lord's time and way. Continual, persevering prayer regarding this
matter is vitally important to a ministry of inner healing prayer.

The Apostle Paul encouraged the Philippians "in everything, by
prayer and petition, with thanksgiving, to present your requests to
God" (Phil. 4:6). If the caregiver believes the promise that the Holy
Spirit will speak to him when helping the hurting, he should ask for
help in recognizing and discerning His voice. The caregiver should
make his request to the Father in joyful expectation, anticipating that
He will help him grow in this area. The Lord has graciously met me
in this way. I still seek more, for I am confident that my capacity to
counsel by the Holy Spirit can increase every time I open to His presence in my life and ministry.

Fill up with God's word so that the Spirit can bring particular scriptures to mind in the inner healing prayer session. The Apostle Paul
admonished Christians to take up the sword of the Spirit, "which is the
word of God" (Eph. 6:17). This principle is very important for the person ministering through inner healing prayer. Paul says that the sword
the Holy Spirit will use is the word of God. Often in inner healing
prayer the Holy Spirit will bring a specific scripture to the caregiver's
mind either to direct ministry or speak to the person being helped.
When He does, the scripture will be both relevant and powerful for
helping and healing the broken person the caregiver is serving.

I cannot encourage a caregiver enough to familiarize himself with
scripture. God's word is "living and active...sharper than any double-

edged sword" (Heb. 4:12). Isaiah said that the word that proceeds from God's mouth will never return empty, but will instead accomplish the purpose for which He sent it (Isa. 55:11). Of all that is spoken in an inner healing prayer session, nothing is as powerful as a specific scripture delivered by the direction and empowerment of the Holy Spirit. When an open, vulnerable heart receives a word fitly spoken, transformation takes place.

Knowing scripture helps the caregiver recognize the Holy Spirit's voice at two levels. First, by reading and understanding God's word, the caregiver is better able to discern whether a thought or message is consistent with the teachings of the Lord. The caregiver must remember that there will be more than one voice speaking in the time of inner healing prayer. The message a caregiver receives from God will be consistent with what He has said in the scriptures. Second, having scripture hidden in the caregiver's heart is like carrying a surgical kit full of precision instruments. The Spirit is able to use those tools effectively and efficiently because the caregiver has made them available to Him. God's word is living and active. When the caregiver hides God's word in his heart, he invites that dynamic power and vitality into his life.

Learn to surrender the mind to the Spirit. I must confess to learning this most important principle in a very trying time in my life. For several years following a dark night of the soul I battled anxiety, often on a moment by moment basis. After a long day of such tension I would fall into bed thoroughly exhausted, only to arise the next day to greet the same terrorizing fate. One day, after a time of crying out to the Lord, I read Romans 8:6, "the mind controlled by the flesh is death, but the mind controlled by the Spirit is life and peace." I realized that a large part of my battle was in the mind, which I was obviously allowing to be controlled by my own weak and fear-ridden flesh. Seeing that Paul said that the mind controlled by the Spirit brought life and peace, I began repeatedly a very simple prayer, "Holy Spirit, please take over my thinking." For months I wore a rubber band on my wrist to remind me of that prayer, which I spoke on hundreds of occasions.

At first this exercise was packed with my own emotion, but I did not recognize any response from the Spirit. But one day I prayed those words and actually felt Him stir within my own spirit. It was momentary, yet real and empowering. I soon felt Him move within me each time I sought His control over my thoughts. I became much more sensitive to His presence through this journey, and have grown today to utter that prayer whenever I am in need of His help. I can testify that in most cases He touches me in a very real and powerful way. Knowing that He is there and also willing to help in counseling session is a source of great comfort and hope to me. I have learned that I can be ever asking for help and ever attentive to the moment at one and the same time.

How Does the Holy Spirit Speak?

I feel compelled to speak a word about the Holy Spirit and diversity (1 Cor. 12:4-6). There are a variety of ways the Holy Spirit speaks, different levels of His power that the caregiver may encounter, and diverse ways people will experience His leading. Said more simply, a caregiver should not anticipate the Holy Spirit speaking to him in the same way, or intensity, or frequency that he may in another person. The caregiver's own personality, gifts, and level of maturity must be factored into the equation, as well as the sovereignty of the Spirit's work. A caregiver may find that the Spirit most often speaks to him in one way, while a colleague may find a different manifestation of the Spirit's leading as most dominant in her experience. This diversity is an exciting part of the rich ministry the Spirit brings to the practice of inner healing. What follows is an introductory discussion of six particular ways the Spirit may speak to a caregiver during inner healing prayer. Understanding and being open to each will impact a caregiver in many positive and exciting ways.

Insight and Inspiration

Imagine that the caregiver enters a session after seeking the Lord in prayer and worship. A broken person is now seated before her, and the time has come to seek the presence and power of the Holy Spirit before beginning. The caregiver opens the time with prayer, inviting the Lord to lead and direct every aspect of the time together. The caregiver asks the Holy Spirit to sanctify her mind and imagination. The caregiver presents herself to the Holy Spirit—mind, emotions, body and spirit—as a potential instrument of His healing touch. From this moment forward, whether listening, giving counsel, or engaging in inner healing prayer, the caregiver endeavors to stay focused on the person before her and the Holy Spirit at one and the same time.

Jesus told His followers that the Holy Spirit would lead them into all truth (John 16:13). He also said that they should not worry about what they would say when serving Him, for the Spirit would guide them (Luke 12:11, 12). As the caregiver grows in sensitivity he will find that the Spirit will fulfill that promise each time he serves the Lord. He will do this by inspiring the caregiver's thoughts, giving insights, specific scriptures relevant to the situation, and particular ideas and concepts that the caregiver has learned in the past. He will enable the caregiver to perceive destructive patterns more quickly, and reach deeper levels of diagnosis sooner and with greater consistency. When the Holy Spirit does this, He moves through the caregiver's own faculties. The caregiver will not hear a distinct voice, either internally or externally, but instead recognize a heightened level of awareness in the moment.

When the Holy Spirit inspires and illumines, the caregiver is able to minister with a naturally supernatural degree of insight, attentiveness and effectiveness. In such ministry the caregiver should surrender to Him and humbly recognize what is happening. Any temptation to take all the credit should be resisted. Instead, the caregiver should rejoice in the Lord's faithfulness and minister with a grateful heart. The Holy Spirit seems to love moving through Christ's followers in this way, enabling them to be instruments of incredible help and healing in Jesus' name.

Words of Knowledge

The Apostle Paul identified the word of knowledge as a distinct work of the Holy Spirit (1 Cor. 12:8). It is a spiritual gift that enables a person to know certain pieces of information without receiving them from the one being helped. It is undoubtedly a supernatural work, and given to caregivers for the sole purpose of moving an individual forward toward health and wholeness. As with other aspects of the Spirit's gifting discussed in this section, a caregiver should not operate in this gifting unless and until it has been clearly confirmed as a way the Holy Spirit moves through her. Even then patience and caution must be exercised.

A clear biblical example of this work of the Holy Spirit can be found in the story of Jesus and the woman at the well (John 4:1-26).

The Samaritan woman was amazed at the knowledge Jesus had about her past, even though He had never met her before. This supernatural insight opened the woman to the deeper ministry that the Lord wanted to bring to her. This was not a unique feature of the ministry of Jesus. People through the centuries have also experienced this gifting. For some it has been an occasional occurrence, while for others a consistent way the Spirit speaks to and through them for the well being of others.

A colleague of mine recently shared a story that perfectly illustrates this point. A new client came to see him, complaining of increasing levels of anxiety and panic. As the person shared the symptoms of this problem, my friend suddenly had a clear impression that this person was involved in an extra-marital affair. Having surrendered the thought to the Lord, he found that the impression only intensified. He began to ask sensitive questions that eventually moved the client to talking about her marriage. Under the guidance of the Spirit, he was able to specifically, yet sensitively ask the client if that in fact was the case. She not only confirmed that it was, but mentioned that she had had no intention of sharing that information voluntarily. My colleague told her of the impression he had received from the Lord. This opened the way to deep repentance, healing, and reconciliation. I asked my friend if he would have gone that direction on his own, and he told me no.

Great caution must be exercised. When the caregiver gets such an impression, she should do several things. First, the caregiver should pray and ask the Holy Spirit to clarify what she is sensing. If it is Him, that assurance will be given. If it is just an impression of the caregiver's own making, or interference from the evil one, prayer will reveal it. Second, the caregiver should watch and wait. I have learned that not everything revealed to me is to be shared with the person I am helping. Sometimes it is insight that will better help me serve the person. At other times, it leads me to ask questions that will help the individual self-disclose. There are times when I feel the Lord directing me to hold what I have received, waiting for more information to be revealed later by Him, or for a better time to approach the issue. The word of knowledge is not given so that the caregiver can appear super-spiritual in someone's eyes. It is a work of the Holy Spirit given for help and healing, and should be used only in that way. Only when the caregiver senses direct instructions from the

Spirit should she directly share, and even then she should do it gently and sensitively.

Discernment

A story in Acts 16 illustrates the way the Holy Spirit speaks to Christians through discernment. Paul and Silas were preaching the gospel of Christ in Philippi and being followed by a girl who kept shouting, "These men are servants of the Most High God, who are telling you the way to be saved" (Acts 16:17). Notice, what she was saying was absolutely true. First impressions might lead one to conclude that she was there to work for the Lord. However, Paul discerned that she was filled with an evil spirit, and at one point he turned to the girl and commanded the demon to leave her in the name of Jesus. It did, and as a result the owners of the slave girl incited a riot that led to the arrest of Paul and Silas.

Jesus told His followers that many would come in His name, and would work signs and wonders, all the while being evil (Matt. 24:24). He admonished believers to be watchful. He also sent the Holy Spirit to help Christians discern what lies beneath a persons actions and words. Discernment is the voice of the Holy Spirit warning a person to be careful about what he is seeing and hearing. That voice may come through a stirring in the caregiver's spirit, an impression or thought, or a conscious awareness that something is not right.

Whenever the caregiver begins to think or sense that things are not as they appear to be, she should take it as a signal to be watchful, allowing the Spirit to speak more about the situation. Scripture affirms the possibility that darkness will disguise itself as light. Knowing when this is true will help the caregiver and the person being served embrace all that God is doing, while resisting and rejecting anything that comes from the evil one, regardless of how deceptive or concealed that work may be. Discernment is a critical gift of grace that the Holy Spirit gives to those who serve the broken. I recommend asking for this gift regularly. Growing in it will reap great benefits in the ministry of inner healing prayer.

Intercessory Pain and Feelings

I must admit that I at first questioned the notion that the Holy Spirit would speak through physical and emotional feelings. But by watching

and weighing I soon saw fruit that was pointing to a root firmly planted in Jesus Christ. Through this unusual manifestation of the Spirit, I saw
that Christ was glorified and people were healed, a standard of evalua-
tion that will always open my heart to what is beyond my comfort level
and experience.

My first exposure to this came while attending Fuller Theological
Seminary in a course on spiritual renewal. The professor invited John
Wimber to speak to our class. He spoke of an understanding of the
Holy Spirit and healing that was well beyond my experience. At one
point he went beyond teaching to actually ministering to people in the
class. He called out specific needs, and in several cases even identified
the person who struggled with the issue. Invariably the individuals
confirmed what Wimber was saying. He then prayed for healing and
the Spirit's infilling.

Afterward I asked Wimber how he perceived these needs. He said
that one way was through an intercessory identification with the person.
He would feel what they were dealing with, and then move forward to
pray for the person. I was both amazed by his answer and challenged.
If I suddenly felt anxiety or fear or back pain while ministering, I always
assumed it was my own, even if nothing in the circumstance seemed to
initiate the feelings. I never considered the possibility that it was an
intercessory identification. Nor did I have a format for understanding the
difference. Yet, over time and with strong accountability, I have experienced this avenue of guidance in my ministry.

If the caregiver is sitting with a hurting person and begins to experience a degree of emotional stirring or physical pain, he should not
rule out the possibility that it is intercessory. The Holy Spirit may be
speaking to the caregiver about the person he is helping, identifying
a specific issue he or she is facing. The caregiver should pray, asking
the Lord if it is a signal coming from Him. If the feeling or pain is one
the caregiver often struggles with, it is most likely his own. But if it is
unusual, or if he has difficulty linking it to a personal issue, he should
seek more of the Spirit's guidance and direction.

The caregiver might ask the person if he or she is struggling with
the particular issue the caregiver is sensing. If the counselee is not, the
caregiver should not impose the feeling upon him or her. But if the person is experiencing what the caregiver mentions, the caregiver should
consider that the phenomenon is the Spirit's guidance. He might be

pointing to a specific issue where He wants to touch the hurting person the caregiver is serving.

A Sanctified Imagination

When God called Jeremiah, He touched His imagination and made it a place where He would speak to him. As the Lord was laying out the nature of Jeremiah's ministry, He asks this question: "What do you see, Jeremiah?" The prophet responds, "I see a branch of an almond tree." Immediately God asks Jeremiah a second time, "What do you see?" This time Jeremiah says, "I see a boiling pot tilting away from the north" (Jer. 1:11-13). Each of these images contained a distinct and important message to the Israelite people. God could have simply spoken straightforwardly and directly to Jeremiah. But He chose to use symbols and visions. Throughout scripture God often used the imaginative and symbolic as means of communication.

Has God stopped doing this in our day? My experience, and that of many people I know and have studied, lead me to say no. If the caregiver is open and aware, the Holy Spirit will present pictures in his mind that will help him perceive what God is doing in the lives of the people He loves. A colleague and good friend was recently ministering to a woman who was experiencing deep levels of despair and self-hatred. In one session my friend saw while praying the following scene in his mind. A celebration was taking place in a large, ornate ballroom. Many people were there, as well as Jesus, and the woman who was sitting before my friend. At one point, Jesus went over to the woman, took her by the hand, and invited her to dance with Him. Everyone there stood and joyfully watched as the Lord tenderly danced across the ballroom floor, focused solely upon the one held within His loving embrace.

My colleague waited prayerfully, and at an appropriate time spoke to the client of the Lord's great love and tenderness towards her, concepts consistent with what he saw in his mind. She seemed touched by the thought, yet not visibly moved to any great extent. After seeking the Spirit's permission, he went further to share the details of the visionary image. As he described what he saw, the woman began to weep deeply, and encountered the Lord powerfully. She later said that she always felt like an undesirable wallflower in life. The constant thought of being left out and overlooked brought a great sense of

shame and self-contempt. The image of Jesus choosing her was transformational. Words were inadequate to communicate to her, but the
image spoke with power and depth.

I am convinced that the Holy Spirit uses mental pictures and symbols to guide people toward healing and new life. But learning how to
appropriately understand and use such insights is critical. A safe environment and mentoring by mature Christians will help, as well as reading material on the subject, such as the books listed at the end of this
chapter. Several foundational guidelines will help. First, the caregiver
should ask the Lord to sanctify his imagination, offering it as an instrument of His power and healing. Second, when a picture or image does
take shape, the caregiver must wait and watch prayerfully. He should
not move quickly to share what he sees, instead patiently allowing the
Spirit to unfold the origin of the picture. Is this from Him or could it
be simply a construction of the caregiver's own imagination? When
the caregiver feels sure that the picture is of the Lord, he should seek
its meaning. Finally, the caregiver should ask the Spirit to lead in how
much and what to share with the person. Sometimes the picture will
be for the caregiver alone, to direct prayer with a person. At other
times, as in the example above, the picture can become a window to
an entirely new experience of God for the person. At all times the
caregiver must move patiently.

I also try to open the people I am helping to this ministry of the
Spirit. When having difficulty with a particular issue in prayer, I encourage them to ask the Lord to use their imagination, giving pictures and
images that will help them move forward in the process. Granted,
some people find this easier than others. But I have found it an invaluable instrument of the Spirit's work. I simply help people present their
imaginations to the Lord, and then wait patiently with them to see if
He will speak that way. I have discovered that it is even more helpful
to people when they receive such an insight, than when I do and then
tell them about it. Caregivers must remember that the setting of inner
healing is one of hope and healing. Messages from the Holy Spirit, I
have found, are not only consistent with scripture and good theology,
but are most often edifying and upbeat. If one sees or hears that which
is condemning or judgmental, he should be cautious. Jesus comes to
save and free people, not condemn.

Dreams and Inner Healing Prayer

When the Holy Spirit was poured out upon the disciples at Pentecost, Peter told the onlookers that it was the fulfillment of Joel's prophecy (Acts 2:16), which he then quoted: "And afterward, I will pour out my spirit on all people. Your sons and daughters will prophesy, your old men will dream dreams, and your young men will see visions" (Joel 2:28). Peter explained to the crowd that the phenomenon they were witnessing, tongues of fire, was the result of the Holy Spirit as Joel had predicted centuries earlier. And from that moment on, Christians have experienced His presence as a constant in their lives, with accompanying signs and wonders often present as evidence of His power. Dreams are one of those witnessing signs.

Dreams have always been listed in scripture as one way the Lord communicated with his people. The record of such encounters includes many heroes of the faith. What child has not learned of Jacob's dream of a ladder extending to heaven or Joseph dreaming of his brothers bowing before him. When Jesus was just an infant, His earthly father, Joseph, had a dream in which an angel warned him of Herod's savage plan and as a result he fled with Jesus and Mary to Egypt. But God's use of dreams did not end with Bible times. One recent example comes from Roberta Hestenes, respected educator, author and pastor. In a *Christianity Today* article, she wrote:

> Sometime in the night of May 8 this year, Pat Hornberger was awakened by a dream in which she saw an automobile accident. She was so concerned, she spent the rest of the night praying for 16 members of her church, Solana Beach (Calif.) Presbyterian, who were on a two-week long trip to Ethiopia. Two other members of the same church also woke up and were moved to pray for the team.
>
> There had, indeed, been a car accident involving the Ethiopian missions team, one that injured three people. And this accident, it turned out, became a turning point for the trip, for Solana Beach's 55-year history, and, we trust, for a little known people in East Africa, the Afar.[2]

Without apology or explanation, Dr. Hestenes, a Presbyterian pastor, speaks of a dream as a window to God's work among a lost and broken people.

Those who regularly practice inner healing prayer should consider the possibility that the Holy Spirit can and will use dreams to direct His purposes. I have experienced this means of guidance only a few times. Yet in each case what I learned through a dream opened the way to deeper and more effective ministry to a broken person.

Dreams demand mature discernment. Whether the caregiver is a regular dreamer, or only experiences dreams occasionally, it is important that she grows to understand their origin and purpose. The vast majority of dreams are reflections of a person's active unconscious. Others can be the result of eating before bed, late night movies or disturbed patterns of sleep. It is unwise and immature to assume that each and every time a person dreams it is the Lord speaking. There are occasions, however, when the message contained in a dream is rooted in the work of the Holy Spirit, speaking when the caregiver is least defended and more open to His voice. It is important that the caregiver learn more about this activity of the Lord, writing down dreams that seem to be more indicative of His voice, and prayerfully seeking their meaning. Though this form of divine guidance seems to occur less frequently, there is immense value in learning to listen when He chooses to speak in this ancient and mysterious way.

There are few places for caregivers to learn about the ministry of the Holy Spirit in and through inner healing prayer. I am not personally aware of counseling or pastoral care programs that seriously address this matter. Yet, His presence and power are dynamically important to helping broken people find freedom. The Holy Spirit is present each moment of every day, there to help the caregiver live as Christ intended, and minister with an empowerment that goes far beyond her own abilities. Learning to recognize and respond to His voice is a great privilege and serious responsibility for someone interested in the ministry of inner healing prayer.

Notes

1. David Pytches, *Does God Speak Today?* (Minneapolis, MN: Bethany House, 1989), 19.

2. Roberta Hestenes, "Meeting Noah's Other Children," *Christianity Today* 44 (No.9, 2000), 50-53.

For Further Reading

Surprised by the Voice of God, by Jack Deere
Hearing God, by Peter Lord
*Christianity with Power: Your Worldview and Your Experience of the
          Supernatural,* by Charles Kraft
When the Spirit Comes in Power, by John White
The Gift of Prophecy in New Testament Times and Today, by Wayne Grudem
Hearing God: Developing a Conversational Relationship with God, by Dallas
     Willard.

Six

Structures of Inner Healing

Imagine a scene in which a man suffering from periods of panic and anxiety walks into a room full of people and asks for help. These are not just any people, but instead gifted and trained professionals who are genuinely concerned for hurting men, women, and children. In the room there is a psychiatrist, a psychologist, a marriage and family therapist, a biblical counselor, a person skilled in inner healing prayer, a pastor, a nutritionist and, finally, a personal trainer. As the hurting individual describes the nature of his problem, each person begins to formulate a recommendation for addressing the anxiety disorder.

The man first goes to the psychiatrist to see what she has to offer. The psychiatrist talks to him about chemical imbalances and the possibility that medication will eliminate the symptoms and allow him to move freely through life with limited periods of debilitating anxiety. The psychologist speaks up and tells the man that he has had success treating anxiety disorders through cognitive-behavioral psychotherapy, which includes cognitive principles for reorienting an individual's thinking patterns and exercises for breaking established dysfunctional behavior triggers. The marriage and family therapist, trained in a systems approach to therapeutic care, asks several questions about the man's family, trying to identify the role his symptoms play in maintaining the current family system of interrelating.

Also in the room is a person who received a degree in biblical counseling at a conservative Christian college. Believing that issues like anxiety are rooted in sin, he asks the hurting man to consider the possibility that his troubles are symptomatic of being out of relationship with God. The person trained in inner healing prayer believes that God must be a part of the solution, but is far more oriented to asking the Lord to identify core wounds and then pray for the Lord's strength and healing for those wounds. The pastor, who has a more charismatic orientation, asks the man if he has ever heard of demons, suggesting that he is under attack and in need of deliverance.

All of this sounds impossible to the nutritionist, who asks about intake of sugars, caffeine, and chocolates, knowing that any one of these can bring on unusual amounts of anxiety in some people. The personal trainer, frustrated by how complex everyone is making this, assures the hurting man that a regular routine of exercise is all he needs, and begins to lay out a daily program that he believes will quickly address the issue.

For the hurting person, all the different options only add confusion and frustration to an already tense situation. To whom should the man turn for help? Which person holds the key to helping him overcome this debilitating problem? Is one approach more viable than the other? Having suffered from this very problem and having experienced as many different options as presented in this scenario, I know the answer is not easily determined. In fact, I think the response, "That depends," has more integrity than many are willing to admit. The problems that people face are often very complex—an interrelated series of issues that can be confusing to even the most experienced caregiver. Carefully diagnosing the problem and identifying all the contributing factors is essential to offering holistic care to hurting people.

The fact that caregivers are trained in such a wide variety of methodologies can be a blessing or a curse to a hurting person. When caregivers have been schooled in one dominant approach to helping people, they easily see all problems through the limited lens of their own training. Imagine that the scenario described above was just a little different. Let's imagine that, instead of walking into a room full of people, he goes to a marriage and family therapist for help. He describes the problem, which initiates a series of sessions in which the therapist examines family of origin and systems issues. The therapist, well skilled in these matters, works to identify and resolve the anxiety by addressing matters faithful to his training and school of thought. So the therapist tends to see everything as a systems problem.

Granted, there can be help in such an approach. But what if there are biological factors or chemical imbalances causing the anxiety? Could there not also be issues of caffeine intake, or work-related stress, or even spiritual factors? There very well may be, yet many specialists approach solutions only through the viewfinder of their own educational bias. This can leave very important matters unexamined and unaddressed.

I was golfing recently with a friend who works in psychiatry. He shared in passing that his daughter, in her mid twenties, had experienced a few panic attacks. I am sure he told me this because of my own struggles with the same problem. He said that he asked a colleague to see her, and was pleased that she prescribed an anti-depressant with characteristics for fighting anxiety. I certainly understand that medication might help, but could there not have been other factors that led to her problems? I believe so, which demands a more holistic approach to diagnosis and treatment. I am not saying medication is not a potential solution, but I am convinced it is not always the first or only solution to the significant emotional problems people face. For some in the psychiatric community, a fifteen-minute med-check is the scope of care needed for most of the people who struggle with emotional issues.

Let's look at the situation presented from a broader frame of reference. A man fighting anxiety enters a psychologist's office seeking help. The professional feels confident that he can significantly help the man overcome panic and anxiety. He will try to identify life stressors and reorient the gentleman's approach to problem solving, as well as help him develop skills in relaxation and behavioral modification techniques. However, the psychologist knows that there may be other contributing issues outside his area of expertise.

He asks the man to do three things: get a complete physical exam, take some standard psychological tests, and complete a life script. He wants him to get a physical examination to see if there are any unidentified medical issues that could be either initiating or contributing to the problem. A physical done by a good general practitioner can serve as a tremendous diagnostic tool in helping those who battle issues that at first glance appear to be more psycho-spiritual. He may also ask him to take some standard psychological tests, as a way of gathering additional data. And the psychologist requests that he fill out a rather extensive life script that will help him identify relevant personal background information, including relational, lifestyle and spiritual issues.[1]

All of this will be evaluated to help the hurting person attack anxiety from every reasonable angle. The psychologist may be able to see the primary causes of the problem, as well as identify other contributing factors. I am convinced that the more significant the presenting problem, the more important it is that a thorough intake be available for analysis, diagnosis and treatment planning. A good professional, like our fictitious psychologist, will treat the person as best he can, as well as refer him to other caregivers who can treat matters he feels less capable of addressing. If the patient needs medication, a psychiatrist is consulted and engaged. If there are significant spiritual issues beyond the therapist's expertise, a pastor can be brought into the picture. If diet and lifestyle are problematic, a nutritionist or trainer can be consulted. The client's problems must be looked at from the broadest view possible, and addressed as thoroughly as possible, with the primary caregiver coordinating the treatment. Narrowly focused caregiving is set aside for a more helpful and broad-based approach to problem solving.

The ministry of inner healing prayer fits into this framework of caregiving. I am convinced that there is power and healing available to deeply hurting people through inner healing prayer, and that it is a ministry of the Holy Spirit open to every responsible believer who learns to move in His presence and power. But from the very start, four truths must be understood. First, inner healing prayer is one of several tools that help hurting people; it is not the only tool. It is critically important that a person know when to move forward with inner healing, and what specific issues are best addressed by it. The remainder of this chapter will focus upon this very issue, helping the caregiver identify the structures of inner healing prayer. Here it is enough to remind the caregiver that some issues, such as biological factors that lead to medical treatment or lifestyle and nutritional matters, are not within the bounds of this approach. The caregiver must know both the limits of his own training and the complex nature of the problems people may bring his way.

Second, the caregiver must know when to refer people. The best caregivers are those who not only know where they are gifted to serve, but also where they are not. As mentioned previously, there are people who specialize in very specific methods of care. When people come to the caregiver for help and, after careful prayer and analysis, he senses that, at the very least, aspects of their problems are beyond him, the caregiver must send them to others who can help. I work in a community where there are several capable and godly doctors, counselors, psychologists and pastors. If an individual comes to me for inner healing prayer and I see that all or part of their problem is beyond me, I contact the appropriate caregivers and enlist their help. Knowing that they share the same Christian philosophical base is important to me, as well as knowing their specific strengths in psycho-spiritual care.

Third, the caregiver should consider working in partnership with one or two other caregivers who have strengths that he may not have. I seldom see an individual for inner healing prayer alone. Far more often than not I have a colleague in the session with me, offering both prayer support and specific help in the area of their expertise. Earlier I mentioned Dr. Judy Allison, a psychologist who is on the teaching faculty at Ashland Theological Seminary. She is gifted in several areas of care, particularly with regard to people struggling with personality disorders. If someone comes to me for prayer who has symptoms of that category of disorders I am quick to enlist her help in the session. Her insights enable me to be more specific in prayer, as well as facilitate greater understanding and involvement from the person receiving care. If I sense that an individual may be struggling with some level of demonization in conjunction with the deep wounds of the past, I would ask Dr. John Shultz to join in the session, trusting his experience and gifting with reference to spiritual warfare and bondage. Jesus sent his followers out to minister in groups of two. That is not a bad way to approach inner healing either, recognizing that there is strength as members of Christ join to help the lost and hurting of the world.

Fourth, the caregiver should remember that the greatest gift a hurting person can ever receive is Jesus Christ. Nothing compares to Him and the journey to His embrace is the privilege of every single believer. I am convinced that everything that comes our way, be it light or dark, easy or difficult, can become a doorway to experiencing more of Him. When a hurting person sits before the caregiver for inner healing prayer it is important to remember that there is something even more important than helping them solve problems. Granted, much of what has been said, and more yet to be said, will focus upon healing and deliverance for hurting people. I believe that is possible and important. But there is more to life than living "limp free."

The greatest treasure of life is experiencing God in the storms of life's difficulties. It is important that the caregiver does not so intently focus on solving problems that he misses helping people experience Jesus. For me, meeting the Lord while struggling with an anxiety disorder has been far more important than overcoming it, though I continue to position myself for complete healing. Through the darkness Jesus has shown Himself to be closer and more tender than I would have ever imagined. There are experiences of His love and embrace that I would never have known had I not walked this way. I am grateful to have learned that having His presence is even more vital than experiencing His healing touch.

Caregivers that singularly focus upon overcoming problems overlook the important possibility that Jesus is present to empower hurting people in the very center of the storm. Caregivers will do well to encourage people to offer their own circumstance and pain as a doorway to experiencing more of Jesus. I will say more about this later, but keep in mind that the structures of inner healing position an individual for more than healing. They enable the caregiver to help people meet Christ in deep and transforming ways. From the very first moment a hurting individual comes for help, the caregiver should offer himself as an instrument of the Holy Spirit's power. A transformational encounter with Christ should be the number one priority for the caregiver and that of the dear person seated before him. When that is true, inner healing is well on the way.

A Framework from Which to Begin

I want to approach inner healing prayer from two different, yet interrelated perspectives. First, I will share an actual account of a person who came for prayer, detailing the issues that brought her and the various components of her problem. The case is not in any way extraordinary, but it does help illustrate the many-layered nature of emotional problems. Once described, I will move on to break down the anecdote into specific structures that provide a framework for understanding and addressing the issues that had to be faced in the counseling sessions. This framework will then serve as a foundation for the ministry of inner healing to be described in the remainder of this book.

Connie had set up an appointment to consider inner healing prayer, and specifically asked that my wife, Cheryl, be there for the session. Having reviewed all the background information provided through her life script, her choice to meet with my wife and me seemed more than appropriate. She was the wife of a local pastor serving a small, yet growing charismatic fellowship. They had been married for five years and were in many ways enjoying favor both in the community and within their congregation. However, there was growing tension within her marriage and it was hard pretending that all was well when the stress was so great at home. What follows is not a session-by-session description, but instead a general overview of what happened. It is important to mention that we met with Connie weekly for almost two months.

In the initial session Connie shared that she and Dave were experiencing tensions in their relationship. She also mentioned that they had sought marriage counseling, yet saw little improvement in the situation as a result. A friend, knowing both the nature of the problems they faced and the power of inner healing, suggested that she see us. Somewhat hesitantly she agreed, and arrived with the blessings of her husband. It seemed strange at first to consider talking to Connie alone about the tensions in her marriage, but time soon bore out the importance of this arrangement.

After the usual introductory comments and opening prayer, Cheryl and I encouraged Connie to share the reasons for her coming. Nervously, and with obvious embarrassment, she began to unfold her story. She told us about her love for Dave and how blessed she felt to have him in her life. Connie told us that she had met Dave when she, a newly converted college student, began to attend the church where he was youth pastor. In time they fell in love and were married, both believing that the Lord had lead them to each other. They were equally committed to a life in ministry and were excited to move forward into the future together.

On many levels Connie and Dave had a solid Christian marriage. They loved the Lord deeply and dearly loved each other. But in one area of the relationship there was ongoing tension and disappointment: sexual intimacy. Since their first night together, sex was a source of disagreement and at times heated discussions. Initially, from Connie's perspective, Dave wanted sexual intimacy far more than she was willing to engage. For a long time she pointed to Dave as the one with the problem, and wanted him to just back off. However, after much discussion Connie was willing to admit that she was actually resistant to sexual intimacy and seldom found it enjoyable. They had tried marriage counseling, but Connie said that it did not help her feelings about the matter. Assuring us that it was not about loving Dave, she said that she struggled with physical intimacy and would get tense and upset whenever Dave approached her, regardless of how gentle he might be.

Connie told us that she had employed various methods to keep Dave at a distance. However, in time she would be aware of his desire to connect and Connie would either suffer through the moment or simply say no to Dave. His disappointment and unhappiness were then equally hard for Connie to face, only adding to her already shameful feelings about this part of their marriage. The resulting distance between them affected many other aspects of their life and ministry.

We encouraged Connie to talk about her feelings. Obviously there was significant inner turmoil about the entire situation. We sought to draw her out at two levels: her feelings about the tensions in her relationship with Dave, and the feelings she struggled with whenever he approached her sexually. Talking about feelings was not easy for Connie, but it held the key to deeper issues related to her sexual difficulties. Eventually she shared a combination of emotions regarding her relationship with Dave. On the one hand, she felt relief whenever he would back away. Somehow she felt safer and better about herself whenever they did not engage in sexual activity. But she also felt sadness over Dave's unhappiness, as well as deep disappointment that her sexual issues were harming their relationship.

The harder issue for Connie was talking about the feelings that would arise whenever Dave approached her sexually. Convinced that feelings tell us a great deal about what we believe about our world, our God and ourselves, I pressed on to help Connie articulate these very painful feelings. Connie talked about fear, shame and guilt more than any other emotions when it came to their sexual relationship. We began to see the path that we needed to walk with her. But it was important to be patient and very supportive through the process, so we waited for the Lord to help Connie open up about what was yet hidden beneath her struggle with Dave.

The Holy Spirit enabled us to take the journey to a deeper level, as He revealed serious distortions that fueled the emotional upheaval in Connie's life. Pointedly, yet sensitively, I asked Connie to share what she believed to be true of herself with reference to her sexual relationship with Dave. In time she revealed that she felt dirty and sinful to be engaged sexually, and that she always felt worthless after the two of them were intimate. We talked with her about God's design for marriage and His invitation for a husband and wife to delight in sexual intimacy, but it never made the trip from her head to heart. Something significant was blocking the path for Connie. While we could surmise various possibilities, it was critical that we allow her to open up on her own timetable. For now she was touching deep pain as she admitted that sexual activity simply amplified her own sense of unworthiness and shame. Prayerful support and love would open the door, enabling us to see beneath the distortions to the wounds that lay deeper still.

At one point, with a combination of courage and great hesitation, Connie spoke of what she had told no one before, not even Dave. Listening in prayer, the painful truth long hidden in darkness began to come forth. Connie shared that she had not been allowed to date until she was sixteen years old, a restriction placed upon her by loving parents who wanted to protect her as much as possible. Sadly, they were not able to shield her from another's ugly sin, for on her very first date she was raped. Connie had gone out with a friend of her older sister and his aggressive behavior caused Connie to experience sexuality in a way God never intended. Full of fear, rage and shame, she told her sister about what happened. While sympathetic, her sister demanded that Connie say nothing, which only made things worse for her. For Connie the silence only amplified the voices crying out within her own wounded soul.

This event caused Connie indescribable pain, which she chose to address in a most unfortunate way. She became sexually promiscuous for several years, on the one hand believing she had little reason left to be chaste, and on the other trying to convince herself that she was not undesirable. By moving in and out of short-term sexual relationships she was seeking a level of acceptance from others that she was unable to offer herself. Every time she engaged in relationships of this type she came away feeling used, unworthy, and covered with guilt and shame. The cycle would then repeat itself as she tried to kill the pain with yet another unhealthy relationship.

Upon finding Christ, Connie experienced a level of strength she had not had before. She began to attend church, learn about Christian principles of living, and grew in her newfound faith. In time she met Dave and was delighted by his interest, a sign, she believed, that God had forgiven her and was pouring out special blessings through Dave. She did not talk to Dave about the past, partly out of embarrassment and to some degree because she feared he would reject her. Connie simply buried it all as deeply as she could, believing that everything would be fine once she and Dave were united in Christ. Marriage followed a season of dating, and the rest of the story is already laid before us. What Connie hoped was far in the past was very much affecting the present. The time had now come to invite the Lord into every pain-filled part of her life.

I share this story to illustrate the basic structures of inner healing. It is not my intention at this point to describe the process of healing prayer, but rather to identify the different layers of pain and wounding that must be addressed along the path to well being. Connie's story provides a narrative that follows the structures of healing. By recognizing the pattern, the caregiver will be able to apply the same structure when helping the hurting people who will turn to her for help. The diagram below illustrates the first part of the pattern, showing the cause and effect relationship between the various components of emotional ill health.

The caregiver should think of the structures of inner healing as the layers of an onion. At the outer layer is the individual's life situation, the context where the person experiences his or her pain and difficulty. For Connie, the life situation was her sexual relationship with Dave. It was there that she experienced deep pain and heartache. In some cases, changes will need to be made in a person's life situation. For example, if someone is experiencing abuse in a relationship, boundaries will need to be set that protect the victim. In Connie's

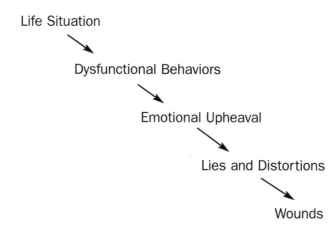

case the changes needed in the life situation were minimal, for the problem lay at a much deeper level. However, identifying and understanding the nature of a person's life situation is important to the healing process, a step we will discuss more thoroughly in upcoming chapters.

The layer beneath the life situation is that of dysfunctional behavior. In Connie's story, the dysfunctional behavior was the unhealthy way she responded to her husband's desire for sexual intimacy. Connie initially projected the problem onto Dave, complaining that he had unreasonable expectations. She also employed various avoidance behaviors, as well as repeatedly refusing Dave's advances. Her response, while appearing to offer short-term relief, was actually planting the seed for long-term heartache in their relationship.

If the caregiver has spent even the shortest time helping the broken, he is already well schooled in the nature and scope of dysfunctional behaviors. Some, like destructive addictions, are easily identifiable. Other behaviors, like workaholism, performance addictions and people pleasing are less offensive, yet do in fact lead to the same level of brokenness. People employ dysfunctional behaviors as a way of coping with great pain. Connie was in pain and tried to medicate herself by avoiding sexual intimacy with Dave. People will have their pain-killers of choice, each of which will need God's healing grace in the inner healing process.

Why did Connie embrace a level of dysfunctional behavior? Because she was experiencing emotional upheaval in her life situation. Sexual intimacy brought bad feelings to the surface for Connie. She experienced powerful feelings of fear, shame, guilt and anger whenever she was expected to be sexual with her husband. No one wants to regularly face such horrible and haunting emotions, so it is understandable that one would devise ways of escape. Connie hated the feelings that sexual intimacy unleashed. She tried to kill the pain the best way she knew, whether by blaming Dave for being oversexed or finding ways to avoid the moment. Most important here is the fact that her behavior was driven by something much deeper: emotional upheaval. It is not enough to address her reaction to sexual intimacy without recognizing the emotions that drove her actions. To do so could lead to solutions that might help a little in the short term but be useless over time. Inner healing keeps looking to what lies behind a person's unhealthy actions.

Feelings are not independent parts of the human psyche that fire off at will unless there is some biological breakdown. Emotions are linked to the thoughts that we have about ourselves and the people in our world. Connie felt upheaval when Dave approached her sexually because of what she believed about herself and about the meaning of sexual relations. Past experiences had shaped several powerful lies that Connie had grown to accept as absolute truth. She believed that she was damaged goods as a result of the rape she had experienced years earlier. She also believed that to give herself to Dave in that way meant that she was easy and worthless. These thoughts had taken shape years earlier and were still very much alive at the core of her being. They were in no way based upon the truth of who she was in Christ, yet she subconsciously embraced these distortions whenever Dave approached her. These distorted beliefs created great emotional pain and drove her to dysfunctional behaviors that steadily compounded the pain.

By now it is possible to see what shaped Connie's distorted beliefs about sex. She had been deeply wounded, first by rape and later by repeated affairs outside the bonds of marriage. These wounds were deep and filled with pain. Having never dealt with the matter in counseling, Connie stuffed a great deal of grief and heartache. She may have moved beyond the events and people who hurt her, but the unaddressed wounds were still creating great turmoil within her. Wounds that are not properly addressed can cause a person to hide, to pretend to be someone she is not, to embrace any kind or number of painkillers, and to adopt protective strategies that keep her isolated and alone. Broken people, like Connie, must open themselves to the healing touch of the Lord at the deepest level of their lives.

I want to restate the structures I have just discussed. Only this time I am going to move from the inside out. Unaddressed wounds create a great deal of deep pain in a person's life. They also often give shape to distortions in the way people view themselves, others and God. These lies give birth to emotional upheaval that is debilitating and distracting. In an effort to control or kill that pain, hurting people adopt various dysfunctional behaviors as a way of coping with the pain they are experiencing. These behaviors are then employed within a particular life situation.

This pattern can be identified in most of the stories that broken people will bring. I encourage the caregiver to listen to those stories with this structure in mind. It will provide a way for the caregiver to place the various components of emotional ill health in proper perspective. I instruct my students to take a piece of paper and write down these different layers with space beneath for note taking. Whenever they identify something about the life situation, they are to write it down. They do the same with everything they discover related to dysfunctional behaviors, emotional upheaval, distortion and deep wounds. Their ministry of inner healing prayer will then be directly related to each level of pain the person is experiencing.

I want to re-emphasize that there is a cause and effect relationship going on in people's psycho-spiritual issues. To treat the outer layers without identifying and ministering to the deeper issues will not lead to long term healing and transformation. If a caregiver only addresses a dysfunctional behavior, helping a person say no to that behavior, he or she is not addressing what drives the problem in the first place. All a person will do is set aside one dysfunctional behavior and pick up another. The issues lying beneath the behavior must be touched by the power of the Holy Spirit. The structure of healing presented here is meant to help the caregiver see the cause and effect pattern and address it at each and every level. Life situations will need changes, dysfunctional behaviors identified and addressed, emotional upheaval healed, lies exposed and reversed, and wounds grieved and healed. All this is to be done in the presence and power of the Holy Spirit, who guides and directs each step along the way. That process is the heart of inner healing prayer, as we will discuss in more detail in the chapters that follow.

Completing the Structure of Healing

The goal of inner healing prayer is to position people for a transforming encounter with Christ in the places of their deepest pain and greatest dysfunction. I want now to suggest what that change will look like within the structure we have just defined. Before encountering the Lord through inner healing prayer, person's issues moved from wound, to distortion, to emotional upheaval, to dysfunctional behavior, which was related to the life situation.

Through the ministry of the Holy Spirit a significant change takes place in this pattern. The wound becomes a place where the person meets the Lord and experiences His empowering grace. The lies are then replaced by the truth of who they are in Christ Jesus, which brings a significant amount of comfort and peace even in the midst of life's difficulties. This peace then enables one to experience empowerment in his or her life situation. The healing progression can be diagramed as follows:

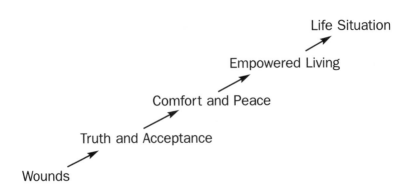

Notice that the broken person is able to choose an entirely new path in response to the wounds that have occurred in his or her life. This change takes place because of the encounter he or she had with the Holy Spirit through the ministry of inner healing prayer. The wounds, instead of leading to a destructive series of cause and effect reactions, become a place of strength and healing, which then births an entirely new way of responding to the hurt and pain. This healing is deep and it is lasting, all because it is the Lord who does it through his servant.

Let's return again to Connie's story to illustrate this change. Over time Connie experienced inner healing prayer at each level described in the structure given above. Connie was deeply hurt when she experienced the violation of sexual abuse. She also was repeatedly wounded when she engaged in premarital sexual relationships over several years. Through inner healing prayer she encountered the Lord's love and acceptance. There she was encouraged to grieve her losses as well as receive the cleansing and renewal that comes from the blood of Christ. From there Connie was guided by the Spirit to confront the lies that she believed about herself and her world. This process, as with all that took place, required time and patience. It was also critical that the Holy Spirit was present and free to move at all times. The Spirit enabled Connie to hear and accept the truth. The Lord spoke of His deep affection for her, as well as the truth that she was his beloved child, gifted, holy, totally forgiven, and free in Him. He also reinforced the message of His cleansing, which established Connie as both pure and worthy in His sight.

Connie had fought to forget all about the wounds that she had received those years before. Unfortunately, the pain was powerful and the voices very loud and debilitating. But through inner healing prayer Connie was able to hear a new word in the very place where lies had once kept their evil vigil. Truth opened the door to His comfort and peace and the storm that raged inside was stilled by the presence of Jesus. Connie actually pictured in her mind a stream of love cleansing her of all the past, and empowering her to move on to an entirely new place in life. This reality birthed feelings entirely different from those she previously knew. There was joy, a sense of worth and freedom, replacing negative feelings that had harassed her for a long time.

Connie's encounter with the Lord had done more than touch the wounds of the past. It empowered her to move out in life with a newfound strength and grace. Granted, there were still issues to be discussed with Dave, and the sexual relationship they desired still needed to be faced. But now Connie felt that she was not alone in the situation. With the need to hide and kill pain gone, Connie was able to tell Dave what had long remained a secret. Certainly there was nervousness and more than a few unknowns. But her confidence helped Dave respond with grace and tenderness, a sure sign that Jesus was right in the middle of this entire situation.

Connie also confronted her feelings and reactions to sexual intimacy. She and Dave determined to move slowly, prayerfully and intentionally. But they did in fact move. Connie continued to meet with Cheryl for some time after we ended the inner healing prayer sessions. She wanted a place to talk about what was happening with her in the pursuit of healthy intimacy and sexuality. In some ways Connie was beginning the honeymoon phase of her marriage for a second time. Only now she was not carrying the baggage that had weighed so heavily upon her the first time. In time Dave spoke of a new joy and excitement in their relationship, the true test of healing brought straight into their own life situation. Connie was not just helped through the Spirit's ministry in inner healing prayer, she was transformed.

Conclusion

The structure of healing presented in this chapter serves as a foundation for all the remaining chapters. Inner healing prayer is best applied when the caregiver can see and identify the interrelationships in the life of a broken person. This structure is a concrete way to identify what is being heard in a session and then to intentionally apply inner healing prayer through the Spirit's guidance.

Before concluding there is one point that I want to emphasize. Ours is a society that sees little use in suffering, and works diligently to either eliminate the cause or silence the symptoms. I believe this trend is not entirely in line with the greater purposes of the Lord. As stated previously, there is something more important than solving people's problems. The caregiver must position them to encounter the living Lord in the midst of life's difficulties. More than a few people have stated through the years that suffering has actually been a doorway into an entirely new and more vibrant relationship with Jesus Christ. Frank Laubach spoke of this in a letter he wrote to some friends while he was a missionary in the Philippines. In that correspondence he commented that he was experiencing a newfound intimacy with the Lord. He then wrote:

> And yet, how was this new closeness achieved? Ah, I know now that it was by cutting the very heart of my heart by suffering. Somebody was telling me this week that nobody can make a violin speak the last depths of the human longing until that soul has been made tender by some great anguish. I do not say it is the only way to the heart of God, but I must witness that it has opened an inner shrine for me which I never entered before.[2]

There is a very important point related to all this with respect to inner healing. The priority of inner healing prayer is the encounter a person can have with Jesus Christ. Nothing is more important than the wonder of His embrace. Healing, as necessary and critical as it may be, is secondary to that reality. Having walked my own dark path, I know that a message like that is not what a person necessarily wants to hear. She wants out, and fast. But the caregiver must patiently keep Jesus Christ central to every session, and help a person position herself for His touch. For me that presence was the Treasure offered to me above instant healing. Many times people will experience the power of His healing touch. That will be wonderful. But many times Jesus will not heal instantly, but will instead give the person the strength to stand firm in the midst of trial and difficulty.

I often think of Joni Erickson-Tada, whose life is a testimony to grace under the pressure of loss and pain. She always points people to Jesus as her strength and joy, all the while facing life with extreme difficulty. Through her wounds Joni has become a healer to countless people across the face of the earth. Some people will be similarly called. It is vital that we recognize that possibility, and point the broken to the potential ministry of being a wounded healer. There is great power in this calling, as well as a wonderful privilege.

I believe in a God who heals, not only because scripture testifies to that reality, but also because I have experienced it. I also know first hand that there are times when the Lord gives something greater than healing. He draws a broken person into a new and exciting relationship that empowers as little else can, all the while strengthening him

or her to stand in a difficult place. I certainly did not anticipate that
for my own life, but having experienced it, I know there are deep
riches to be mined from such an encounter with Christ. Add to that
the potential of touching the broken through one's wounds, and the
Kingdom becomes quite dynamic and exciting.

Inner healing prayer is a powerful ministry of the Lord's grace to
the broken. When the caregiver begins to move in this channel of the
Spirit, broken people will see in her a source of hope and healing.
That is both a special grace and an incredible responsibility. May we
all keep our eyes fixed on Christ, for He is both the means and the
end to all we do in His name.

Notes

1. You can find an example of such a life script in the appendix.

2. Brother Lawrence and Frank Laubach, *Practicing His Presence* (Beaumont, TX: Seed Sowers, 1973), 10.

For Further Reading

Wounded: How to Find Wholeness and Inner Healing Through Him, by
   Terry Wardle
Deep Wounds, Deep Healing, by Charles Kraft
Homesick for Eden, by Gary Moon
The Transformation of the Inner Man, by John and Paula Sanford
The Healing Presence: Curing the Soul through Union with Christ, by
   LeAnne Payne

Seven

Dysfunctional Behaviors and the Cross of Christ

For years I had little appreciation for the place of pain in my life. I hated discomfort, physical or emotional, and wanted it eliminated as quickly as possible. Furthermore, if I anticipated that something I would do or would be done to me could result in pain, I worked hard to avoid it whenever possible. Dentists and doctors were not my friends unless they were able to assure me that what they intended to do would be pain free. Pain was an enemy to be avoided or overcome whatever the cost.

Far too many times in life my response to pain has been unhealthy. Take, for example, the pain that comes with feeling unworthy. On more than a few occasions deep sadness and fear has risen up within me because I believed that I did not measure up. Any one of a number of situations could initiate these feelings, but I was unaware of the real cause that lay just beneath the surface. All I knew was that I did not like the way I felt, because it hurt deeply. So what did I do? I killed the pain. Sometimes I would do this by engaging in something as seemingly harmless as getting lost in a good movie or book. I would not touch the need behind the pain, but instead anesthetize the discomfort. At other times I would numb out with far more destructive behaviors. I responded to pain but never identified or touched the need. As long as I did not hurt I was not really concerned about the unaddressed primary need causing the pain. Unfortunately the deep need not only remained, it grew, increasing both the discomfort I was experiencing and the corresponding need for a painkiller.

My problem with dysfunctional behaviors has not been limited to pain killing. At times I have tried to go ahead and meet the need beneath the pain. But I addressed it in an unhealthy way. Consider for example the matter I mentioned earlier regarding my feelings of unworthiness. I am convinced that we all have a desire to be special and unique. I believe it is one of the core longings present within us from the moment we are born. God has provided that such deep needs be met in and through Him. However, we often attempt to fill those needs in ways that are both ungodly and destructive. In my case, I tried to satisfy my sense of unworthiness through performance. I had concluded that if I could accomplish things I could gain worth and then receive acceptance and approval. This led to a workaholic attitude that contributed to my own dark night. No matter how hard I worked, the need remained untouched, which caused me to increase the level of performance in order to meet that deep-seated desire. My behavior was unhealthy and dysfunctional. It not only hurt me, it negatively impacted most of the significant people in my life.

Every day caregivers meet people who try to eliminate pain through dysfunctional behaviors. The list of these unhealthy responses can be extensive, including a variety of addictive behaviors, such as:

Sexual Addictions	Drug Abuse
Alcoholism	Eating Disorders
Obsessive Gambling	Excessive Television
Shopping Addictions	Over Sleeping
Avoidance Mechanisms	Kleptomania

This list is only a sample of the many different ways that broken people may try to kill pain in their lives. The hurt that they are experiencing is often excruciating and, like me, they want the pain to go away. But they choose a path of short-term relief that never touches the need beneath the discomfort; indeed, it only leads to greater long-term destruction.

Even if the broken want to touch the need deep within, they often turn to solutions that are equally unhealthy. Lonely people might turn to affairs, the unloved to people-pleasing or performance, the fear-filled to manipulation and control, or the insecure to some level of co-dependence. The world offers countless options, promising great satisfaction through hollow solutions that ultimately lead to breakdown and emptiness. Hurting people walk along like visitors at a carnival midway, where slick hawkers lure them to spend what they cannot afford, to get what they in no way need or want. In the end all they have bought into is another remedy that leads away from healing and into deeper bondage and brokenness.

The men and women who turn to inner healing prayer are most often caught in the destructive patterns I have described. Most of them are worn out and desperate for change. They probably have already tried other avenues of help, yet discovered that a level of heartache and brokenness remains. By God's grace and through the power of the Holy Spirit, the caregiver will be a critical part of a most exciting and transforming journey to well being. But he must know that the pilgrimage will not be easy. It might be especially difficult in the early stages. Why? Because broken people must relinquish their painkillers in order to discover the deep needs that lie beneath the heartache. They will also need to set aside the short-term solutions they have embraced if they hope to experience the Lord's provision where the needs are greatest. For many the very thought will be frightening, because unmet needs do produce pain. But identifying and confronting dysfunctional behaviors is part of the healing process. This understanding opens the way for people to truly know what the unmet needs are, thus positioning them for an encounter with Jesus that brings both hope and healing.

The caregiver will need to prepare people for things to get worse before they get better. If someone is killing pain with a sexual addiction, that dysfunctional behavior will need to be laid down before the Lord. Not only is it out of line with the Lord's design for life, it can block the pathway to the deep needs that are causing pain in the first place. Broken people will soon begin to see what they did not want to see, feel what they did not want to feel, and admit what they hoped would never need to be known about their lives. That is difficult and will demand a great deal of prayer and support from the caregiver.

When the level of pain increases, the desire for relief, albeit short term, becomes great. But when the broken step forward by the leading of the Spirit, they will meet Jesus in ways they never knew possible, and soon discover that He is in fact loving and full of grace. He is able to touch the greatest and deepest needs in ways that are indescribably satisfying and freeing. People will experience the reality of Christ's words, "Come to me, all you who are weary and burdened, and I will give you rest. Take my yoke upon you and learn from me, for I am gentle and humble in heart, and you will find rest for your souls. For my yoke is easy and my burden light" (Matt. 11:28-30).

Starting with Dysfunctional Behaviors

Let's review the structures of inner healing for a moment. When the caregiver is moving from the outer layer toward the core wounding, he begins with the life situation. This represents the context from which a person tends to act out. Beneath that is the particular dysfunctional behavior(s) that the broken person has embraced to kill pain and/or try to meet needs in his or her life. In inner healing this is often the place where work begins. Broken people often are not always in touch with the deep needs that drive their behavior, but they do tend to recognize at least some aspect of their behavior that is out of order. For many, this will be what brought them to counseling in the first place.

Take Karl for example. He was heartbroken, humiliated and embarrassed as he told me about his problem. He was a respected pastor within his community who had a secret that was destroying him. The matter caused him to feel horrible about himself and led him repeatedly to question his place in Christian ministry. He tried to address the issue on his own, but his solutions had been ineffective and short lived. Finally, after years of bondage and great shame he turned to somebody for help. It was obvious from the flow of tears that Karl was desperate, deeply sorrowful, and emotionally exhausted. Clearly he did not want to admit the struggle, which he felt was too ugly, too dark, and too humiliating. But the isolation had become overwhelming to him and he was now at the end of a fraying rope.

Karl was caught in a sexual addiction. A man nearing his sixties, he had, since adolescence, been obsessed with dressing in women's nightgowns and engaging in auto-sexuality. His wife knew nothing about this behavior, though they had been married for over thirty years. Karl said that he did this most when under stress or during those times when he was not connecting with his wife. Whenever she was not home, Karl would invariably turn to this activity and then afterward experience indescribable self-hatred and shame. Karl had prayed much about this problem and tried to fight the temptation. He wanted to be free, but when the turmoil arose he soon found himself going yet again to the place that he despised yet needed at some deep level.

As Karl shared his story it was obvious that a great deal of pain in his life was driving this behavior. Initially I could only guess at what might lie beneath the behavior. Whatever it was, I knew that Karl was never going to find satisfaction through this addiction. He needed help in confronting this problem through the power of Christ, and then receive support in tracing the pain to the true need that was deep within his life. That was not going to be an easy proposition. But in this case it was clear that the place to begin was with the behavior itself. Only in setting it aside would the Lord move to the lies, wounds, and core needs that were yet to be touched by His love and grace.

I emphasize again that identifying and confronting dysfunctional behaviors is the logical place to start. After all, if the "peeling the onion' analogy is accurate, unhealthy behaviors are the first unhealthy matter to be revealed in the inner healing model. But even as I say that, I am well aware that with the things of the Holy Spirit there is no readily predictable pattern. He alone determines where the work is to take place. In each session the caregiver must be sensitive to His leading and be ready to do what He directs. To minister otherwise would be to move contrary to the foundational teachings on the ministry of the Holy Spirit previously discussed. Session by session the caregiver should wait upon His leading. There will be times when he will lead one to deal with lies before behaviors or wounds before emotional upheaval. If that is the case one must do what He says.

But for the purposes of our discussion and in anticipation of what might most often occur, it is critical to be prepared to address dysfunctional behaviors early in the process. After all, if people are hurting themselves or others as a result of pain or unmet needs, the caregiver will want to stop them. Even while the caregiver is seeking to identify and understand the deep lies and wounds that are yet to be exposed, he should be vigilant to lovingly yet intentionally call them away from dysfunctional responses to pain and unmet needs. Only in Christ will people find fulfillment and strength to endure. Setting aside sin to rest in His embrace is the first step to wholeness and new life.

Whatever Happened to Sin?

At this point I want to move slightly away from the language of psychology and counseling to concepts more consistent with practical theology. We have already seen that dysfunctional behaviors are ultimately rooted in deep pain and unaddressed needs. I also accept the fact that much of this is at some level symptomatic of horrible woundings and loss, suffered at the hands of others. As such, caregivers must do more than help people step away from destructive behaviors. They need to point people to the healing presence of Christ at the deepest level of need and heartache. The caregiver should support and encourage people to go well beneath the behavior and identify the need that has ultimately driven the unhealthy choices being made by hurting people.

But it is also very important that these dysfunctional behaviors be identified for what they are; sinful responses to pain and unmet needs in people's lives. Whenever people kill pain and try to meet needs in unhealthy ways, they are falling short of God's desire for them. And the simple definition of that set of choices is sin. Failure to identify this truth takes away the personal responsibility for their actions that people must accept. Even when a person is in pain or facing a genuine need, choosing to address it in a way that is hurtful to themselves or to others is a sinful response. The presence of underlying wounds does not absolve people from responsibility for the unhealthy choices they make. Having been wounded by others does not give people the right to react in a way that wounds anyone else, even themselves. It was sinful when I chose to deal with feelings of unworthiness by harmful painkilling, and sinful when I tried to meet my deep needs through self-centered performance. It was also sinful for Karl to engage in a sexual addiction, even though there was deep pain and genuine need deep beneath this behavior. Sin must be recognized and dealt with before the Lord as an integral part of the inner healing process.

I am well aware that it is not popular in our day to talk about sin. To do so is to risk accusations of being a hell-fire fundamentalist who enjoys threatening others with punishment and condemnation. That does happen in some churches, and it often does far more damage than good for people. That is not my intention or my heart. I am opposed to that approach and find it inconsistent with the testimony of scripture. I am overwhelmed by God's good grace and have experienced unbelievable acceptance, forgiveness and hope in the midst of my own problems. However, the starting place for experiencing His matchless grace is recognizing why we need His mercy in the first place. We are like straying sheep, wandering away from God's best, feeding in places that ultimately lead to our own destruction. Many times this happens because we do not know better. At other times we make bad choices consciously, either unconcerned or unconvinced that the consequences are really that serious or sinful. But they are, and there is no responsible way to detour around that reality on the path to inner healing.

In 1973 psychiatrist Karl Menninger spoke to this matter in his book, *Whatever Became of Sin*. Though renowned for his work in the field of psychology, Menninger was deeply concerned that people were trying to address problems without reference to sin. He pointed to the obvious issues being faced within society, including great social ills like the raping of the environment, oppression of minorities and the consumption of the world's resources by a mere fraction of the global population, leaving a great majority to struggle in abject poverty. Menninger also described individual behaviors that were hurting people yet were redefined in such a way as to minimize the serious violation taking place before God. His question then was, "Whatever became of sin?"

> In all the laments and reproaches made by our seers and prophets, one misses any mention of "sin," a word that used to be a veritable watchword of prophets. It was a word once in everyone's mind, but now rarely ever heard. Does that mean that no sin is involved in our troubles—sin with an "I" in the middle? Is no one any longer guilty of anything? Guilty perhaps of a sin that could be repented and repaired or atoned for? Is it only that someone may be stupid or sick or criminal—or asleep? Wrong things are being done, we know; tares are being sown in the wheat field at night. But is no one responsible, no one answerable for these acts? Anxiety and

depression we all acknowledge, and even vague guilt feelings, but has no one committed any sins? Where, indeed, did sin go? What became of it?[1]

Menninger's concern should be ours as well. As Christians we must never forget that we live our lives before God, who has called us away from sin and into holiness through Jesus Christ. Communicating this truth is not the responsibility of preachers and pastors alone. All who desire to follow Christ and serve the broken should remember that sin is a serious matter. The Christian caregiver should be prepared to admonish people to turn toward God for help, healing, and deliverance. It is irresponsible, as well as unbiblical, to minimize the seriousness of the wrong choices people make by staying away from the word sin because it is an unpopular concept. People in the behavioral sciences certainly have valuable insights into the human condition. But the trend in that field to distance the discussion from theological considerations is wrong. It is ultimately keeping people in serious bondage.

Sin Defined

What precisely is sin? Menninger defined it as "transgression of the law of God: disobedience of the divine will; moral failure. Sin is failure to realize in conduct and character the moral ideal, at least as fully as possible under existing circumstances."[2] More simply stated, Menninger is rightly defining sin as the failure to live according to what God expects. This involves not doing what God has told people to do, and/or doing what he has expressly forbidden. Theologians and biblical scholars have often referred to the Greek word hamartia which in the New Testament is simply translated as missing the mark. In other words, God has set before us a standard of character and behavior and to fall short of that is to miss God's mark. And to miss the mark is to sin. Dysfunctional behaviors aimed at killing pain or meeting needs in unhealthy ways do in fact miss the mark.

I find the words of Jesus most helpful and pastoral on this topic. He defined the purpose of life as "loving the Lord your God with all your heart, mind, soul, and strength, and loving your neighbor as yourself" (Matt. 22:37-39). He said that all of the rules and laws contained in the Bible hang on these two commandments (Matt. 22:40).

Expanding on an Old Testament text, Jesus was telling all his followers that they are to live according to the rule of love. How does one know what is right and wrong? According to Jesus that is really quite simple. Do what is loving to God, loving to other people and loving toward oneself. Every action that is rooted in the law of love hits the mark of God's expectation, dead center. Conversely, if any thought or action is not loving toward God, another person, or oneself, it is sinful. Scripture goes on to give more detail regarding what specific actions are sinful, but it all relates to this central teaching of Jesus. Therefore, with reference to our topic, pain killing and meeting needs in any way that is unloving toward God, hurts another person, or which at any level compromises the well being of an individual, is sin.

Once again allow me to illustrate that from my own life. What really is the concern about trying to meet the deep need I have for acceptance and worth through performance? Can it truly be a problem, given that I can accomplish a great deal while I am addressing my own need? Let's look at that in light of Jesus' teaching regarding the law of love. First, by turning to performance in order to gain a sense of worth, I am in fact creating an idol. God has made provision for that need through the work of Christ. To seek worth apart from Him is unloving toward God and clearly misses the mark He set before me. As for others, it was very easy to subconsciously use people to meet my own deep needs. They became an unhealthy means to an end, which devalues and invalidates. That is not loving either. And as for myself, one trip to a psychiatric hospital was more than enough evidence that performance and workaholism are both damaging and depressing. Simply said, my behavior was more than dysfunctional. It was sinful and had to be addressed as such on my pilgrimage to personal wholeness.

The Problem with Sin

I believe it helpful to be reminded yet again about the seriousness of sin, as described by Paul. In doing so the caregiver will be motivated all the more to address sin as part of the inner healing process, for she will recognize it as the destructive force that it truly is in people's lives. In Romans Paul wrote:

I put this in human terms because you are weak in your natural selves. Just as you used to offer the parts of your body in slavery to impurity and to ever-increasing wickedness, so now offer them in slavery to righteousness, leading to holiness. When you were slaves to sin, you were free from the control of righteousness. What benefit did you reap from the things that you are now ashamed of? Those things result in death. But now that you have been set free from sin and have become slaves to God, the benefit you reap leads to holiness, and the result is eternal life. For the wage of sin is death, but the gift of God is eternal life in Christ Jesus our Lord. (Rom. 6:19-23)

Consider what Paul is saying about sin in this text. First, he repeatedly uses the term slavery with reference to sinful actions. This is very important for the caregiver who will be involved in inner healing prayer. The Holy Spirit will move her to lovingly confront sinful choices because of the slavery that comes from such actions. Paul was well aware of the practice of slavery and knew its terrible cost. Slaves had no freedom to go where they wanted to go, do what they wanted to do, or become what they wanted to be. They were in bondage, forced to live according to another person's demands and desires. They were often mistreated, dehumanized and deval- ued. They had become the property of another, enslaved to spend their lives serving people who had little care or concern for them as human beings.

Sin leads to slavery. A hurting person has a pain and need deep within that becomes too much to bear alone. Misguided, the thought comes to him to try some way to alleviate the ache inside his soul. Whether out of ignorance or rebellion, he stumbles upon a short-term solution to his problem. Initially it is a conscious act that he initiates and controls in order to feel better. But over time, the action turns into a habit, less conscious, more impulse driven. Slowly the habit sets deep talons into the flesh of the wounded soul and he becomes enslaved to a behavior that begins to rip and tear at his life on every level. The behavior has turned into the beast, and the broken person becomes a slave to sin's dark design. This slavery is a constant result of sinful choices, and if the caregiver has any level of concern for people, she will call it the ugly taskmaster that it is.

Paul also challenges people to consider the results of the sins for which they are now ashamed (Rom. 6:21). I recognize how important it is that he linked the word shame to sin, for it is unquestionably one of the most devastating consequences of behaviors that fall short of God's commandments. I have not only personally struggled under the weight of shame, but faced it in others while helping experience the Lord's healing. Broken men and women often wear shame like a dead skin that should have been shed long before. It is ugly, heavy and carries with it the most horrible feelings of self-contempt.

Sandra Wilson has defined shame as:

> ...a soul-deep sense that there is something uniquely wrong with me that is not wrong with you or anyone else in the world. Because I am not perfect and problem free, I felt hopelessly, disgustingly different and worth less than other people. I view myself as, literally, worthless. It isn't that I make a mistake when I make a mistake; I am a mistake when I make a mistake. This is shame's message.[3]

This definition cuts to the core of shame's dark nature. Inevitably people who are caught in sin wrestle with its suffocating presence. Often that battle occurs in silent hiding because few people want others to see what they live with day in and day out. While sinful choices seem at first to offer some relief to deep need, in the end they bring a covering of shame that only heightens an already difficult inner battle.

Paul does not end there, but speaks to a third consequence of sin: death. He says quite clearly that the ultimate and most devastating consequence of missing God's mark is destruction. Paraphrasing his words, "death is the final payoff of sin" (Rom. 6:23). Even a short time caring for broken people will be enough to convince the caregiver of this biblical principle. Enslavement to dysfunctional behaviors has the potential to emotionally, mentally, relationally, spiritually, and at times physically kill. Who has not seen this with those trapped in various addictive behaviors? Though people may think such choices are harmless, long-term bondage rips and tears at people until they begin to die deep within their souls. It is often a slow demise, as dark forces, bit by bit, steal the life that God intended for His people. Most devastating of all is the eternal death that comes to those who never respond to God's offer of forgiveness and redemption through the work of His Son, Jesus Christ. Should caregivers be concerned about such things? How could a person ever claim to follow the Lord and not challenge the broken to turn away from sin and to the wonderful grace that comes to all who believe?

The Good News of Jesus Christ

So far I have pointed to the reality of sin and its deep and devastating consequences in the lives of the broken. But this is far short of the entire story that surrounds the question of sin. There is good news, which has come to us through Jesus Christ. I am writing these words while on Christmas break from my responsibilities at the seminary. Could there ever be a more appropriate time to discuss the gospel that is ours because of Jesus? It is in these days that we celebrate the coming of the Son of God, heralded by angels who declared:

> "Do not be afraid. I bring you good news of great joy that will be for all people. Today in the town of David a Savior has been born to you; he is Christ the Lord. This will be a sign to you; You will find the baby wrapped in cloths and lying in a manger." Suddenly a great company of the heavenly host appeared with the angel, praising God and saying,
> "Glory to God in the Highest, and on earth peace to men on whom his favor rests." (Luke 2:10-14)

Even as the caregiver admonishes the broken to take sin seriously, the message of joy should spring forth from her heart. Jesus Christ, God the Father's unconditional gift of love, has provided a way for people to be free from sin and its devastating consequences. Through the cross, every man, woman, and child has the opportunity to experience forgiveness and reconciliation with God. Sinful choices need no longer plague people with slavery, shame, and death. Jesus gave His blood so that all who believe can be saved. And that salvation definitely includes the element of healing, reconnecting lost people with God, and empowering them to move forward in the power of the Spirit.

The Apostle Paul has clearly revealed all that is possible for the broken because of the work of Jesus on Calvary. In Colossians he wrote:

When you were dead in your sins and in the uncircumcision of your sinful nature, God made you alive with Christ. He forgave us all our sins, having canceled the written code, with its regulations, that was against us and that stood opposed to us; he took it away, nailing it to the cross. And having disarmed the powers and authorities, he made a public spectacle of them, triumphing over them by the cross. (Col. 2:13-15)

To call this good news is an understatement. As people turn to a caregiver for help, Jesus stands before them with fantastic news. As Christians they have been forgiven all their sins. Jesus fulfilled all the requirements of the law and paid for sin at the cross. Through His shed blood, Jesus has disarmed all the dark forces aligned against them, giving them authority by His powerful name to defeat their evil foe. Because of this, Christians are now alive with Jesus, held securely in His eternal embrace.

In his letter to the Ephesians, Paul assures believers that they receive every blessing they need through Christ, and that even as they struggle, Jesus has made a way for them to be holy and blameless in God's sight (Eph. 1:3, 4). He assures Christian people that through Christ they are sons and daughters of God, recipients of great gifts, redeemed by His blood, and heirs to glorious riches of God's grace (Eph. 1:5-8). And let there be no question about the grace-based faith that Paul declares. All of this comes, not because someone has worked hard or lived right, but as gifts, freely given to all who believe in the wonderful work that Jesus did at Calvary. They are not, according to Paul, given stingily, but instead lavished upon those whom God calls into His eternal family (Eph. 1:8).

What I have said here about the matchless grace of God, through Jesus Christ, is but a small representation of all that he offers people. The gospels and epistles of the New Testament are full of descriptions of the unsearchable riches of Christ. The responsible caregiver would do well to know the texts that speak of these benefits in order to help the broken feed regularly upon that life-giving bread. For the good news of Jesus is at the very heart of what inner healing has to offer: hope and wholeness for broken people everywhere.

When those who are outside of Christ come for healing prayer, the message of sin and salvation should be presented as an invitation

158 HEALING CARE, HEALING PRAYER

to faith. Such an offer should be made gently and sensitively, without manipulation or forceful confrontation. I am convinced that inner healing prayer is a ministry of the Lord to those who have received Him into their lives. It is based on the presence of the Holy Spirit in a person's life and involves confronting evil, as well as delivering people from the bondage of sinful behaviors. I do not believe it possible to bring such healing to people who do not know Christ. For this reason the caregiver will find herself as a proclaimer of God's message of redemption, which is in fact the single greatest healing God offers.

Given that the deeper levels of inner healing build upon the work of new birth in people's hearts, the caregiver will often be praying with believers who are caught in destructive behaviors. The message of Christ is a word of hope and acceptance to His hurting children. Many will come fearing the Lord's rejection and punishment for what they have been doing. Granted, they must know that their choices are sinful and ultimately destructive. But they should also be made aware of God's steadfast love and acceptance in spite of their actions. He has no punishment left for them, having poured it out upon Jesus who died on their behalf. No behaviors could have qualified people for His love, and none can cause Him to stop loving His own. He looks toward the broken with divine compassion and understanding. While He in no way minimizes sin, God offers people the power to be set free and thoroughly forgiven. He longs to love and touch his sinful, wounded children.

People need to hear that nothing can separate them from His love, and that even on their worst day He is thoroughly crazy about them. God rejoices as every prodigal turns toward home, meeting them long before they expect Him to be there, welcoming them with great joy and providing the healing they need. As He calls people to set aside their painkillers and dysfunctional behaviors, He opens the way for them to have their deepest needs met in Him. And where pain continues to be present, He comes to strengthen and equip the broken to move forward in the power of His enabling grace. This is the message of hope that the caregiver holds out to the broken. While on the one hand she helps them see the seriousness of sinful choices, on the other she extends to them the matchless love of the God who desires to free them from all that is dark and evil. As she does this, people will be more attracted to God's love than they are to sinful painkillers and behaviors. When that is true, the path to inner healing opens wide before them.

How to Approach the Issue of Sin

As the caregiver begins to approach the issue of sin with people, she needs to remember five principles. First and foremost is the importance of following the leading of the Holy Spirit. As we have already seen in two preceding chapters, waiting upon the leading of the Spirit is the key to every step in the process. Do not address the matter of sin before He opens the door, and never fail to do so when it is clear that He has prepared the way. The Holy Spirit prepares people to hear and respond to the call to repentance. He works not only through what you may say, but also through every situation that comes their way during the process. Trusting that truth and being ever watchful for when the time is right, the caregiver will sense God's empowerment to help people say no to sin and yes to the Lord's invitation to new life.

Second, the caregiver should keep in mind the relationship between sinful choices and inner healing. Dealing with the issue of sin is very important, but it is not the end of the process. It is the beginning of a deeper work. If a person comes for prayer and the caregiver is able to help him lay down a dysfunctional behavior, the caregiver must remember that the underlying issues have yet to be touched by Christ. Failure to do that will only set a person up for future problems. Something deeper, be it pain, need, or rebellion is driving the unhealthy choices being made. If the caregiver only addresses the choice, the broken person will more often than not be tempted to find yet another sinful response to fill the driving need. Or eventually he or she will turn back to the initial behavior. Inner healing prayer always moves to the place of deepest need, allowing Jesus to heal and strengthen the broken person.

Third, the caregiver should have an attitude of gentleness and humility when helping people deal with sin. As we discussed in chapter two, Henri Nouwen presents the thesis that ministry to the broken should flow out of one's willingness to be a wounded healer. He proposes that people are effective at touching the hurts of others when they are, before Christ, aware of and attentive to their own wounds.

Nouwen reminds us that this was the position Jesus took in the ministry of healing, and should be emulated by all Christian caregivers.

Practically this means the caregiver must be on his own pilgrimage to well-being. When this is true, he is likely to be gentle with people who are broken, extending the type of care he would most like to receive in a similar circumstance. He will also be more humble when dealing with sin, keenly aware that there is nothing that another person has done or is doing that he could not also do given the same background and circumstance. This attitude is consistent with the teaching of Paul when he said, "Brothers, if someone is in sin, you who are spiritual should restores him gently. But watch yourself, or you also may be tempted" (Gal. 6:1). Rather than speaking down to the broken, the wounded healer will stand with them in a place of honest vulnerability and hope.

Fourth, the caregiver should remember his call as a Christian to warn people about the seriousness of sin. The more in touch the caregiver is with his own sinfulness, the more hesitant he may be to speak about sin to others. Many times I think, "Who am I to challenge someone else regarding sin?" After all I am prone to wander at times and know there is yet much room for growth in my own walk with Jesus. However, silence about sin only allows the problem to grow. Sin must be exposed to the light of Christ, and the caregiver should not fall back from that responsibility. James, the brother of Jesus, admonished Christians to help people turn away from sin when he wrote: "My brothers, if one of you should wander from the truth and someone should bring him back, remember this: Whoever turns a sinner from the error of his way will save him from death and cover a multitude of sins" (James 5:19, 20). The word of God gives the caregiver authority to serve the broken in this way, providing a clear reminder of the seriousness of sin. Warning people about sin is a ministry of rescuing that he cannot fail to do if he intends to be a channel of the Lord's healing power.

Finally, when dealing with sin, the caregiver must keep Jesus at the center. One easily gets bogged down in the bad news of slavery, shame and destruction when addressing dysfunctional behaviors. While that discussion is important, the power in the gospel message centers upon Jesus Christ. People should hear far more about the ability of Christ to free them, than the power of sin to break their lives. People know about brokenness, but freedom and healing may be a foreign concept. It is important to emphasize all that Jesus has done for them at the cross, with special attention to His cleansing, forgiveness and unshakable acceptance. I want the people I serve to be overwhelmed with the message of grace, assuring them that God's love is far greater than their sin.

Many people who seek care believe that their sin has so angered God that He does not want to have anything to do with them until they have straightened out their lives. The caregiver must help them see that God never turns His back on His own, but is instead always positioned to love them lavishly. Some Christians fear that such emphasis will give license to sin, but I have experienced just the opposite. When people finally glimpse and begin to experience the matchless grace of God, they turn from sin and run into His embrace. They find in Him the answer to their greatest need. They find freedom and healing that the painkillers and short-term solutions could not provide. The message of grace, far from giving license to sin, promises the broken a level of strength and wholeness that only God can provide.

Some Practical Advice

How does all of this fit together in the context of inner healing prayer? At one level there is an element of unpredictability as to how this will look when ministering to a broken person. After all, each person is different, and every session is affected by the unplanned. This is especially true when the Holy Spirit is leading the time being spent with people. He certainly has an order to the process, but it does not necessarily match a textbook description of inner healing. However, I follow some practical guidelines that help me anticipate the appropriate time to address dysfunctional behaviors.

I usually begin by discussing the structures of inner healing, explaining the cause-and-effect relationship between the various ingredients present in brokenness. I usually define and describe each level, starting with the deep wounds and moving through to the lies, emotional upheaval, dysfunctional behaviors, and into the life situation. Far more often than not, this discussion helps people see what is happening within their lives and instills both understanding and hope.

Once this is generally covered, one can move forward to help the broken understand the nature and character of dysfunctional behaviors. I talk to those I serve about what the term means, why people turn to such behaviors, and the relationship between behavioral choices and unmet needs. At the appropriate time I discuss this with specific reference to sin, a discussion that should be bathed in prayer and conducted under the anointing of the Holy Spirit.

When the time is right I help the broken person address sin in his or her life. This best begins by encouraging the individual to meet God in prayer, asking Him to reveal areas where there are sinful responses to pain and unmet needs. I want the individual to be open and honest before the Lord, allowing the Holy Spirit to show him where he has gone astray. I most often lead the person in such a prayer in my office, fully aware that the process of recognition proceeds on a very unpredictable timetable. Sometimes a great deal is discovered right there and then. More often than not, this prayer time initiates a season of discovery that can cover several days, weeks, and at times months.

I have found it helpful for people to deal with the issue of sin one step at a time. I first ask them to seek God's help in identifying obvious sin in their lives, actions that clearly fall short of God's design as described in scripture. People may be hesitant to look at these actions before God, but deep within they already know that what they are doing is wrong. They are just hesitant to admit that what they have been doing is sinful. I find it important to encourage a symbolic activity as a way of dealing with sin. I send them off for the week with the assignment to listen for God's voice regarding sin. When they experience His work of revealing, I ask them to find a stone that represents a particular sin, and then bring it to the next session. I encourage them to carry it with them through the week as a way of remembering the burden this action has been upon their lives. When they return, I then pray with them, as described in the following section, and challenge them to lay it down before the Lord as an act of submission and surrender.

After dealing with obvious sin, I pray with people to seek the Lord regarding unresolved past sin. Be assured I believe that all past sin has been forgiven before Christ. But many Christian people have moved away from sinful behaviors without ever dealing with them before the Lord. Not only is that a matter of confession, but also an issue of closing the door completely on what has happened. For example, if a Christian had cheated someone in a business deal, he or she may need to reconcile with the person and repay what was taken. If someone had dealt with occult practices in the past, specific prayers of deliverance and release may be necessary. An individual may have practiced sexual immorality years before, but did not break the spiritual bonds that occurred as a result of these unhealthy relationships. These unresolved issues may need attention before the Lord. Having defined unresolved sin, I encourage people to stand before the Lord and see what He reveals. If unresolved sin is revealed, I pray with them for direction and empowerment from the Lord.

Finally, I suggest that we pray about unknown sin. Few people think of pain-killing as sin, especially when it involves things like television, food, shopping or similar socially acceptable activities. Most people do not consider that there may be harm in turning to such things or that this type of pain-killing can become a kind of idolatry. Nor are there many who understand that actions like performance and people-pleasing are wrong. It becomes my obligation and opportunity to talk about the relationship between such choices and sin. I gently talk about pain-killing and meeting needs in unhealthy ways, relating this to the biblical topic of sin. My words are not always enough on this matter so, again, I encourage the broken to seek the Lord and to be open to the Spirit's work of convincing and convicting. Soon, over time and in His presence, people see that the choices they are making are far more destructive than once thought. They become open to the touch of Jesus, which is always the proper response to their deepest needs.

Once people have identified the specific actions in their lives that are sinful, they can be led carefully and slowly through a six-step process. I do this in prayer, knowing that the work of the Holy Spirit is the true means of healing and deliverance for broken people. All that has been said and done only serves this important transaction. These steps, listed below, have been alliterated to help people remember them as a simple yet biblically faithful path to freedom.

Recognize. Encourage individuals to come before the Lord, fully admitting that specific choices and actions that the Holy Spirit has identified are sinful. Help them to speak out before the Lord all that these actions have cost, reminding them that these short-term solutions bring long-lasting destruction to their lives.

Repent. This is a two-fold response involving turning away from sin and turning toward God for help and healing. The word repentance carries with it the connotation of agreement. In this case, the individual is agreeing that sin is not part of God's plan, and admitting that what God has identified as sin is just that, sin.

Renounce. Sinful choices open the door for the oppressive and harassing work of the evil one. Much more will be said about this in the final chapter. Here it is enough to say that a person should renounce any involvement the evil one may have in this problem, bringing himself thoroughly under the blood-bought victory of Christ Jesus. Help people do this whether there is overt evidence of demonic activity or not. Reclaiming ground for the Lord is a good strategy and more often than not helps set them free.

Receive. Encourage people to audibly accept the forgiveness and cleansing that is theirs in Jesus Christ. Voicing the benefits of grace helps take the Lord's provision to all the deeper areas within the life of the broken person. Such declarations, made not only on earth but through the Spirit in the heavenlies, solidifies the redeeming work that Jesus does for the Father's children.

Realign. This prayer involves two steps. First, encourage people to seek the Lord's help in making specific changes in their lifestyle related to the sin they are confessing. For example, if pornography is an issue, being accountable to stay away from the sources of such behavior is important. Second, help broken people look to God as the strength of their lives and the true source of all they need. This realignment turns them around to seek God for all they need, rather than an unhealthy and sinful behavior.

Rejoice. There is power in praise. Paul admonished believers to "rejoice in the Lord always" (Phil. 4:4). The writer of Hebrews encouraged people to "continually offer to God a sacrifice of praise" (Heb. 13:15). Giving thanks for the cleansing work of Christ Jesus opens the heavens for an even greater shower of blessings from the Father. It is good to help people practice praise as a lifestyle, for the presence of Christ will be an experienced reality in their lives.

The healing work of Christ happens at every level of our lives. By helping people identify sin and choose into Christ, the way is opened for the broken to experience a powerful encounter with the Lord. It is in many ways the unlocking of the first door leading into the deepest places of pain and heartache. Dysfunctional behaviors have stood guard, keeping individuals locked away from the places where Christ has wanted to meet and free them. The caregiver should be encouraged to take this step both seriously and joyfully. As sin is surrendered, the light will begin to move into the hidden recesses where wounds have festered and lies have remained unchallenged. These are the places of inner healing and the committed caregiver will be the servant of the Lord who leads the way.

Notes

1. Karl Menninger, *Whatever Became of Sin?* (New York: Hawthorne Books, 1973), 13.

2. Ibid, 18.

3. Sandra D. Wilson, *Shame Free Parenting* (Downers Grove, IL: Inter-Varsity, 1992), 14.

For Further Reading

Whatever Became of Sin? by Karl Menninger
The Cross of Christ, by John Stott
What's So Amazing About Grace? by Philip Yancey
The Search for Freedom, by Robert McGee
The Christ Life, by A. B. Simpson

Eight

Emotional Turmoil and the Lies that Drive It

As a small boy I spent many hours watching my father and grand-father practice archery behind our home. Hour upon hour, night after night they would shoot brightly colored arrows at targets placed at varying distances throughout the yard. They seemed tireless, repeat-edly drawing their bows, taking aim and sending arrows on a straight course toward the red bull's eye far out in the distance. On most evenings my dad's friends would join him, all of them trying to improve their skills in preparation for upcoming tournaments. The men stood together in a row, much like soldiers in review, each tak-ing his turn at shooting. Once all the arrows had been fired, they walked to the target, counted up the score and retrieved all the arrows for yet another round. My father was undisputedly the best archer of all, and I still have his trophies and medals to prove it.

I loved those evenings behind the house. I was enamored with the fine leather quivers, beautiful bows uniquely decorated for each archer, and all the special pieces of paraphernalia that accompanied the sport. I also reveled in the harmless bragging and tall tales that these colorful characters told, often with a special wink directed my way at just the appropriate time. To me, becoming an archer was a rite of passage.

Somehow I believed that manhood would be mysteriously conferred whenever I finally took my place in that line. I pestered my dad repeatedly about getting my own bow, convinced that something primitive and magical would happen, transforming me from an awkward kid into a modern-day Robin Hood. I could not wait.

In time my father did buy me a bow and arrow and set out to teach me some basics of archery. I thought that unnecessary, but humored my dad and tried to listen. My dad assured me that, of all that he said, two pieces of advice were more important than everything else. First, dad instructed me never to shoot a wooden bow without having an arrow set upon the string. He said that if I "dry fired" a bow it could break the limbs. I didn't understand the basic principles of physics behind his admonition, but I knew I did not want a broken bow. The simple truth is that, without an arrow, all the energy created from drawing and firing a bow stays within the limbs. This pressure can weaken a bow and cause it to snap. With an arrow on the string, however, the energy leaves the bow and enters the arrow, sending it on its way. The limbs release all the power into the arrow and return to a state of rest without the slightest damage.

Second, my father told me that I was to shoot at nothing but the target set out in front of me. He assured me that if I failed to listen, I would lose my privileges, and worse, possibly hurt myself or someone else. The arrow was to fly to the appropriate target and nowhere else. With those words I began a love affair with archery that continues to this very day.

Expressing emotions is like shooting an arrow. The internal energy created from deep wounding is expelled when an individual releases the feelings of hurt. Such release may be initially difficult, but it enables one to rise up and function appropriately once again. Certainly the intensity of feeling and length of grieving varies with each wound; but expressing the emotional turmoil is both positive and healthy. However, when the emotions are killed, denied or stuffed, the powerful energy remains trapped within the individual. This ongoing tension often leads to levels of breakdown. Unexpressed feelings eventually produce symptoms of ill health in a person's body, mind and spirit. When the breakdown does occur, a person may not initially realize what has happened. But the truth is that a lifetime of stuffing has ultimately fractured their lives.

Martha came for inner healing prayer because of repeated seasons of depression. She had received some help through medication, but the reoccurring nature of the problem motivated her to seek another kind of help. Over time I discovered two very important facts about Martha. She rarely expressed what she was feeling, which contributed to a chronic sense of anxiety; and, years earlier, she had been sexually molested by her father. While she had talked to a counselor about the event, she had never allowed herself to feel the anger, sadness and fear that resulted from her molestation. Instead Martha told herself to move on, given that she had now talked about it. But the pent up emotions were taking a serious toll on her well-being, manifested through the despair that she regularly battled. For Martha to experience healing, she would have to discharge her emotional energy just as the bow discharges an arrow. Granted, helping her do that was not easy, but the Lord enabled Martha to finally connect with her feelings and express them in ways that complemented the healing process.

Not every person who struggles with emotional upheaval responds by bottling his feelings. Some people have no problem expressing their negative emotions, but do it in ways that are harmful to themselves and to others. Mike is a gifted surgeon who serves as a member of the teaching faculty at a major university hospital. He is sought after by residents in his specialty, and delivers papers at conferences around the world. Anyone meeting Mike for the first time is immediately drawn to him, attracted by his generous spirit and caring attitude. But Mike has a serious problem. He regularly rages at those closest to him, particularly family and members of his office and surgical staff. His outbursts are unpredictable, often triggered by incidentals that most people would not even notice. Mike has regularly lost staff members who tire of his behavior. But until recently he did not consider that the problem was his own, blaming anyone and everyone for making his world more difficult.

Only after conversation and prayer did Mike come to see that long-standing anger toward his withholding father was being unleashed at the people around him. Mike had never confronted his father, and had a difficult time admitting that years of disapproval had left him disappointed and upset. He certainly did not stuff his feelings; rather he fired them off indiscriminately, hurting others with his misdirected anger. The outbursts may have offered temporary relief, but he was not touching the real problem that was generating the rage in the first place. Mike was shooting the arrows of his feelings without concentration or aim. As a result, things were only getting worse. This gifted man needed guidance to clearly identify the source of his anger and then express it in ways that were consistent with God's word and helpful to the healing process.

Helping People Understand Emotions

Many people who come for inner healing prayer will be battling a torrent of unpleasant feelings, but remain unaware of the relationship between what they are experiencing and the healing process. It is part of the caregiver's responsibility to help the broken understand human emotions and guide them to respond appropriately. I have found that one or more of the following three steps enable people to embrace their feelings more positively: instruction, permission and prayer.

Instruction

People know they have feelings, but seldom understand why. As a result, they act out their feelings in ways that compromise their health and well-being. A caregiver should be sensitive to instruct people about the role emotions play in their lives. Dan Allender and Tremper Longman III have written an important book about emotions called *The Cry of the Soul* (NavPress, 1994). In this book they discuss the link between emotions and personal health. Feelings serve as signals to a person's spiritual condition, telling him a great deal about what is happening inside of him. If a person learns to listen, he will be able to discover potential questions, misbeliefs, and weaknesses relative to faith. Allender and Longman write:

> We can...view our emotions from the perspective of whether they lead us to engagement with God or move us away from greater dependence upon Him. We can listen to what they tell us about our struggles. Emotions are like messengers from the front line of the battle zone. Our tendency is to kill the messenger. But if we listen carefully, we will learn how to fight the war successfully.[1]

I can easily illustrate this truth from my own process of healing. As anxiety began to dominate my life, I sought every way possible to kill the pain, but all I did was further compromise my life. But when I learned that emotions were messengers, I began to listen. I found that my feelings were trying to tell me that there was a deep insecurity within that only Jesus could touch. By His grace, and with the help of my own caregiver, I began to follow the cry of the soul to the source of pain, and there met the Lord as never before. My experience can be the experience of every person who turns to a caregiver for help. Feelings are not enemies. Granted, people must not base all their decisions or actions upon feelings. But they must learn to listen, for the message feelings carry is critical to personal well-being.

I have also found it important to instruct people on ways to identify and label their feelings. Many people who come for help will be quite out of touch with their emotions. They will have learned to spend a great deal of time in their head, trying to respond to their environment rationally and objectively. As products of the Enlightenment that may sound good, but it keeps people away from the deepest part of what it means to be human. The feeling part of who they are is closely connected to a sense of personal identity. Only by accessing feelings will they be able to move deeper to discover who they are as God's unique and gifted children. But when asked to talk about their feelings, the broken often are unable to do so with much accuracy. Or they will generalize all their emotions into the categories of happy, sad or angry. Their emotional center remains an unexplored region that the caregiver must help them traverse. Providing definitions of specific feelings and helping the broken accurately identify what they are experiencing is a giant step toward release and deep inner healing. Numerous books and resources provide help with this process, including, *Emotions: Can You Trust Them?* by James Dobson.

Finally, I recommend that the caregiver emphasize the importance of a safe place where the broken person can express negative feelings, free of condemnation and judgment. Two things can complicate this. First, if support people are prone to move quickly in an effort to resolve a person's feelings, they may compromise the process. Safety means that the caregiver must be patient, allowing time for the pain and heartache to be experienced. Second, a context can be unsafe if the people who are helping have a personal investment in the situation. "Safe people" are able to empathize yet not react out of their own personal involvement.

Initially the caregiver should not encourage a broken person to vent feelings directly toward those who have hurt or offended him. There will be a time for that, but later. I believe it best to first open up the torrent of feelings before the Lord. He alone is able to bring the deep healing necessary to freedom and well being. Unleashing feelings without first meeting the Lord can result in more hurt. But when an individual resolves much of the internal turmoil in an honest encounter with God, he or she can move forward to take action that enhances greater wholeness for all concerned. Specific steps in that process will be discussed in a later section of this chapter.

Permission
When I began to work with Martha I discovered that she believed that negative feelings were sinful. Raised in a Christian home, she was taught that believers do not show anger, grieve losses or admit fear. To do so would be reason for discipline and potential disqualification. She was taught that Christians were happy, forgiving, optimistic people who always see the bright side of life. One of the tragic consequences of all this was the fact that, after revealing childhood molestation, Martha had no opportunity to release the deep cry of her wounded soul. She was admonished to forgive her offender as Jesus would and move on. By the time I saw Martha, she had suppressed the pain for years and was suffering as a result. One of my first tasks was to convince her that expressing negative feelings was an important and permissible Christian response to deep pain.

Christians may teach that expressing emotions is wrong, but they cannot support that idea from God's word. Jesus certainly did not suppress His feelings. In numerous places in the Bible we find Jesus responding with deep emotion to the events in His life. This was not just true of positive feelings, but also of the negative. The following passages (emphasis added) provide examples:

Filled with compassion, Jesus reached out his hand and touched the man. (Mark 1:41)
He looked around at them in anger and, deeply distressed at their stubborn hearts, said... (Mark 3:5)
He was amazed at their lack of faith. (Mark 6:6)
When Jesus saw this, he was indignant. (Mark 10:14)

...He was deeply moved in spirit and troubled. "Where have you laid him?" he asked. "Come and see, Lord," they replied. Jesus wept. (John 11:33-35)
"Love each other as I have loved you." (John 15:12)

Jesus did not deny, kill or stuff his feelings. He expressed his emotions openly and appropriately, an example to all who would grow to become healthy and mature Christian people. Furthermore, the Psalms are full of virtually every emotion known to humankind. The writers express love, joy, delight, wonder, awe, amazement, anger, sorrow and despair repeatedly. The psalmists also unleashed dark feelings that were oppressing them, crying out openly in times of deep depression and utter hopelessness. Often they admitted feelings of doubt, disappointment and deepest fears. At times it seems that their feelings of frustration and rage bordered upon the disrespectful, yet God heard their cries and reached down to meet them in the midst of heartache and feelings of abandonment.

> How long, O Lord? Will you forget me forever?
>   How long will you hide your face from me?
> How long must I wrestle with my thoughts, and
>   every day have sorrow in my heart?
> How long will my enemies triumph over me?
> Look on me and answer, O Lord my God.
>   Give light to my eyes or I will sleep in death;
> My enemy will say, "I have overcome him,"
>   and my foes will rejoice when I fall.
> But I trust in your unfailing love;
>   My heart rejoices in your salvation.
> I will sing to the Lord,
> For he has been good to me. (Psalm 13)

Abandonment, compulsive thoughts, depression and enemy attacks are taking a toll on the psalmist. But instead of hiding, he cries out to the One who can help him find freedom and deliverance. So it must be for the broken. A caregiver will serve people well whenever he helps them see that expressing emotions is not only permissible, but is a biblically correct response to life.

Prayer

Even after careful instruction and permission, people will often find it difficult to express what they are feeling in ways that enhance healing. At that point, a caregiver should help the broken person lean into the Lord for help. She can pray with the individual, seeking the presence and empowerment of the Holy Spirit, asking Him to heal the emotional fabric of the person's life. It may even be beneficial to anoint the person with oil, as a sign of the Lord's touch. More than once I have prayed with people in this way, specifically asking the Holy Spirit to help the person release the pent-up emotion. Movement invariably occurs when such a prayer is offered patiently and in faith.

It may also be valuable for the caregiver to encourage the broken to write out their feelings as a way of accessing what is locked deep within. People who have difficulty identifying and expressing emotions are often able to begin the process with pen and paper. Once again I want to illustrate this process with reference to Martha. Even after time explaining the purpose of emotions and pointing to scripture, I found her hesitant and self-conscious about touching her feelings. I sent her away with an assignment to write a psalm of lament.

I explained to Martha that in the Psalms prayers of lament outnumber songs of praise. Though the Christian tradition has largely ignored the lament psalms, they are acts of worship that remind us that we are fragile people and needy in most moments of our lives. The act of lament flows from our weakness and distress; it is the cry of the soul when God seems far away. The psalm of lament is the honest, uncensored expression of the heart that is broken, disappointed and powerless. The psalmists who wrote the scriptural laments invite us to weep before the Lord, presenting our offerings of pain and our complaints that "life isn't right." Lament is an act of admitting our barrenness and surrendering our hurt to God, ultimately acknowledging that it is God himself that we need most of all.[2]

The requirements for Martha were simple. She was to sit down and pray for the help of the Spirit, and then write a lament to the Lord, expressing, without censoring, whatever she was feeling at the time about her molestation. I assured her that there was no pressure to make something happen. She simply needed to be honest. Here is her very first lament:

Lord, I am afraid!!! I don't think I can do this. There is no way that I can convince myself that it is okay to be as angry as I think I am inside. I hate my dad so much. It is difficult to know how that can get turned into something good!! I feel sick to my stomach. I cannot breathe. I am way too anxious...It feels like I will not survive this. Lord, please can't you just take these feelings away.... all of it, the anger, the fear, the anxiety, the sadness... please God, please!! Lord, please help me. That is what the cross is all about, isn't it? May I not forget that you love me; that you will never leave or forsake me. Lord, I love you so much, but I feel like what I am doing is so wrong. Help me see the truth. God, please forgive me for my unbelief. I hate my dad, he has no guts to do anything. It is like he is a nonperson, silent, always silent. I hate that he has silenced me and has been silent all his life. I hate you dad. I hate you for what you have done to me and left me with. You are so stinking weak. Can't you say anything for yourself? For what you did to me? Don't tell me you have nothing to say to me! You have something to say. Don't be silent...it feels awful, like I am a terrible person, like I did something wrong, like I am bad, like I am worthless, and YOU are ashamed of me. I hate feeling this way. I hate you. You are supposed to love me like a daughter, not like an object to take advantage of. You are supposed to love me, hold me, accept me, and tell me you are proud of me. You not only did not protect me, you violated me. God, please help me understand all of this. I feel awful, ugly. Oh God, I hate my family, I hate them so much. But I love them too. I feel like my heart is torn in two, part love, and part hate. God, please love me like I am supposed to be loved. Please love me.

When Martha returned, her emotions were close to the surface. She had never allowed herself to even think bad thoughts about her dad, let alone express her hurt and anger. But this exercise, done before the Lord, opened the way for her to feel and express what had long remained hidden and silent. She came ready to work, and after a brief discussion, we went to prayer. I asked the Lord to be present with us, and then instructed Martha to read what she had written, remembering that God was there. With the very first words, Martha became emotional. Tears flowed as anger and disappointment began to pour out of her wounded soul. I tried to be supportive and encouraging, all the while asking the Holy Spirit to help her unleash the deep despair that was compromising her spiritual and emotional health. He came and Martha was well on her way to experiencing the Lord's healing touch. There were many more laments for Martha, but with each one came the healing presence of Jesus. As the heartache poured out, His love rushed in to fill her as never before.

This exercise will help many people who have been locked in emotional turmoil. It is critical that the caregiver instruct the broken to complete the assignment before the Lord and to be absolutely honest. She should remind him that it does little good to edit words and feelings in an effort to make them proper and acceptable. The caregiver should tell the person that it might take several tries before the psalm of lament takes shape. That is normal. However, the caregiver should be clear that, once the lament begins, it is likely that feelings will begin to surface. While this may be initially uncomfortable for the individual, the caregiver should help him lean into the Holy Spirit and release the pain that has compromised his health and well-being. All of this instruction, permission, and prayer will enable the caregiver to position the broken for an encounter with the Lord that brings freedom. And, as an instrument of the Lord, the caregiver will clear the way for the broken to identify and confront the dark distortions and lies that have long empowered emotional turmoil.

Dark Distortions and Destructive Lies

Before moving forward to describe the next step in the process of inner healing prayer, a brief review is in order. Thus far the effective caregiver would have helped the broken person consider realistic changes in his life situation, identify and repent of sinful behaviors embraced in an effort to kill pain and temporarily meet deep needs, and release emotional turmoil in ways that are healthy and healing. All of this would have taken place under the leading of the Holy Spirit, experienced in an environment that is both safe and instructive. Significant and noticeable changes may already be taking place in the person's life, which would provide tremendous encouragement. These changes should be identified and celebrated. But there is still important work

to be done by the Lord at the level of destructive lies and then, ultimately, the place of deep wounding. Each step along the way is to be
approached prayerfully, with the clear knowledge that it is the touch
of Jesus that truly heals and frees the broken in Christ.

Remembering the structures of inner healing, it should now be
obvious that the next step will be to identify the destructive lies that
drive much of the emotional turmoil people experience. Seasons of
emotional and spiritual upheaval are often fueled by unchallenged false
beliefs. Like every strategy of the evil one, these false beliefs invariably
remain hidden, where they grow stronger and more destructive. For
most people these distortions were shaped during childhood as a result
of bad experiences, poor teaching by significant others, or as the out-
come of significant woundings in their lives.

Regardless of the cause, these lies must be brought into the light
where they can be exposed and renounced through the power of
Christ. Jesus said that the truth will set people free (John 8:32), and that
principle is a foundational part of the inner healing process. Transformation takes place whenever an individual exposes lies in the light of
Christ's presence. Such "truth encounters" supernaturally snatch power
away from the evil one and, as a result, reduce the emotional upheaval. The Lord then empowers people to align their thoughts and
beliefs with God's word, which inevitably brings strength and peace
where turmoil once reigned.

The Holy Spirit, as stated many times previously, guides this
process. Paul said that where the Spirit is, there is freedom (2 Cor.
3:17). The caregiver must recognize His leading in the process, helping the broken surrender to His internal search. This work does not
normally happen as a result of a single spiritual experience. It comes
about through the ongoing work of the Lord as He reveals the dark
lies, enables people to break free of their grasp, and then empowers
them to rest in the truth of who they are in Christ. This process is often
lengthy, demanding intense prayer and hard work. But transformation
awaits those who step into such an encounter with Christ.

This process can be well illustrated in Martha's experience of
inner healing prayer. As we have seen, she came for help because of
recurring seasons of depression. Within a short period of time it was
clear that she had never properly grieved the loss she had experienced
as a result of sexual molestation. All the anger and sorrow had been

locked within and even the slightest situational crisis would initiate an unbearable amount of anxiety. The turmoil needed to be released, but the process was not without problems. Martha was bound up inside because of dark and destructive lies. Several of these had been taught to her when she was little. Martha was raised in a Christian home where negative emotions were seen as bad, and as such were hidden away or denied. She told me that her parents repeatedly stressed that it was important for her to behave as a good Christian. This meant that problems had to be covered over with sweet smiles and pious platitudes. It also required that she never show anger, fear, or despair, because "good Christians" never experience such things.

These lies had become rules to Martha, which kept her locked in deep bondage. She told me that she had feared the Lord's wrath if she would express negative emotions. Martha lived by these dark principles that her parents had imposed upon her from childhood. The distortions had to be identified, exposed to the light of Christ, and renounced as strongholds of the evil one. Martha needed to hear the truth, and then be empowered by the Holy Spirit to rise above the lies. The process took time and the help of the Holy Spirit. But, as evidenced by the lament shared earlier, Martha was able to move toward health and wholeness.

The most destructive lies in Martha's life were the result of her molestation. As the Holy Spirit brought light into the dark place of her abuse, several false beliefs were exposed. Unable for years to confront the matter in a healthy way because of a dysfunctional family system, Martha was left to draw her own conclusions regarding what happened. She lived every day convinced that she was defective, unlovable and worthy of rejection. She believed that if anyone really knew what had happened to her they would judge and reject her. She lived with a nagging fear that she could never be safe. And, possibly worst of all, Martha felt that somehow she was to blame. All of this was brought to the surface as we sought the Spirit's direction and help through prayer. It was not pretty or easy, but out in the light the evil one was no longer in control. Jesus was positioning Martha for great healing.

It is easy to see how these lies created significant turmoil within Martha. Not only was there the pain of molestation, but there was the emotional upheaval generated by believing so many dark things about herself. Who would not experience despair, given the same belief system? Add to that the fact that it was "wrong" to express negative emotions, and depression becomes the only realistic consequence. If there is any serious desire to bring emotional balance, such lies must be confronted by the power of Christ through inner healing prayer. This took place with Martha, which opened the way for her to unleash years of anguish that had been bottled up within her soul. On the other side, she began to experience the promised peace of Christ, and new truths about her identity and value as God's precious child.

False Beliefs

My first exposure to the role of false beliefs came through the teaching and writing of Robert McGee. He is the founder of Rapha, a nationally recognized health care organization that provides in-hospital care for people suffering from psychiatric and substance abuse problems. He also authored the best-selling book, *The Search For Significance* (Rapha Publishing). McGee rightly contends that God intended for people to find their basis for self-esteem in their relationship with Him. He teaches that men and women can only build this through an experience of the love and forgiveness of Jesus Christ. But because of deep wounds and poor teaching, people experience self-contempt rather than self-love. According to McGee, this self-contempt is created by false beliefs, which then generate tremendous emotional turmoil in people's lives. Individuals then, as suggested earlier, try to address that upheaval in very destructive ways, which leads to emotional and psychological breakdown. Freedom comes, according to McGee, when the broken recognize the lies they believe, then replace them with the truth that comes from God's word.

In *The Search For Significance*, Robert McGee suggests that there are four main false beliefs that handicap emotional well-being. They are:

1. I must meet certain standards in order to feel good about myself. He calls this "the performance trap," and states that it leads to such things as the fear of failure, perfectionism, drivenness, manipulation and avoidance.

2. I must be approved (accepted) by certain others to feel good about myself. McGee refers to this as "the approval addiction." He says

that this false belief leads to trying to please others at any cost, fear of rejection, being overly sensitive, defensive and withdrawing from people.

3. Those who fail are unworthy of love and deserve to be punished. This is labeled as "the blame game" by the author, and causes people to live in fear of punishment, blaming others for personal failures, running from God and people, avoiding new opportunities and inflicting self punishment.

4. I am what I am. I cannot change. I am hopeless. This he calls "the shame trap," which brings feelings of shame, hopelessness, inferiority, passivity, loss of creativity, withdrawal from relationships and pretense of many kinds.[3]

Whenever people live according to one or more of these false beliefs, they compromise emotional, spiritual, and relational development.[4] The pain of all this drives them to embrace dysfunctional and addictive behaviors which eventually destroy their lives. Helping people experience freedom demands that the belief system be identified and replaced by the truth. And, as McGee so ably concludes, the only truth powerful enough to do that is found in the person of Jesus Christ. McGee identifies specific scriptural teachings that correspond to the four false beliefs:

> *The Performance Trap.* God's answer is justification, which means that God has forgiven me of my sins, but has also granted me the righteousness of Christ. Because of justification, I bear Christ's righteousness and am, therefore, fully pleasing to the Father. (Rom. 5:1)
>
> *The Approval Addiction.* God's answer is reconciliation, which means that although I was at one time hostile toward God and alienated from Him, I am now forgiven and have been brought into an intimate relationship with Him. Consequently, I am totally accepted by God. (Col. 1:21-22)
>
> *The Blame Game.* God's answer is propitiation, which means that Christ satisfied God's wrath by His death on the cross; therefore, I am deeply loved by God. (1 John 4:9-11)
>
> *The Shame Trap.* God's answer is regeneration, which means that I am a new creation in Christ. (John 3:3-6)[5]

When the Rapha hospital system was at its height, people all across America were being taught about the destructive consequences of the four false beliefs, and then helped to embrace the truth of who they were in Christ. McGee's network of trained counselors and psychologists were helping people find freedom from addictive behaviors and emotional turmoil, encouraging them to base their self worth on the love and acceptance of God. I count myself as one who benefited, both professionally and personally, from Robert McGee's pioneering work through Rapha and his book, *The Search for Significance*. His work first convinced me that the responsible caregiver must help people identify destructive lies, and then point them to the truth of all that is theirs in Christ Jesus. This is the only way to find lasting peace where emotional turmoil once went unchecked.

As important as McGee's contribution is, my personal and professional experience has taught me that a caregiver must take this matter further than he did. It is not enough to teach people about the four false beliefs and then help them replace the lies with truth. This is a great beginning, but will not always impact the healing process as deeply as necessary. A caregiver should be prepared to help the broken deal with lies in three additional ways.

First, a caregiver must encourage the broken to identify the specific lie(s) that have compromised personal well-being. While the four false beliefs are helpful categories, they are often too general for people to identify in their own lives. Julia came for inner healing prayer because she was full of self-contempt. Time and prayer revealed several causes for this, including a very painful lie that had been spoken into her in childhood. Julia's mother was a seamstress, and on one occasion had made a beautiful pink dress for a neighbor's daughter. Upon seeing it, Julia asked her mother to make one like that for her. Her mother said, "You are not feminine enough to wear pink. I'll make you an orange dress." These words devastated Julia, affecting her sense of self-worth and her attitude about her own femininity. This specific lie, while possibly categorized under McGee's fourth false belief, the shame trap, needed to be exposed and directly addressed.

Many of the lies a caregiver encounters will be like that. Here is a list of some that I have heard when praying with the broken:

I am stupid.

I am ugly.

Girls are not as important as boys.

It is wrong to be angry.

I have horseshit for brains.

I am plain.

Others are more important than I am.

I can't make decisions on my own.

I can never be safe.

I will never amount to anything.

I can't do anything right.

If people knew the real me they would reject me.

I am permanently defective.

I am damaged goods.

Boys should not express emotions.

I am on my own.

It is not safe to be alone.

God is angry at me.

I am responsible for how others feel.

I am not capable of succeeding.

This list could go on and on. Obviously believing such things could generate a great deal of emotional turmoil in a person's life. More often than not, these lies were caused by the words and actions of significant others, and left deep wounds that compromised a person's sense of well-being. While the distortions may be categorized in the general list of four false beliefs, healing happens best when the work is specifically applied. This includes not only identifying the specific lie, but also the corresponding truth that is found in God's word. This is the work of the responsible caregiver, who understands the nature of emotional upheaval and the wonderful promises found in scripture.

Second, a caregiver should recognize that it is not enough to simply tell a broken person the truth. They need to experience the transforming touch of the Lord. I would like to believe that understanding the truth intellectually brings freedom to people. But it is often only the beginning of the healing process. Rachel came for prayer after a long and destructive relationship with an abusive husband. Years of mistreatment had severely damaged her self-worth. Rachel believed that she was worthy of being walked over by everyone and anyone. In prayer she revealed that her husband had regularly called her a "fat, ugly pig." For years he had screamed these words into her soul until Rachel believed they were true and accepted his rejection and abuse. When the time came to work on the lies, this phrase came forth quickly. I pointed out numerous scriptures that spoke of Rachel's worth before God. That did help some, but did not go deep into the place where these words took root.

I determined, through the Holy Spirit's guidance, that we would go to prayer and ask the Lord to help Rachel hear the truth. I asked Rachel to tell the Lord what she believed about herself. With tears and shame she did as requested. I then encouraged her to ask the Lord how He saw her. I waited, and prayed during the silence. Suddenly Rachel's face began to glow, with tears of joy beginning to run down her cheeks. I sensitively asked her to share. Rachel told me that she heard the Lord call her "His special Princess." These were not words I had ever used, but they were certainly consistent with the testimony of scripture. Rachel was overjoyed. The voice of God became louder and stronger than the words of her abusive husband. The "Truth" had set her free. The caregiver should be prepared to both speak the truth to the broken, and to also position them in prayer to hear God whisper life into a dying soul.

Third, the caregiver should consider the possibility that a level of demonization has occurred as a result of the lies. Once again I direct the reader to the last chapter, which will treat this subject in some detail. Here it is enough to comment that the evil one will stand on any ground he is offered. If a person has believed lies about himself and about God, Satan is quick to capitalize upon that darkness to harass and afflict the broken. A caregiver should be aware of that potential and guide the broken through prayers of renunciation and deliverance. This process need not be complicated or frightening for the caregiver or for the person being helped. Christ has won the victory, and has given power to believers to set the captives free.

Practical Guidance for the Caregiver

There are five final considerations that a caregiver should know related to the lies that keep people in bondage. First, the caregiver must know the truth in order to share the truth. Scripture is inspired by the Holy Spirit and contains God's word of hope and healing to all the broken and lost. It is critically important that the caregiver know and believe what the Bible says. When it comes to freeing those in bondage, personal opinion and popular thought do little good. It is the Truth that sets people free. If the caregiver intends to speak the Truth into people's lives, he must know that Truth.

I appreciate the work of Neil Anderson, who has written several valuable books that teach Christians about their identity in Christ. In virtually every volume, Anderson writes about the glorious inheritance that God has given to his children. Like McGee and numerous others, Anderson believes that people suffer because they do not know and believe this truth. He describes in detail what God's word teaches regarding the provision that Christ has made for the broken. Included in most of his books is a list of texts that Anderson encourages Christians to claim for their own. He personalizes them as follows:

> *I am God's child (John 1:12)*
> *I am Christ's friend (John 15:5)*
> *I have been justified (Rom. 5:1)*
> *I am united with the Lord and I am one spirit with Him*
> *   (1 Cor. 6:17)*
> *I am a member of Christ's body (1 Cor. 12:27)*
> *I am a saint, a holy one (Eph. 1:1)*
> *I am complete in Christ (Col. 2:10)*
> *I am free forever from condemnation (Rom. 8:1, 2)*
> *I am a citizen of heaven (Phil. 3:20)*
> *I am God's workmanship, created for good works*
> *   (Eph. 2:10)*
> *I can do all things through Christ who strengthens me*
> *   (Phil. 4:13)*[6]

This representative list is an excellent way to use scripture with people caught in destructive false beliefs. The caregiver would do well to develop a thorough collection of such verses, familiarize herself with them, and speak them into broken people in the context of inner healing prayer. The caregiver would also be well served by remembering that the best way to recognize a lie is to thoroughly know the truth. Fail here, and the process of helping broken people find freedom is seriously jeopardized.

Second, the caregiver must listen carefully to a person's story, with an ear for recognizing destructive lies. While it is true that there is usually a specific time to deal with false beliefs in the counseling process, a caregiver should be listening for them from the first meeting. If the caregiver is well versed in the truth, she will recognize them even when they are carefully camouflaged by the evil one's darkness. When I meet with a person for inner healing prayer, I keep a pad close at hand. One reason for this is to record any lies that I hear the person speak in the midst of his story. More often than not, I simply record what I hear and then let it wait for the appropriate time. But, after looking at a person's life situation, dysfunctional behaviors and emotional upheaval, I refer back to the list. I give some instruction to the person regarding the nature of false beliefs and lies, and then encourage him to think about what may be beneath the surface of his own emotional turmoil. My list is always at hand, a ready guide for further work and Spirit-filled prayer.

Third, the caregiver should be prepared to help the broken identify the lies they believe. I use an exercise that invariably helps people discover the false beliefs that have driven them. After some basic instruction about lies, regarding how they are shaped and the affect they have, I send them away to work. I give them two strips of white bandage, then ask them to seek the Lord's help in identifying the lies that have been spoken into them since childhood. Many of these will already be apparent. But the exercise always unveils more and keeps the broken focused upon the work of identifying their lies.

Once discovered, they write all the lies upon the two bandages. I encourage them to include any specific incidents related to the lies. They are also asked to find two sticks, one to represent the dominant lie that they were driven with as a child, and the other to represent the most powerfully destructive lie they have driven themselves with in life. I pray before they leave, and encourage them to trust the Lord to point the way to truth. Regardless of how apprehensive or unconvinced, people return with the specific sticks and the bandages covered in ink. The sticks are normally very different from each other, of various shapes and sizes, symbolically meaningful to the individual. Upon their return I ask them to describe their feelings and experiences while doing the assignment. Then, with all this in hand, I move forward to pray about everything that has been discovered.

Fourth, the caregiver should help the person pray for freedom and deliverance from all destructive lies. I believe that prayer makes things happen, even moving spiritual forces in heavenly places. I am particularly convinced that the prayers and declarations of the wounded individual himself are most important to the process. With this in mind, it is necessary that the broken bring all that they have learned before the Lord and, by faith, seek His touch. I ask people to hold one of the two sticks, and begin to pray a simple four-step process.

First, I ask them to describe to the Lord the specific lie; second, to tell Him all that this distortion has cost them; third, to renounce that lie and any level of demonization that has occurred as a result of it; and fourth, to declare in the heavenlies the corresponding truth that is theirs in Christ. Once completed, I encourage them to take the two sticks and bandages, and shape a cross. This then becomes a symbol of their newfound freedom and deliverance. This process has proved to be powerfully freeing for literally hundreds of people. The caregiver, whether using the exercise or not, should help people pray to the Father, exposing the lie, describing the cost, renouncing its power, and announcing the truth. This act takes the process well beyond the intellect to the spiritual center of life.

Fifth, the caregiver should equip people to continue to walk in freedom from destructive lies. There are two ways for this to happen. First, the process of prayer modeled in the session can be taken home by the person being served. Just recently I received a note from someone I had prayed with well over a year ago. He not only thanked me for the time we spent together, but commented that he was able to do lie work on his own. He had recently discovered another false belief, and knew to pray as he had done in my office. This is a valuable tool that any caregiver can give to the people he serves.

Equally important is helping people hold fast to the truth. The caregiver should know that, even after a person has identified and renounced a particular lie, he can fall prey to it again if not careful. The antidote for this is spending time each day declaring God's promise and provision for one's life. The caregiver should provide a list of specific scriptures, much like the example given earlier. I have identified nearly one hundred such truths, and give them to people as a guide. I also encourage them to highlight those that refer specifically to the issues they have addressed, and to carry a notebook or card that contains such texts for easy reference. I keep such a list in my Bible, and pray through it regularly as a way to enfold specific truth deep within my soul. While the bondage has been broken, such scriptures serve to fill the heart with much needed nourishment.

Emotional upheaval and the lies that drive it are serious issues for the broken. But through inner healing prayer, God has provided a way for people to experience His transforming touch. It is possible to see people move from turmoil to peace and from deep despair to hope. Lies can be exposed to the light of Christ and replaced with the one Truth that sets people free. This work is a gift of the Lord, available to all who reach out for His powerful touch. It is hard work, but an exciting invitation to new life for every broken person who longs for freedom. The caregiver has the opportunity to be an instrument of this wonderful healing process, a calling that anyone would be humbled to follow. With all this completed, there is one place yet to go on this healing journey, where deep wounds still bring pain and heartache. That is the focus of the next chapter.

Notes

1. Tremper Longman III and Dan Allender, *The Cry of the Soul* (Colorado Springs, CO: NavPress, 1994), 24.

2. On the function of biblical lament, see Walter Brueggeman, "From Hurt to Joy, from Death to Life," *Interpretation* 28 (1974), 3-19.

3. Robert McGee, *The Search for Significance* (Houston: Rapha, 1990), 40, 41.

4. Ibid., xiv.

5. Ibid., 40, 41.

6. Neil T. Anderson and Rich Miller, *Freedom from Fear* (Eugene, OR: Harvest House, 1999), 340-342. Other books by Neil Anderson include: *The Bondage Breaker; Walking Through the Darkness; Living Free in Christ;* and *Victory Over Darkness.*

For Further Reading

The Cry of the Soul, by Dan Allender and Tremper Longman III
Emotions: Can You Trust Them? by James Dobson
Shame and Grace, by Lewis Smedes
The Search For Significance, by Robert McGee
The Search For Peace, by Robert McGee and Donald Sapauh

Nine

Healing Deep Wounds

I am sure that there are people who believe that the wounds of the past do not impact the present. I, though, am not one of them. Regardless of how forgotten or hidden, old wounds shape the way people think, feel and respond to life. Without the Lord's healing touch, those wounds affect people in negative and destructive ways, often sending individuals into deep spiritual, emotional and relational crisis. The caregiver will invariably find that beneath the presenting problem are wounds that compromise the well-being of people who come for help. He must help them identify these hurts and then invite the Lord to touch each wound with His healing power.

I understand why people want to forget hurtful memories from the past. Wounds are ugly, dark and destructive. They often bring with them feelings of shame and fear, and no one wants to re-experience such negative emotions. As a result people develop elaborate mechanisms to distance themselves from any remnant of what occurred. Memories are locked away, denied, minimized or marginalized. All the while these untouched wounds continue to bring harm to people's lives. Though hidden far below conscious awareness, they remain powerful and destructive. They must be remembered and addressed by the Lord if the broken are to experience freedom and wholeness. Henri Nouwen wrote:

It is no exaggeration to say that the suffering we most frequently encounter is a suffering of memories. By not remembering them we allow the forgotten memories to become
independent forces that exert a crippling effect on our functioning as human beings.[1]

Also, when our memories remain covered with fear, anxiety, or suspicion the word of God cannot bear fruit.[2]

The caregiver who seeks to minister inner healing prayer will
repeatedly encounter people who have worked hard to forget. Many
will be able to describe the symptoms of their problem, yet be out of
touch with the real cause. Trying to help a person without getting to
the wound is like cutting the leaves to an ugly weed while leaving the
hidden roots untouched. The symptoms will return, because the cause
remains deep in the darkness of the wounded soul. Inner healing
prayer attends to such wounds, revisiting the memories that the Holy
Spirit identifies in order to invite Jesus into the pain. This chapter
focuses upon that process.

Preliminary Considerations

A caregiver should understand three foundational considerations
before moving forward to pray for deep wounds. First, inner healing
prayer, as we have seen, is at every level a ministry of the Holy Spirit.
A critical aspect of this ministry relates specifically to the process under
consideration in this chapter. As mentioned previously, many wounds
are hidden away in the subconscious. Broken people are often
unaware of the specific incidents that have compromised their well-
being, and as a result need help identifying deep wounds. While I have
heard of techniques some caregivers use to "retrieve" what is hidden,
I recommend trusting the Spirit with that process. He can bring to mind
every wound and hurt that remains untouched by the Lord. He is able
to reveal them in the way and order that best serves the inner healing
process. Experience tells me that if the caregiver helps the broken person ask, the Spirit will answer that prayer. The Holy Spirit might bring
memories to mind during the session, while working, walking, cook-
ing or watching television. What needs to be addressed will be brought
into the light, and the wise caregiver will trust that process.

Second, the caregiver is best to remember that the primary goal is
to help a person meet Jesus in the painful memory the Spirit identifies.

His presence brings change that cannot be experienced in any other way. For most people, that change will include the release of powerful grief, followed by powerful healing and deliverance. They will move forward in life with newfound freedom, unhampered by the wound or the resulting lies, turmoil or destructive behaviors. However, there will be times when Jesus will enter the wound, not to heal immediately, but instead to strengthen a person to become a wounded healer. Much like Paul's admonition of 2 Corinthians 12:8, the Lord's grace will be enough, enabling the person to experience Christ's power through weakness.

I have experienced this in my own journey to wholeness. While the Lord empowered me to repent of sinful behaviors and renounce destructive lies, the symptomatic anxiety lingered. I found that this weakness became a doorway to the Lord's presence, enabling me to experience Him in the midst of the pain. From this experience He enabled me to help others who are similarly broken. His grace has been enough as the healing continues to progress in my life. The caregiver should be open to this possibility, always helping the broken to seek Jesus even more than personal healing. Healing will flow, but the process will vary according to His purposes for each individual.

Third, it would be wise to revisit the structures of inner healing prayer, with particular reference to deep wounds. Referring once again to the metaphor of peeling an onion, the work progresses from what lies at the surface to deeper, more serious problems.

Consider our simple diagram again:

Life Situation

Dysfunctional behaviors

Emotional Upheaval

Lies and Distortions

Wounds

Once the healing process has begun, a person experiences an entirely new cause and effect relationship relative to their wounds. It can be illustrated as follows:

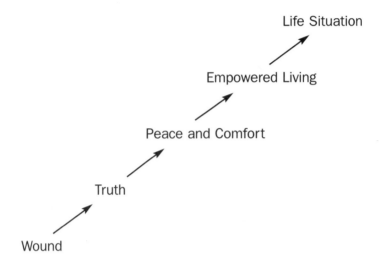

The changes are easily identifiable. The wound touched by Christ enables people to believe the truth of who they are in Him, which creates peace and comfort even in the midst of life's storms, and opens the way for them to experience Spirit-empowered living in the specific life situation. This is an entirely new way of life for the wounded, a transformation that takes place as the caregiver follows through on the Spirit-directed process. The specific steps to completing this healing will be discussed later in the chapter.

The Biblical Foundation of the Process

My interest in inner healing prayer did not begin out of mere professional curiosity. It came as the result of a dark and debilitating time in my personal life where I desperately needed to meet the Lord. After years of performance-driven ministry, my emotional and spiritual reserves were depleted. I had worked to achieve great goals, all the while compromising my own psycho-spiritual heath. Though symptoms of my problems had been present long before breakdown, I simply killed the pain and moved on to accomplish more "for the Lord." But all I really did was position myself for a long and difficult struggle with debilitating depression and chronic anxiety, which ultimately lead to hospitalization. Counseling and medical care helped, giving me some much needed cognitive and behavioral skills. But even after I began to function in ministry again, recurring symptoms made it clear to me that there had to be more healing than I was experiencing. With desperation and determination, I repeatedly turned to the Lord, crying out for His touch in the place of my deepest pain.

Even though I did not receive immediate healing as a result of my plea, I did at times sense the love and compassion of Christ. The battle was intense for a long time, and I often wondered if I could hold on. Yet there were those moments when I somehow knew that He was there and that He cared about me, even when the night was dark and the storm too powerful for me to endure. I especially experienced the tender presence of the Lord where the wounds were most painful. The words of Isaiah became an experienced reality, where he wrote of the Servant of the Lord, saying, "A bruised reed he will not break, and a smoldering wick he will not snuff out" (Isa. 42:2). I was that bruised reed, that smoldering wick, and I can testify that Jesus deeply cares for the broken hearted.

My journey toward the Healing Christ took me to the passion narratives of the gospels. I read the stories of His suffering repeatedly in order to better comprehend my own difficult times. It became increasingly clear that Jesus experienced far more emotional, relational, spiritual, and physical suffering that I ever did or would. I also saw at a deeper level than ever before that His passion was for me and every other broken person of the world. Jesus, the Son of God, clothed himself in humanity in order to bring salvation and healing to all who believed. Through the ministry of the Holy Spirit, I found that two particular passages held keys to my own inner healing. Both were about the suffering of Christ, and each held clear promise for my own healing.

> They went to a place called Gethsemane, and Jesus said to His disciples, "Sit here while I pray." He took Peter, James, and John along with Him, and he began to be deeply distressed and troubled. "My soul is overwhelmed with sorrow to the point of death," he said to them. "Stay here and keep watch." Going a little farther, he fell to the ground and prayed that if possible the hour might pass from him. "Abba, Father," he said, "everything is possible for you. Take this cup from me.

Yet not what I will, but what you will."

Then he returned to his disciples and found them sleeping. "Simon," he said to Peter, "are you asleep? Could you not keep watch for one hour? Watch and pray so that you will not fall into temptation. The spirit is willing, but the body is weak."

Once more he went away and prayed the same thing. When he came back, he again found them sleeping, because their eyes were heavy. They did not know what to say to him.

Returning the third time, he said to them, "Are you still sleeping and resting. Enough! The hour has come. Look, the Son of Man is betrayed into the hands of sinners. Rise! Let us go! Here comes my betrayer." (Mark 14:32-42)

Two other men, both criminals, were also led out with him to be executed. When they came to a place called the skull, there they crucified him, along with the criminals—one on his right and one on his left. Jesus said, "Father, forgive them, for they do not know what they are doing." And they divided up his clothes by casting lots.

The people stood watching, and the rulers even sneered at him. They said, "He saved others; let him save himself if he is the Christ of God, the Chosen One." The soldiers also came up and mocked him. They offered him wine vinegar and said, "If you are the king of the Jews, save yourself. There was a written notice above him, which read: THIS IS THE KING OF THE JEWS.

One of the criminals who hung there hurled insults at him: "Aren't you the Christ? Save yourself and us!" But the other criminal rebuked him. "Don't you fear God," he said, "since you are under the same sentence? We are punished justly, for we are getting what our deeds deserve. But this man has done nothing wrong."

Then he said, "Jesus, remember me when you come into your kingdom." Jesus answered him, "I tell you the truth, today you will be with me in paradise." (Luke 23:32-43)

These texts, as well as the entire passion narrative, demonstrated the extent of suffering that Jesus endured on my behalf. But I also came to see that they showed me how Jesus endured that suffering. I came to find within the verses a road map of sorts, plotting out the course toward my own encounter with Christ where I was hurting most deeply. By the guidance of the Holy Spirit, I found a way to approach the inner healing I so desperately needed.

Consider what these scriptures teach, by implication and design, about dealing with suffering. To begin with, it is clear that Jesus was experiencing great emotional turmoil. The scripture says that he was "deeply distressed and troubled," overwhelmed with sorrow to the point of death (Mark 13:33, 34). Luke wrote that Jesus was in such anguish that He began to sweat drops of blood. And he recorded that the struggle was so great that an angel appeared to help him (Luke 22:43, 44). Right away, anyone experiencing heartache can see that Jesus understands suffering. Because He felt the storm of emotional upheaval, He can help the broken embrace the chaos and darkness of their own distress. This is one reason I turned to Christ for inner healing, and why I bring the broken before Him for strength and freedom.

When it came time to deal with the deep issue in Christ's heart, He went before the Father and asked for help. He wanted his friends there for support, which they failed to offer. But Jesus knew that true help came from above. And so He prayed to His Father, unleashing His feelings without censure. Whatever was stirring within His soul came pouring out through His tears. He was also quite clear about what he wanted God to do for Him. The text records that three times Jesus asked God to take the cup away from Him. It seems that at some time during the process, Jesus heard from God, and surrendered His own will to the greater plan of God. With that, He arose in the Father's strength to face what was coming.

Christians know that Jesus defeated the evil one at Calvary, as described by Paul (Col. 2:13-15). This victory is one of the most important truths that the broken can embrace. But the gospel narrative quoted previously takes us beyond theological considerations to the actual events that took place at the cross. Jesus forgave all the people who were hurling insults, mocking, and laughing at him, praying, "Father forgive them, they do not know what they are doing" (Luke 23:34). He could have called down fire from above or asked for legions of angels to descend upon the people with a vengeance. Instead, even while in great pain from their wounds, he appealed to God's love and grace and extended forgiveness.

Jesus also ministered life to the unworthy even at a time when He was giving up His own. The people taunted Jesus, asking Him to prove His authority by saving Himself. He chose to ignore their pleas, for He knew that by doing less than they wanted He would provide more than they could ever need or imagine. By staying on the cursed cross, He brought the possibility of eternal blessing and rest to all who believe. How grateful I am that He did not do what they wanted, but instead gave what I so desperately need. Jesus also gave hope and promise to the thief, who in death expressed simple faith in Jesus as Savior and King. In response to a criminal's brief declaration of faith, Jesus assured him of paradise. Jesus was tender and compassionate to the broken and lost, even in extreme suffering.

These wonderful truths, briefly recounted here, have shaped my understanding of inner healing at the place of deep wounding. Over the years I have seen simple, yet profound principles take shape in my mind and practice from the passion of Christ. They now serve as a guide for praying with those who have been significantly hurt and wounded in life. I have walked this path with hundreds of broken people, and have taught it many times to caregivers. The Lord has used this process to transform countless lives, an act of His guidance and grace.[3] The steps are as follows:

Step 1: Bring the Broken Person Before their Heavenly Father

Step 2: Ask the Holy Spirit to Identify the Wound to be Touched

Step 3: Help the Broken Person Grieve His Loss Before the Lord

Step 4: Position the Person to Experience Infilling and Truth

Step 5: Encourage the Person to Extend Forgiveness

Step 6: Enable the Person to Embrace the Victory of the Cross

These concepts are not a blueprint that demands unwavering obedience to every step, precisely in sequence and identically applied. They are more like road signs that give direction along the path to inner wholeness. Landscape, weather, and unexpected obstacles demand much of the attention of a careful traveler. So it is for the caregiver, who must be carefully attentive during the inner healing process. Broken people will feel most vulnerable when the work gets to the level of deep woundings. They are usually vulnerable, fearful, and ashamed of what has been hidden away for so long. They will feel like the bruised reed and smoldering wick spoken of earlier. It is the caregiver's responsibility to keep the process focused and centered upon Christ. I believe the steps mentioned above serve that process well. Each will be discussed in detail in the section that follows.

Deep Wounds and Inner Healing Prayer

This whole book has been leading up to this part of the process. The core of the problem people face is the unaddressed wounds hidden away behind layers of protection and pretense. These wounds generate the great pain people experience and feed the lies, turmoil and dysfunctional behaviors that compromise well-being. Much work will have been accomplished by the client and the caregiver to get to this point. All of it has been important and necessary. But now, the heart of the problem must be brought into the light of the Lord's presence and touched by His matchless grace. Only then will true and lasting transformation take place.

Before detailing the specific steps that enable this process, several foundational reminders are in order. The caregiver must be spiritually and emotionally prepared to lead people through to strength and healing. This means, as stated from the very beginning, that the spirituality and emotional well-being of the caregiver matter. He must be intentionally leaning into the Lord, and trusting the Holy Spirit to guide each step along the path. Not only does that require being Spirit-filled, but it demands that the caregiver be Spirit-directed.

Throughout this final stage of healing the caregiver must continue to rely upon the Holy Spirit's insight and inspiration from scripture. He should be open to a potential word of knowledge that will open new doors of understanding, and be discerning about what is not seen, yet real. The caregiver should watch for possible intercessory feelings, as well as Spirit-inspired pictures and images that may serve as guides along the way. In addition, the caregiver should encourage the person who is receiving prayer to be equally watchful for the Holy Spirit's presence and power. True strength and healing will come because He is present. Neither the cleverness of the caregiver nor the hard work of the broken person can substitute for what Jesus can and will do for those who position for His touch.

Step One: Bring The Broken Person Before the Heavenly Father
When Jesus was in great emotional and spiritual pain He went to pray before the Father, wanting support from those closest to Him. The caregiver will do well to serve as that support for the broken. But the answers Jesus needed, and the strength He desired, rested with God alone. This point must not be lost when dealing with deep wounds. A great deal of discussion, instruction, and hard work will have preceded this moment. But once wounds begin to surface, horizontal conversation must surrender to the vertical. The caregiver will become less counselor and more priest, serving as a bridge between a broken person and a healing God. As John the Baptist so ably stated, "he must become greater; I must become less" (John 3:30).

The caregiver must never forget the role he has to play at this stage of the process. Like the friends who carried their paralyzed friend to Jesus for healing, the caregiver is there to bring the broken to the Lord. Conversation that aids and leads to that encounter is good. But there is no substitute for the connection between the wounded heart and the healing touch of Christ. By saying this I am not suggesting that the caregiver continue to talk about Jesus or describe His love or teach about healing. At this point the caregiver is there to help position the person to actually speak to the Lord, experience His love, and receive His healing touch. That, I believe, happens through focused prayer, initiated by the caregiver and continued by the person who is seeking healing.

When people reach this stage in the process, the caregiver should bow to pray, inviting the Holy Spirit to be present and asking Him to guide. After that, the caregiver should ask the person to tell the Lord why he has come before Him, describing as specifically as possible what he wants. The prayer does not need to be long, grand, or theologically deep. It can be a simple as, "God, I am hurting badly, and I need your help. I can't seem to get better on my own, so You are going to have to touch me. I need you." With that prayer, the final part of healing begins. The broken will be positioned before the only One who could set him free, waiting for God to heal the wounds that have long brought despair.

Too many Christian counselors do not help clients meet the Lord during the counseling session. The conversation is limited to words spoken between the professional and the broken person. Granted this is valuable and an important part of foundational work. But if inner healing is to occur, the dialogue must shift from the caregiver talking with the client to a broken person dialoging with the Living God. This is the course of true healing. And it is the responsibility of the caregiver to instruct people regarding how and when to make this shift.

I often share Psalm 142 as a way of preparing people to open their hearts to the Lord. King David was experiencing a great deal of opposition and rejection when, while hiding in a desert cave, he wrote this psalm.

> I cry aloud to the Lord;
> I lift up my voice to the Lord for mercy.
> I pour out my complaint before him;
> Before him I tell my trouble.
> When my spirit grows faint within me,
> It is you who know my way.
> In the path where I walk
> men have hidden a snare for me.
> Look to my right and see;
> No one is concerned for me.
> I have no refuge,
> No one cares for my life.
> I cry to you, O Lord;
> I say, "You are my refuge,
> My portion in the land of the living."
> Listen to my cry, for I am in desperate need;
> Rescue me from those who pursue me,
> For they are too strong for me.
> Set me free from my prison, that I may praise your name.
> Then the righteous will gather about me
> Because of your goodness to me.

In reading and describing this portion of God's word, I attempt to help the broken see that it is right and good for them to cry out to the Lord. He alone knows all about their pain, and is ready and able to help them find refuge, strength and healing in His name.

Step Two: Ask the Holy Spirit to Identify the Wound to be Touched
What are the specific wounds that have generated all the multi-dimensional problems experienced by the person being served? This is a vitally important question that I believe is answered best with the help of the Holy Spirit. By this time in the process the caregiver should have clearly explained the relationship that exists between deep wounds, lies, emotional turmoil, and dysfunctional behaviors that have compromised an individual's well-being. The caregiver should have led the individual through the preceding stages of healing, positioning him for this final and most important process. The wounds that have compromised the person's life must now be identified in order to present them to the Lord for healing.

Most people who come for help will have three categories of wounds. There will be those they have always known were present, those that they have hidden away and forgotten, and experiences that were hurtful but considered incidental and insignificant. All of these have the potential of causing significant problems, and should be considered during inner healing prayer. The very best way for this to happen is by inviting the Holy Spirit to reveal and direct the process.

Laura was a pediatrician and well-respected in her community as a caring Christian doctor. She regularly attended church, served on various community service organizations, and was well known for her generosity. Laura was married, with three young daughters, and appeared to be a happy and productive person. But below the surface of right behavior and professionalism, Laura struggled. She would regularly experience periods of self-hatred, often brought to the surface by interpersonal conflict. If she perceived that someone significant was not pleased with her behavior, Laura would begin a slide into a dark place of self-contempt. She did not just think that she had done something wrong, but that she was wrong. Able to maintain appearance, few would know that Laura had a problem. But she recognized that more and more she wanted to run and hide from everyone. The time had come for her to receive help.

After several sessions dealing with behaviors, emotions and lies, Laura began to focus upon deep wounds. As I generally do, I ended a session by suggesting that Laura ask the Holy Spirit to help her remember the unresolved events of the past that had wounded her. I told her to simply write down what came to mind throughout the week. She did not need to detail the event, but simply record a sentence that would bring the memory to mind when asked. I told Laura that she did not need to sit and think about it or work to remember periods of her life. I simply wanted her to trust that the Spirit would lead the way into her past. He might do that while she was driving, watching television, talking with a friend, or sitting in prayer. But I wanted her to make an initial list of what He brought to mind.

When Laura returned she was amazed by what she had remembered. Many of the events centered on her dad, who was explosive and verbally demeaning when angered. She remembered him tearing up little hearts she had made to decorate her room, pushing her away when she tried to kiss him goodnight, and repeatedly telling Laura's mother to "get her out of my sight." There were many such incidents on Laura's list, which would convince any person that he or she was undesirable and worthy of rejection. Laura said that she had forgotten most of these events, but felt the heartache as soon as they came to mind.

The time had now come for Laura to begin inner healing prayer that was focused upon deep wounds. I prayed, inviting the Lord to be present, and then encouraged Laura to ask the Father for help in the process. I then encouraged her to ask the Holy Spirit to bring to her mind the specific wound he wanted to address. I asked Laura to trust Him to lead the process, and soon she was focused upon a very specific incident. With that, we moved forward to meet the Lord through the remaining steps. I repeated this process with each memory the Holy Spirit brought to mind for Laura. Some were resolved in a relatively short period of time, while others were more difficult. In some sessions we covered several wounds, and at other times one session was not enough time to complete the process. In all, the Holy Spirit was in charge.

The principle behind this step is based upon allowing the Holy Spirit to identify the wound that needs to be addressed. Granted, people will already have memories and often want to work on them immediately. I recognize the sense of urgency this can create for a person, but believe that the caregiver must allow the Spirit to direct the process. The Holy Spirit knows what needs the touch of Christ and the order that best serves the inner healing process. This is an act of surrender that I believe leads to ultimate victory for the wounded person.

Finally, I want to say a word about hidden memories. People are able to lock painful events away from the conscious mind, dissociating from what happened. If a child is severely wounded, this can actually help him or her survive severe trauma. But in adulthood, such wounds will increasingly compromise a person's well-being. The wounds will likely need healing, and to do that these events will need to be remembered. But there is great disagreement as to how this should take place. I follow two guidelines. First, let the Holy Spirit guide. And second, trust Him to help a person remember, rather than give a "memory" to an individual.

Recently, a woman told me that God revealed that she had been molested by her grandfather when she was three. I asked her if she remembered that event, and she said no. I asked her if any family member remembered such an event, and she responded negatively again. I then asked her how she knew this took place, and she said the thought came to her mind while praying, and she believed God was revealing it to her. She then went on to tell me when God said it happened, where He said it occurred, and how many times. While I know God is able to do this, such claims make me nervous. It is very easy to be deceived and sent on a rabbit trail in this process. The evil one and our own creative subconscious minds are able to produce false memories. I believe that the Holy Spirit does help us remember, but when He reveals, we or others are able to recall the events. The idea that no one would remember what He is revealing raises a red flag for me. I would move forward with extreme caution and great prayer, leaning heavily upon the discerning work of the Holy Spirit in order to stay on track with the process.

Step Three: Help the Broken Person Grieve His Loss Before the Lord
There is a tragic incident of sexual abuse recorded in 2 Samuel 13. Amnon, one of the sons of David, lures his sister Tamar into his bedroom and wants to have sex with her. She begs her brother not to do such a shameful thing and tries to resist. But Amnon overpowers and rapes her. Afterward, he hurls verbal abuse and hatred at Tamar, and forcibly removes her from his presence. Devastated, Tamar runs away weeping loudly, and her brother Absalom sees her. He follows, learns what happened, and then gives his sister this horrible advice. He said, "Be quiet now, my sister....Don't take this thing to heart" (verse 20).

In other words, "stuff your feelings and forget your wound." Tamar follows his instructions, and the final word about her life was that she lived her life as "a desolate woman" (verse 20).

Every loss we experience needs a corresponding period of grieving. The length of time and depth of grief should correspond to the nature of the loss. When a person is small and someone breaks his favorite toy, he is right to cry for a while. Tears help the child process the loss and help him to let go and move on. The worst thing that could happen at this time is for an adult to say that the little one is being silly or childish. He is actually responding appropriately, unleashing disappointment, sadness and anger. When an adult loses a job or is betrayed by a friend or experiences the death of a loved one, it is right and healthy to grieve. How, where, when and how long a person must grieve will vary from person to person. But the process is important to everyone.

Jesus grieved before the Father in Gethsemane and received strength for the upcoming suffering. The disciples did not deal with feelings that night, but instead slept through the dark hour. As a result, when the pressure became great, they denied Christ, ran in fear, or lashed out in anger. So it is with broken people. Failure to grieve can set a person up for long-term problems, including depression, denial, avoidance behaviors and many other unhealthy reactions. The more ungrieved losses one has, the more powerful the internal tension the individual will experience when new losses happen. It is as if all the previous emotional upheaval attaches to the most recent event, driving the person into deeper and more devastating despair.

Wounds must be grieved, regardless of how far in the past they occurred. During the inner healing process, the caregiver should help the broken person feel the pain and express grief before the Lord. As already stated, the caregiver brings the person into the presence of the Lord, encouraging her to tell God why she has come. Next, the Holy Spirit is asked to identify the specific wound to be addressed. Once identified, the caregiver should encourage the broken person to describe the details of the event to the Lord. I asked Laura to tell Jesus about the time her dad up ripped all the decorations she had made for her room. She described the details of her room, the way she cut out hearts and stars, and where she placed them around the room.

Laura also told the Lord about her dad entering the room, calling her special artwork trash, and ripping it apart.

The caregiver should be supportive and affirming throughout. A gentle word or affirming touch when appropriate can help the person know she is not alone in the moment. I tend to ask three questions that help the individual open up to the grieving process. While I propose the question, the person is to answer it to the Lord.

How did you feel when this happened? I try to keep the individual focused on feeling words, which usually unleashes much of the pent-up emotion.

What did you believe as a result of this event? I ask this to identify any lingering lies, as well as to help the individual discover why the loss was so great. People interpret losses individually, and the meaning of the event varies according to personal perspective. For Laura, her father's actions meant that she was trash, had wasted time making artwork, and should be punished. Someone else may have interpreted the event differently, which is important to know in the process.

How did you react as a result of this event? This question helps the person see how he or she changed personal behaviors and attitudes, in response to another person's hurtful actions. This helps them let go of lingering dysfunctional behaviors and embrace life as the Lord intended.

The caregiver should be patient with this process, all the while keeping the dialogue directed to the Father, and spoken from the heart. Experience tells me that, with the Holy Spirit's help, people will pour out feelings that had been long hidden away. It is important to validate those feelings, and give room for the person to emote openly before the Lord. This step helps the person express feelings, and then let go. Too little or too much can compromise the process. The caregiver will need to be attentive and intentional.

Step Four: Position the Person to Experience Infilling and Truth
Wounded people often live alone in their pain, believing lies that continue to destroy their lives. In the earlier stages of the process the caregiver should have helped the broken person unleash feelings and recognize lies. That would have been helpful. But at this point, as the deep grief has poured from specific wounds, the time has come to invite Christ into the place where darkness and pain generate destruc-

tive power. Instead of being filled with pain, shame, and despair, Jesus is invited to bring peace, love, and comfort. That is the inner healing that most transforms people, and the caregiver should carefully guide the person into the divine encounter.

Once again, I will review the steps taken to this point. The caregiver will have brought the person before the Lord, and encouraged her to ask God for His presence and strength. With the help of the Holy Spirit, a specific wound would have been identified and described in detail to the Lord. With the support of the caregiver, pent-up feelings will begin to flow, as deep grief is expressed before the Lord. At the appropriate time, the caregiver will help the person ask the Lord to fill the wound with His presence and strength. A simple prayer is sufficient, as long as it comes from the heart of the person. When necessary, the person can repeat the following:

> Dear Father, I thank You for being here with me now. I ask to be filled with Your peace. Please bring Your light to every dark place where fear, anger, shame, and despair have built up within me. Please touch me with Your healing power, and help me experience Your presence. Speak Your truth to me, chasing all destructive lies out of my life. Empower me to live according to Your provision and promise. In Jesus' Name. Amen.

The caregiver should continue to sensitively guide the person through this step of inner healing. Once again I find three questions helpful:

What are you sensing? After a person has prayed for the Lord's touch, the caregiver should wait in prayerful expectation. After a period of silence, he should ask what the person is sensing. Hopefully, the presence of the Lord is beginning to flow into the individual's life. If so, the caregiver should bless that grace and ask for more. Possibly the person will tell the caregiver that there are negative feelings. If so, he should find out what is causing them and intensify prayer. Many times the person will feel little, so he and the caregiver should wait in expectant prayer.

What are you seeing? By this time the person should have been encouraged to offer his imagination to the Lord. This was discussed in detail in chapter five. The caregiver should find out if the person is having any images of the Lord touching him. The caregiver would also do well to sensitively share what he may be seeing, as it is lead by the Spirit. There are times when I direct the process, asking the person to revisit the memory, seeing it in the imagination. Then, I ask her to invite Jesus into the picture, in order to show her where He is in the moment and how He has come to help. Remember Laura's decorations? I walked her back through the memory and upon inviting Jesus into the moment, she saw Him grieving with her, and then hold her close as she wept about her father's brutality. She saw Jesus smoothing her crumpled hurts and treasuring them. Such pictures can take the truth of Christ's love deep into the place of wounding.

What are you hearing? God's word, spoken to the heart, brings great healing to people who have been trapped in painful wounds and destructive lies. As such, the caregiver should encourage the person to listen for His voice during the process of infilling. The woman who had been repeatedly called a "fat, ugly pig," heard the Lord call her a Precious Princess. That word was louder than all the shouts of her abusive husband, and caused great joy in her heart. Such words can come through the Spirit, speaking into the person's heart, or through the caregiver who gives a truth from scripture that speaks into the moment. This is a very important part of healing, giving the person an anchor of truth to hold her fast in the future storms life may bring.

The caregiver must not rush this step, for it lays the foundation of healing for future health and blessing. People need to meet the Lord, experience His infilling, and hear the truth about His love, protection, and provision. When they do, new life and freedom begin to flow.

Step Five: Encourage the Person to Extend Forgiveness
Forgiveness is one of the clearest requirements of kingdom living. Jesus taught it to His followers (Matthew 18:21-35), and clearly modeled it from Calvary (Luke 23:34). He required that forgiveness be extended mercifully and repeatedly, and said that those who fail to forgive will only end up prisoners of their own condemning heart (Matthew 18:35). Anyone who has lived with unforgiveness knows that it leads to deep bitterness and anger. When they try to exact payback and protection by withholding forgiveness, wounded people only add more destructive darkness to their already broken lives.

At this point in the inner healing process, the caregiver should encourage the wounded to release and forgive the person(s) who offended them, and rest in the provision and protection of Christ. This will not be easy for most people, even after they have been touched by Christ in the place of deep wounding. That is often true because of some misunderstandings about the nature of forgiveness itself. For this reason I briefly explain several important truths before asking the person to forgive.[4]

Forgiving is not forgetting.

Forgiving does not release the offender from responsibility.

Forgiving does not mean the offended must be positioned to be re-injured.

Forgiving is not pretending that it never happened.

Forgiving does not mean it did not matter.

Forgiving does mean that I release any desire for revenge, repayment, or punishment.

Forgiving means that Christ will give me strength to live with the consequences of the offender's actions.

Forgiving others flows from the forgiveness I have received in Christ.

Forgiving means that I recognize my own weakness and sinfulness.

Forgiving happens because of the blood of Christ, shed for me.

Sharing these truths will help the person take the risk to forgive, trusting that the Lord will now be enough. Sometimes forgiveness will need to extend not just to the offender but to the wounded person himself. Self-punishment can be a reality for some individuals, and at this step in the process, the person should be encouraged to forgive even himself.

The caregiver must understand the importance of time and sequence when it comes to forgiveness. Many Christians are pushed to forgive too soon. Jesus extended forgiveness from the cross, but first grieved His loss before the Father. I believe that same sequence of events helps the inner healing process. Wounded people need a chance to feel the pain of the wound and express the heartache caused by the hurt. They need to release before the Lord all that is bottled up inside, rather than stuff all the emotions down into some hidden place.

I have listened many times as broken people shared stories about Christians pressuring them to quickly forgive. When this happens, the process of healing is compromised. It is like covering a deep mud hole with a pretty blanket. The mess may be out of sight, but if anyone gets near, they are going to get stuck. The sinkhole needs to be cleaned out and then filled with solid materials. So it is with deep wounds. Broken people need cleansing, not pretentious coverings. I believe that happens best when the person's heartache is validated and given freedom for expression. Forgiveness needs to be genuine and deep, which comes as people are transformed by the healing touch of the Lord.

Step Six: Encourage the Person to Celebrate the Victory of the Cross
In his letter to the church in Corinth, Paul wrote, "For the message of the cross is foolishness to those who are perishing, but to us who are being saved it is the power of God" (1 Cor. 1:18). This power is greater and more extensive than any force on earth, and is available to all who trust in Christ. Every aspect of inner healing prayer happens because of what Jesus Christ did at Calvary. His sacrifice brings life to all who believe, and healing to our deepest wounds. His blood can cleanse the conscience of sin and bring eternal life to all who accept Jesus as the Lord of life (Heb. 9:14, 15). His death brings reconciliation to God, forgiveness for sin, payment for all debts against God and the power to overcome the forces of darkness (Col. 2:13-15).

With this in mind, the caregiver should help the counselee embrace the provision Christ has made and praise Him for the newfound life and freedom. This can happen in three specific ways. First, the caregiver can model gratitude by thanking the Lord for what was accomplished during the session. Second, he can help the person shape a similar prayer and offer it to the Lord. The prayer does not need to be long, well-developed or extensive. But it should include specific references to the Lord's provision, presence, and healing power. This act of thanks not only seals the work Jesus did more deeply into the person's heart, but it serves as a declaration into the heavenlies that the person has overcome through Christ. The spiritual implications of this small act are significant and should not be taken lightly.

Third, the caregiver can give a simple scripture assignment that will help the person understand the wonderful provision that Jesus has made for them. I encourage people to read the first three chapters of Ephesians, underlining each reference to a benefit that is theirs in Christ. I ask that they make a list of each, similar to the one that follows:

Gifted	Chosen
Blamelessness	Sealed by the Spirit
Adoption	Wisdom
Grace	Hope
Redemption	Forgiveness
Salvation	Great power
Peace	Nearness to God
Knowledge of God's will	Unity with other believers

I then encourage people to spend time each day praising the Lord for one item on the list. Doing this helps root individuals in the awesome provision of Jesus as well as birthing an attitude of thanks and gratitude for all he has done.

Finally, in completing the process of praying for specific wounds, the caregiver should lead the person in a prayer of renunciation. As mentioned earlier, the evil one will work where permitted, standing on whatever ground that is not under the control of Christ. Previously hidden wounds held the potential for just such an activity of darkness. Now, with Christ filling the specific wound with His peace and presence, the person should be encouraged to renounce any influence Satan may have had. The biblical and theological foundation of this will be discussed in the next chapter. Here, I simply encourage caregivers to help people pray such a prayer. It can be as simple as this:

Dear Jesus, I thank you for touching me today and healing the wound I received when _____. I declare your Lordship over that area of my life, and invite You to fill that memory with Your presence. I repent of any unhealthy reactions I made as a result of that wound, and align my life with Your will. I also renounce any level of demonization that may have existed, and offer that very wound as an instrument of Your Glory. In Jesus' Name, Amen.

The six steps discussed in this chapter have been used hundreds of times with broken people. There is nothing especially powerful about them, except that they invite the One who is powerful to move in people's lives. This is not a formula but rather a set of guidelines offered to the Holy Spirit and directed according to His purpose. The caregiver will find that they will help keep the process of inner healing prayer focused and moving forward in the power of Christ. The steps are impacted by the willingness of the person being served, and the prayerful attentiveness of the participating caregiver. And in the end, the excitement does not rest in the method but with the Healer who compassionately moves to set precious people free.

Notes

1. Henri Nouwen, *The Living Reminder* (New York: Harper Collins, 1992), 20.

2. Ibid., 23.

3. I first wrote of this process in my book, *Wounded: How you can find inner wholeness and healing in Him* (Christian Publications, 1994). The steps outlined in that book were not as extensive or biblically rooted as those described in this volume. They have served as the foundation of what is presented here, particularly the material in chapter eight of *Wounded*.

4. A thorough treatment of this issue is found in my book, *Draw Close to the Fire* (Grand Rapids, MI: Chosen Books, 1998), 128-146.

For Further Reading

Healing for Damaged Emotions, by David Seamands
Healing of Memories, by David Seamands
Whispers of Love in Seasons of Fear, by Terry Wardle
Forgive and Forget, by Lewis Smedes
The Search for Freedom, by Robert McGee

Ten

The Relationship Between Inner Healing & Spiritual Warfare

Many people are given to extremes whenever the topic of spiritual warfare is raised within the Christian community. This has been true for centuries and continues to be a reality today, even within the context of Christian counseling. On one end of the continuum are those who dismiss any possibility that demons exist or have anything to do with emotional and mental disturbances. Their training and theology has been influenced by a western worldview that denies the existence of spiritual beings, and as such they do not see or consider supernatural evil as a possible factor.

Some Christian scholars and pastors have sought to advance this position, convinced that the notion of evil spirits is superstitious nonsense left over from a less informed time. Rudolf Bultmann, noted New Testament scholar of the twentieth century, greatly influenced this liberal understanding of spirituality. He concluded that it is impossible for any thinking person to believe in devils and angels in an age of airplanes and electric light. He contended that the scientific age left no room for such naive and ill-informed beliefs.[1]

Some Christians would not go as far as Bultmann in de-mythologizing scripture, declaring themselves biblical and orthodox theists. In practice, however, they function much like deists. They confess belief in God, but in practice make decisions as though He were essentially distant and irrelevant to daily life. In matters of emotional and mental disturbance, they diagnose and treat people according to conclusions consistent with medical and behavioral sciences, without reference to or consideration of spiritual realities. Regardless of how "Christian" such care is called, it is rooted in a humanistic worldview that is inconsistent with scripture. People treated from this perspective can receive help, but transformation and freedom are compromised because a significant part of the problem is left untouched.

On the other end of the continuum are those who see demons everywhere. They spiritualize every event in life, blaming evil spirits for each discomfort or trial they face. Personal responsibility and the normal cause-and-effect relationship between action and reaction in an empirical world are eliminated. For them the devil is the cause, and the only response is aggressive warfare and exorcism. They see emotional disturbances, dysfunctional behaviors and illnesses as symptoms of demon possession, and they treat it accordingly. The thought that there could be biological or psychological considerations is quickly dismissed as unbiblical and unfaithful.

A dear friend of mine, whom I will call Susan, is yet recovering from her pastor's repeated efforts to cast demons out of her. After years of personal struggle she finally shared with him about losing blocks of time with no memory of what transpired. She told him that she would suddenly find herself in a place and have no idea how she got there. Revealing this to him was a huge risk and a desperate plea for help. The pastor immediately gathered a prayer team, and in a public setting led a deliverance session that went on for hours. People shouted at the devil and admonished Susan to display more faith. In the end, Susan lay on the floor, exhausted and afraid. She was finally taken to a person who understands emotional and mental trauma, and received proper diagnosis and treatment. Susan was suffering from Dissociative Identity Disorder, the result of severe abuse and molestation in childhood. Granted, there may have been some demonic element related to her struggle, but Susan needed much more than deliverance to move toward new life and freedom. She needed love, sensitivity and ongoing psychological and spiritual care that kept Jesus Christ at the center. Her pastor's approach was short-sighted and left her fearful, frustrated and ashamed that she did not have more faith. People treated this way are often more traumatized after the treatment than they were before.

In the preface to his classic book, *The Screwtape Letters*, C. S. Lewis made a plea for balance. "There are two equal and opposite errors into which our race can fall about devils," he wrote. "One is to disbelieve in their existence. The other is to believe, and to feel an excessive and unhealthy interest in them. They themselves are equally pleased by both errors, and hail a materialist or a magician with the same delight."[2]

Nowhere is it more possible to see the two extremes mentioned by Lewis than in people's views of emotional problems. And nowhere is balance more important to Christians than when discussing the relationship between spiritual warfare and inner healing. Throughout this book I have referred to demonization and the process of healing. Now, with caution and a concern for balance, I want to discuss this topic and its implications for healing broken people.

An Appeal for Balance

Before discussing the issue of spiritual warfare more directly, I want to consider briefly the matter of proper diagnosis and treatment. When people come to a caregiver for help, they often do not know what is causing their problems. People will spend time describing symptoms and situations, but the root issues are not always clear. The caregiver's responsibility is to do everything possible to identify the cause of the problems, then set forth a treatment plan that will help.

Caregivers tend to approach diagnosis through the lens of their own training and experience. This is understandable. But it can filter out certain contributing factors. Few people who come for help have one issue that is producing their symptoms. While one factor may be primary, other issues most often contribute to the upheaval. Any combination of the following factors can be present:

Family of origin issues
Biomedical factors
Psychological disorders
Life stressors and circumstances
Relational tensions
Lifestyle issues
Diet and nutrition

Sin

Spiritual issues, including the demonic

As most caregivers are aware, many of these causes have similar symptoms. A person can describe suffering from periods of light headedness, shortness of breath, thoughts of being out of control, despair and fatigue. It would be easy for a caregiver to quickly conclude that the person suffers from an anxiety problem, and begin to work on behavioral techniques that help reduce the flight or fight response. However, those may also result from biomedical problems, diet and nutritional factors, deep wounding in childhood, unconfessed sin or demonization.

A responsible caregiver should not jump to the conclusion that any single issue is causing a person's problems. In fact, it is better in my view to consider a combination of factors, and endeavor to determine what may be the primary cause, and what may be contributing to the situation. With this information available, one can develop a plan to address the issue holistically, attending first to primary causes, then to the contributing factors.

The caregiver can gather this type of information in three ways. I recommend that each be used, especially when the person coming for inner healing prayer has significant issues that are not easily diagnosed. First, the caregiver should encourage people to have a thorough physical exam. I did this when I began to suffer from depression and it kept me from obsessing about what might be wrong, and identified a lifetime battle with hypoglycemia that was a contributing, but not causal, factor in my struggle. Hurting people will be well-served by such an exam, and a responsible caregiver will suggest this as part of the healing process.

Second, people with recurring symptoms of emotional and mental disturbance should be tested psychologically. Most every community has licensed professionals available who can administer such tests. Many good instruments are available today to help identify problematic behavior and thinking patterns. Such tests are not 100% accurate, but they are scientifically developed and can reveal very useful information for diagnosis and treatment.

Finally, a caregiver will be well served by asking people to fill out a basic intake questionnaire or lifescript. Judy Allison and I have developed such an instrument that is included in the appendix. It is several pages long and includes questions about family of origin, lifestyle, diet, relationships, faith, and aspects of spirituality. There are questions that identify a person's previous involvement in occult activities. This information helps a caregiver determine if demonization may be related to a person's problems. All the data is important to the caregiver and should be considered when developing an overall treatment plan for the person seeking help.

This now brings me more directly to the matter of spiritual warfare and inner healing. I do not believe demons lurk behind every bush. But I do believe that a level of demonization can be at least a contributing factor and under some circumstances the primary cause of the problems some people face. I look for that possibility whenever people come for inner healing prayer, and I address it as a part of the overall process. This can be done in a way that is balanced, sensitive and not sensationalistic. As a matter of course I encourage people to pray basic deliverance prayers of renunciation at various points in the process of inner healing. Whenever there is evidence of more dramatic demonization, I help them take a more direct and intentional approach to living free from such influences. After defining what I mean by levels of demonization, I believe the concept will be less controversial that some may think. Regardless, the caregiver who intends to minister inner healing prayer should have a developed understanding of spiritual warfare and know how to help people find freedom in Christ.

Developing a Biblical World View

Many naïve people live by the notion that "what you see is what you get." The truth is that many perceptions of reality are not in fact reality. Things can appear to be much different from what they truly are. Every day the sun appears to rise in the east and set in the west. People describe the phenomenon that way, even though their description could not be farther from the truth. In reality the earth actually does all the moving, revolving around the sun every twenty-four hours. What you see is not always what you get.

So it is in spiritual warfare. Just because people do not see spiritual beings, does not mean they do not exist. And simply because a caregiver does not recognize the possibility of demonization does not mean that evil spirits are not playing a role in a person's problems. Most often, the problem lies more in the caregiver's worldview. I believe Charles Kraft's book, *Christianity with Power* (Vine, 1989), should be required reading for any person who ministers inner healing prayer. He provides a thorough treatment of worldview and its related considerations. Kraft writes:

> We will here define worldview as the culturally structured assumptions, values, and commitments underlying a people's perception of Reality. Worldview is the major influence of how we perceive Reality. In terms of its worldview assumptions, values, and commitments, a society structures such things as what its people are to believe, how they are to picture reality, and how they are to analyze. People interpret and react on this basis reflexively without thinking.[3]

Simply stated, worldview determines how an individual interprets what he sees. And that set of interpretive assumptions, values, and commitments is determined by what the person has been taught by the society/culture in which he has been raised. Most western Christians were raised and educated in a society/culture that did not believe in spiritual reality. Their worldview was dominated by a naturalistic and materialistic prejudice that prioritized reason and scientific inquiry. This belief system has filtered into the church and remains the dominant worldview upon which much Christian liberal arts education is based. A caregiver could be educated in a Christian college and never be taught about evil supernaturalism, particularly within the sciences. The entire subject might be essentially ignored, because the worldview says it does not exist. And so a hurting person could be significantly demonized, and the caregiver would not see it or address the problem. But not "seeing" does not mean that evil supernaturalism is not a reality. It simply means that the caregiver has a worldview that limits his ability to perceive reality.

Christian caregivers must be challenged to embrace a biblical worldview, which recognizes the existence of evil spiritual beings that are active on earth, with assignments to harass and hurt people. While this position may be hard for a western person to grasp, it is undoubtedly the worldview of New Testament Christians. Jesus certainly shared this belief and ministered to people accordingly. There are repeated references to the devil, evil spirits, and the ministry of deliverance in the gospel accounts of the Lord's ministry. After Jesus was baptized by John the Baptist, He went into the desert for forty days of fasting and prayer, and was tempted by Satan. Given that no one was there to witness this event, Jesus obviously must have shared the experience with His followers. He did this because He wanted them to know about the opposition that would be a constant part of their ministry to broken people.

Jesus certainly believed in evil spirits. The gospel records often refer to Jesus' confrontation with demonic activity as part of His healing ministry (Mark 1:32-24; Matt. 8:16; Luke 4:40, 41). There are also specific stories about people being delivered from evil spirits, including the Gadarene demoniac (Mark 5:2-20), Mary Magdalene (Mark 16:19), the man who could not speak (Matt. 9:32-34), and the boy who experienced repeated seizures (Matt. 17:14-22). Even the Pharisees who opposed Jesus recognized His ability to cast out evil spirits, but claimed that He used the devil to do it. Jesus responded to their accusations with a powerful teaching about evil supernaturalism. He said:

> Every kingdom divided against itself will be ruined, and every city or household divided against itself will not stand. If Satan drives out Satan, he is divided against himself. How then can his kingdom stand? And if I drive out demons by Beelzebub, by whom do your people drive them out? So then, they will be your judges. But if I drive out demons by the Spirit of God, then the kingdom of God has come upon you. (Matt. 12:24-28)

This text is important for two reasons. First, Jesus says that the ability to drive out demons is from the power of God, and, second, that deliverance is a sign that the kingdom of God is present on earth today.

When Jesus called His disciples, He gave them authority to cast out demons (Matt. 10:1). The book of Acts gives ample evidence that they did in fact include deliverance as part of their ministry (Acts 5:16; 16:16-18; 8:7). One particularly interesting story is found in Acts 19:13-16. It seems that the seven sons of a man named Sceva tried to invoke the name of Jesus in an effort to deliver a man who was demon-possessed. Interestingly, the demon spirit spoke saying, "Jesus I know and I know about Paul, but who are you?" (v. 15) With that, the man with the evil spirit jumped on them and beat them until they ran away bruised and naked. This story certainly encourages a caregiver to know what he is doing when confronting evil spirits!

One of the most important teachings about evil supernaturalism in scripture comes from Ephesians 6:10-19. With reference to spiritual warfare, Paul admonishes believers to,

> *Be strong in the Lord and in his mighty power* (v. 10)
> *Put on the full armor of God against the devil's schemes* (v. 11)
>   *The belt of truth* (v. 14)
>   *The breastplate of righteousness* (v. 14)
>   *The shoes of peace* (v. 15)
>   *The shield of faith* (v. 16)
>   *The helmet of salvation* (v. 17)
>   *The Sword of the Spirit* (v. 17)
> *Remember that the struggle is not against flesh and blood* (v. 12)
> *Pray on all occasions with all kinds of prayer* (v. 18)
> *Be alert* (v. 18)

Paul uses imagery from warfare because he knows that the enemy is real and violent against God's children. He wanted believers to be prepared for battle at all times, and always to look beneath the surface of events to identify the hand of the evil one and stand against him.

Jesus and the disciples held a worldview that recognized the reality of demonic forces. The responsible caregiver should do the same, taking evil supernaturalism seriously and setting forth strategies of healing and deliverance for broken people trapped by their designs. Such a position may not be popular in a modern society, but it is faithful to God's word. The remainder of this chapter provides a basic discussion of spiritual warfare, offering several steps for the caregiver to take in helping people find freedom through the power of Christ. The treatment will be brief, so it would serve the caregiver well to read additional volumes on the topic. Several of the better and more practical of these are listed at the end of the chapter.

Inner Healing and the Demonic

The first questions that most people normally ask are about the origin and nature of demons. "Where did they come from and what are they like?" The work of Fred Dickason, in *Demon Possession and the Christian* (Crossway), provides a balanced and biblical answer.

> There is a problem concerning the exact origin of demons, since it is not precisely stated in the Bible. We can say a few things with certainty. They are not the product of an overactive imagination or the disembodied spirits of a supposed race before Adam. Neither are they the monstrous offspring of angelic cohabitation with women before the flood (Gen. 6:1-4). There is no evidence for these views.
>
> There is good evidence, however, that demons are fallen angels aligned with their leader and chief demon, Satan. In his original rebellion, Satan drew with him a great number of lesser angels, perhaps a third of all created (Ezek. 28:18; Rev. 12:4). They may now be classified as either confined or free. The free have their abode in the heavenlies and have access to earth and its inhabitants (Ephesians 3:10; 6:12).[4]

Dickason describes demons as personal, spiritual and powerful beings, devoted to promoting Satan's destructive plans. He writes that they are working against the purposes of God, opposing people in general, while specifically targeting Christians for destruction.[5] The New Testament explicitly and implicitly teaches that demon spirits:

Are evil (Luke 11:24-26)
Intend to do harm (Mark 9:17, 18)
Accuse (Rev. 12:10, 11)
Deceive (1 Tim. 4:1)
Bring sickness and disease (Mark 5:2-4)
Torment people (Mark 5:1-18)

While this reality may initially frighten believers, Dickason assures Christians that demon powers are limited by God, and are ultimately overcome by the blood of Christ.

> Despite the awesome powers of Satan and demons, believers may confidently rest in their sovereign Creator and Savior. He

defeated Satan's hosts at the cross, controls all things, and
guarantees in His wisdom, love, and faithfulness that he will
never leave us or forsake us. Neither can any demon separate
us from the love of Christ (Colossians 2:15; Hebrews 13:5).
The demons believe and tremble (James 2:19). Believers may
believe and trust.[6]

These words are a comfort to the soul, and encourage the caregiver
to learn more about this issue and the authority that is available
through Jesus Christ.

Demonization Defined

Countless times I have been asked if Christians can be demon pos-
sessed. Certainly many believe that such a notion is impossible. A pastor friend of mine would become almost irate whenever I mentioned
praying deliverance prayers with a believer. He would repeatedly say,
"Impossible! The Spirit of God possesses the soul of the Christian, and
Satan is not welcome." I am convinced that the problem we had was
not one of theology but of translation. Charles Kraft speaks to this issue
in his book, *Defeating Dark Angels* (Vine Books). He, along with many
other scholars, believes that the concept of demon possession comes
from an inaccurate translation of the Greek word *daimonizomai*.

> The word *daimonizomai* occurs seven times in Matthew,
> four times in Mark, once in Luke and once in John. A parallel
> expression, *echein daimonion*, "have a demon," occurs once in
> Matthew, three times in Luke, and five times in John. Luke uses
> the phrase interchangeably with *daimonizomai*. Though the
> scriptural authors may have intended that *daimonizomai* indi-
> cate a slightly greater degree of demonic control than *echein
> daimonion*, translators are simply not justified in rendering
> either term "demon possession." This rendering signifies too
> much control…it is far better to use a more neutral term such
> as "have a demon" or "demonized." Both are more true to the
> original Greek and also run less risk of frightening people.[7]

I am convinced that Kraft's conclusions are balanced, faithful to
scripture, and most helpful in understanding evil supernaturalism.
Simply stated, any level of activity that a demon spirit is bringing to

bear on a person is called demonization. With this understanding the caregiver can position the broken to resist and renounce demons through the authority of Christ, regardless of the intent or intensity of their schemes. I find it helpful to think of types of activity and levels of strength. These conclusions are admittedly based in my experience in working with people, and do not reflect specific scriptural references. But as tools of understanding and practice, I have found them to be quite helpful. I identify demonization as occurring in four distinct ways.

Harassment. Much the same as a hornet flies around a person's head, annoying and distracting him, so it can be with this level of demonization. The demon does not keep the person away from his or her appointed course, but does seek to bother and discourage him.

Oppression. This level of demonic activity is much like a fog that settles in upon a person. The individual finds it more difficult to stay on track, and often battles varying levels of emotional and spiritual oppression. It can be more difficult for a person to keep focused on what is true and right.

Affliction. Jesus often cast out demons when people suffered from physical sickness. At this level of activity, demons seek to bring emotional, spiritual, and physical suffering to a person in an effort to defeat and demoralize them.

Bondage. The demon spirit is exercising a certain level of control in an area of a person's life. This demonization is possible because of personal choices that give room for this type of bondage. Despite personal efforts to move beyond the problem or sinful behavior, the individual finds it difficult to resist and repeatedly fails to find freedom.

The caregiver should realize that demonization usually occurs without the person knowing that the source of the problem is demonic. People can exhaust themselves chasing down other causes without considering any involvement from evil spirits. Each type of demonization can also vary in degree and symptom, depending upon the specific function of the demon spirit. This means that the caregiver must be spiritually prepared to help people resist the work of evil, including the ability to identify demonization and serve as an instrument of freedom through Christ Jesus.

Once again, it would be helpful to revisit the stages of inner healing mentioned earlier. The caregiver should by now know the cause-and-effect relationship that occurs from wound, to lie, to emotional upheaval, to dysfunctional behaviors, to life situation. With reference to demonization, the caregiver must realize that demonic activity in any of the ways described can occur in any or all of these stages. Broken people can experience some level of demonic involvement within each aspect of the complex problems they bring to the caregiver for prayer. The demonization might vary from mild harassment to significant bondage. That can be true of wound issues, lies, emotional upheaval, dysfunctional behaviors and the life situation. When demonic influence is present, inner healing prayer must include prayer for deliverance and freedom, led by the caregiver and declared by the person seeking Christ's touch.

What are the Signs of Demonization?
When should the caregiver help people pray deliverance prayers? I recommend that this happen as a matter of course throughout the process of inner healing prayer. I do this whether I sense demonization or not. In early Christian practice, new converts were cleansed of demonic infestation before they could join the church. People came to Christ from cults and heathen religions, and church leaders wanted them to move toward involvement and leadership free of demonic bondage. I know of few places where this happens today, and yet people enter the church broken and in deep emotional pain. Often this is a result of sinful behavior, including various degrees of involvement in practices clearly influenced by demonic powers.

I encourage people to speak out prayers of renunciation throughout the inner healing process. I then help them make declarations of Christ's Lordship and victory. Specific reference has been made to this in the chapters that dealt with dysfunctional behaviors, emotional upheaval and lies, and deep wounds. The prayers need not be complex, but they should be theologically sound and spoken in the authority of Christ. Often the caregiver will need to lead such a prayer, with the person audibly repeating them before the Lord. There is absolutely nothing wrong with this approach, for it follows a long tradition of liturgical prayer. The important point is that the individual and the caregiver recognize the power of Christ to set people free and declare that truth openly and enthusiastically. Jesus blesses such prayers and will bring His power to bear on any forces of darkness trying to stay connected to the broken person.

The symptoms of demonization are important to discuss. If the caregiver operates in the spiritual gift of discernment, she will sense the presence of the evil one and then move forward to encourage deliverance. It is good for all caregivers to ask the Lord for that level of spiritual sensitivity. However, not every person will be equipped to sense the demonic. When that is true, the symptoms being described by the person can help with diagnosis. Rodger Bufford has provided a list of the more severe symptoms of demonization in his book, *Counseling and the Demonic* (Word, 1988). They include:

> *Knowledge of the supernatural*
> *Supernatural strength*
> *Going about naked*
> *Unable to speak, hear*
> *Seizures*
> *Blindness*
> *Use of "different" voice*
> *Presence of distinct personalities*
> *Bizarre behavior*
> *Fierce, violent behavior*
> *Unusual behavior*
> *Feeling of overpowering evil*
> *Self-report of demonic influence.*[8]

Bufford's list, as well as his book, can be helpful to the caregiver. As he recognizes, however, there are some problems with simply looking at symptoms to determine demonization. First, as anyone schooled in the behavioral sciences knows, these characteristics are also symptoms of various mental disorders and psychological problems. Also his list addresses only the symptoms of severe demonization. Other less extreme levels of demonization could go completely undetected if these characteristics are the standard for diagnosis. That is why I believe the lifescript is so important. It will reveal previous sinful behavior and cultic involvement that could indicate demonization as a likely cause for a person's problems.

What is the Starting Point?
The caregiver must begin and end with complete confidence and trust in Jesus Christ and what He did on Calvary. Inspired by the Holy Spirit, the Apostle Paul wrote these glorious words:

When you were dead in your sins and in the uncircumcision of your sinful nature, God made you alive with Christ. He
forgave us all our sins, having canceled the written code, with
its regulation, that was against us and that stood opposed to
us; he took it away, nailing it to the cross. And having disarmed the powers and authorities, he made a public spectacle
of them, triumphing over them by the cross. (Col. 2:13-15)

There are powerful truths in this text, which the caregiver must
claim, proclaim and celebrate in anticipation of helping the demonized.
Jesus has brought life, forgiveness and cleansing to every believer. And,
by the cross, He has disarmed every demon spirit. His victory is the
Christian's victory, be it broken person or caregiver. James said that this
truth causes demons to shudder, which should encourage believers to
rejoice and move forward boldly in Jesus' name (James 2:19).

The caregiver must believe that Jesus has made it possible for him
to exercise His power and authority when ministering deliverance to
the broken. Jesus twice gave His disciples power and authority over
evil spirits, at the beginning of their ministry and right before He
returned to heaven after the resurrection (Mark 6:7 and 16:17). This
ability obviously extended beyond the original twelve, because several other people demonstrated this ministry in the book of Acts. I am
convinced that every Christian can flow in the power and authority of
Christ since, as Paul said, they are seated with Him in the heavenly
realm (Eph. 1:6). This means the caregiver, as well as the person
receiving inner healing prayer, not only has Jesus in him but is spiritually in Jesus.

What an incredible privilege! Because of Calvary and the shed
blood of Christ, the caregiver can command evil spirits to release people from their destructive grasp. The caregiver is also able to help the
broken exercise power and authority by praying for their own deliverance and freedom. I usually begin such prayers with these words:
"Jesus, I come to you in prayer, and ask that you touch Robert. I do
this, not just from my position here on earth as your servant, but from
my position in the heavenly realm where I am seated with You."
Granted, this truth is in many ways beyond comprehension. But I
encourage the caregiver to accept it by faith and pray with the authority and power of Christ.

Another important consideration for the caregiver is preparation. While Jesus has provided power and authority for ministry, the caregiver should never take that for granted. Spending time in prayer before the session is vital, as is the personal devotional disciplines of the caregiver. It is foolish to try to minister deliverance while living in obvious sin or disobedience. It is equally unwise to try to help others experience freedom when the caregiver is personally cavalier about the Christian life. The powers of darkness will not be passive about such a ministry, launching counter attacks against those who help the broken. This means that the caregiver should be well-armed (Eph. 6:10-18) and supported by a faithful core of prayer warriors. This ministry is not a game. As Paul said, it is a battle with principalities and powers. Christ has given the victory, and the caregiver must align his life with all that is right and good. And so we come back to where this book started: Spirituality matters. Inner healing prayer and the ministry of deliverance are related to the spiritual maturity and vitality of the caregiver. There is no escaping that reality.

Addressing Demonization

Charles Kraft always says that demons are like rats. They are attracted to garbage. If you kick out the rats but leave the garbage, they will come back. Jesus said that when they do return, uglier and meaner rats (demons) will join them (Luke 11:24-26). Things only get worse. But if you clean out the garbage, the rats have nothing to feed on and are easier to chase off and keep out.

Once, as he was praying, St. Francis saw that an evil spirit was surrounding the Place of Portiuncula. The Lord revealed to him that one of the friars was angry with his brother, which had given the evil spirit access to attack the friars. St. Francis went to the brother and told him what God revealed.

> And he, seeing that the holy Father had read his thoughts, was afraid and revealed his wound—all his poison and rancor—and acknowledged his fault and humbly asked for forgiveness and a penance. And when he had done that, he was absolved from sin and received penance, and all of a sudden St. Francis saw the devil fly away.[9]

While one might take exception to some aspects of this story, it illustrates Kraft's point perfectly. People must deal with the sin, false beliefs and wounds that demon spirits feed upon. I am convinced that demonization occurs because a person has given room for demons to work. That ground must be taken back and surrendered to the Lordship of Jesus Christ. So whenever the caregiver helps the broken turn from sin, renounce lies and receive healing for deep wounds he or she is engaging in an aspect of deliverance. Garbage is being cleared, which makes the actual ministry of deliverance more effective.

Once the caregiver has helped a person, through the power of Christ, deal with the garbage of sin, lies or deep wounding, it is time to deal with whatever level of demonization remains. And the very best way to accomplish this is by helping the person with self-deliverance. My earliest experiences with deliverance were well-intended but ill-informed. The person sat passive as a team of Christians prayed to send demons away in Christ's name. Often it took a great deal of time and energy, given the failure to deal with garbage and involve the participant. I am now convinced that the most effective prayers of deliverance are those spoken by the person needing help.

I have been greatly influenced on this point by the works of Neil T. Anderson. Through his books and seminars, Anderson has encouraged the church to help people find freedom in Christ through what he calls "truth encounter." He contends that many people suffer from demonization because they do not know who they are in Christ or understand the wonderful provision that is theirs in Him. To help people experience freedom, Anderson has developed an extensive series of creedal declarations and prayers, which help the broken experience deliverance from demon spirits. These declarations and prayers follow a six-step sequence, built around the themes of:

> *Counterfeit versus Real*
> *Deception versus Truth*
> *Bitterness versus Forgiveness*
> *Rebellion versus Submission*
> *Pride versus Humility*
> *Bondage versus Freedom*
> *Acquiescence versus Renunciation*[10]

Anderson's material is excellent and effective. I have used it with numerous people and have gone through the prayers myself. The material is extensive and designed for use with a support person who leads the person through the written prayers. While the process is not focused on inner healing, it does serve as an excellent resource for further work relative to demonization. The prayers that I have included in this book are briefer, and relate specifically to the issues being addressed through inner healing prayer.

At times people might find it difficult to speak declarations of deliverance. Individuals may feel light-headed, distracted, stuck, fearful or angry. Normally this is a form of harassment from evil spirits, endeavoring to stop the process. The caregiver would do well to inform people of this in advance, instructing them to share such feelings as they arise. When they do, the caregiver should thank the person for sharing, encourage her regarding the victory of Christ, and gently encourage her to continue the process. While that is happening, the caregiver should silently pray for the Lord to intensify His power and presence in the moment.

The caregiver may face times when the level of demonization is such that the person is unable to move on. When that happens the caregiver should attempt to do three things. First, he should stop the process and encourage the person about all the good things God has done and will do through inner healing prayer. He should ask the Lord to seal the work completed and protect the individual as he or she leaves. The intention is then to focus more directly on the specific issue in the next session. Second, the caregiver should prepare during the week, particularly through prayer and fasting. And third, the caregiver might find it helpful to get prayer support during the time he meets again with the person. If the individual does not object, it would be good to have another person actually present.

When the next session begins, the caregiver should return to the deliverance prayers left unfinished from the week before. If the opposition continues, the caregiver should ask the Lord to reveal any existing ground that may be present which is giving the spirit authority to stay. If such ground exists, be it sin, false beliefs, or deep wounds, it should be addressed. This should clear the way for the person to return to prayer. If the opposition remains, the caregiver should take authority and command the spirit to leave in Jesus' name, on behalf of the person.

This type of deliverance prayer is referred to as a power encounter, and can be more animated and intense than other deliverance sessions. It is extremely important that the caregiver stay focused on the truth of Christ and His victory. The caregiver should trust the Holy Spirit to guide the process, and spend far more time pointing to Jesus than wrestling with the evil one. Demons are liars who love to hide, deceive and distract people from the truth, so the caregiver should keep all eyes on Jesus Christ. It is very important in such power encounters that the demon(s) be given no authority to control the situation. The caregiver is in charge as the instrument of the Holy Spirit and must continue to exercise authority in Jesus' Name. There is incredible power in praise, so the caregiver should be quick to worship the Lord and declare the promises of God's word. Again, power encounters will be the exception rather than the rule. Every effort should be made to help people with self-deliverance before considering any other approach.

The material covered in this chapter is only part of inner healing prayer. People often find evil supernaturalism sensational and begin to major in deliverance ministry. That is a mistake, particularly when the caregiver wants to help the broken experience the transforming touch of Christ. The vast majority of dialogue, instruction and prayer will not be directly focused upon demonization. The issue is important and the caregiver needs to understand the process. But inner healing prayer is primarily about experiencing the tender love of Jesus where deep wounds have remained painful and destructive. It is about hearing the heart-cry of the wounded and then listening for the whispers of God.

Inner healing prayer is a ministry that brings a broken person before the Healing Lord, where they can experience love, acceptance and freedom. The caregiver has the privilege to serve as a bridge that joins a ravaged heart with a Ravished Heart. Inner healing prayer is about light in the darkness, comfort in the storm, and loneliness being overcome by Love. Inner healing prayer is a powerful ministry that brings radical transformation, not just to the broken, but to the caregiver as well, God's wounded healer.

Notes

1. Rudolf Bultmann, *Jesus Christ and Mythology* (New York: Schribner's & Sons, 1958).

2. C. S. Lewis, *The Screwtape Letters* (New York: Touchstone, 1996), 5.

3. Charles Kraft, *Christianity with Power* (Ann Arbor, MI: Vine, 1989), 20.

4. C. Fred Dickason, *Demon Possession and the Christian* (Westchester, IL: Crossway, 1987), 25, 26.

5. Ibid, 25-30.

6. Ibid, 30, 31.

7. Charles Kraft, *Defeating Dark Angels* (Ann Arbor, MI: Vine, 1992), 35, 36.

8. Rodger Bufford, *Counseling and the Demonic* (Dallas, TX: Word, 1988), 105.

9. *The Little Flowers of Saint Francis*, trans. Raphael Brown (Garden City, NY: Image, 1958), 93.

10. Neil T. Anderson, *Setting Your Church Free* (Ventura, CA: Regal, 1994), 327-352.

For Further Reading

Defeating Dark Angels, by Charles Kraft
Demon Possession and the Christian, by C. Fred Dickason
Counseling and the Demonic, by Rodger K. Bufford
The Bondage Breaker, by Neil T. Anderson
The Handbook for Spiritual Warfare, by Ed Murphy

Conclusion

I recently completed teaching a three-day seminar on inner healing prayer. Men and women from a variety of caregiving professions gathered for instruction, experiential exercises, and most importantly spiritual empowerment. I am always humbled and overwhelmed by the way the Lord equips people to bring His healing presence into places of pain and wounding. Far more than learning about inner healing prayer at these seminars, people are personally touched by the transforming power of Jesus Christ, and lives are changed.

Let me share one story. Renee had been a licensed therapist for nearly a decade, practicing with a Christian counseling group in southern Ohio. For the past few years she had grown frustrated with her ministry, concerned that she was not connecting people with all that the Lord had available for their healing. She could clearly see that the broken needed His touch, and that Jesus was more than willing to meet them at the place of pain. However, she felt something was missing in her approach to bringing the two together.

Before the seminar Renee was skeptical about the concept, but felt that she could use the continuing education credits, so she came. At the end of the first day she told Dr. Allison about her initial reservations, yet now believed that this was the very thing she had been looking for to empower her ministry. While that was important, God had deeper, more personal things in mind for Renee.

During an exercise the second day Renee profoundly encountered the Lord. Jesus touched her in a wounded place hidden away for years, and as a result of His presence Renee experienced a peace she had never known. Jesus brought her a new level of personal wholeness and a deeper level of intimacy in her relationship with Him. As she considered what Christ had done within her, she became excited about what she believed He could now do through her. Renee recognized that Jesus was positioning her to be a channel of His healing presence. As she left the seminar Renee said, "This past week I met Jesus and His power in a new way. I am changed. Everything has changed."

The ministry of inner healing prayer as developed in this book is all about change. Change will first occur in the caregiver's personal life, the focus of chapters one through three. As the servant of the Lord prioritizes intimacy with Christ, personal well-being, and involvement in spiritual community, his or her life will be transformed. The second change will occur in the caregiver's relationship with the Person and work of the Holy Spirit, which is developed in chapters four and five. The caregiver will consistently grow to be an instrument of His grace: discerning, gifted and divinely empowered to work in harmony with the Holy Spirit in the ministry of deep healing.

Inner healing prayer will also change the way a caregiver approaches care. He or she will help people see the relationship between wounds, lies, emotional upheaval and dysfunctional behaviors, with the goal of addressing each area of compromise in the power of the Spirit. The caregiver will be equipped to offer specific help related to every level of hurt and wounding, as described in chapters five through nine. The caregiver will also be able to help people stand against the evil one, finding victory and deliverance in the power of the cross, as detailed in chapter ten.

The final changes initiated through inner healing prayer will occur in the lives of the broken. The Holy Spirit, using the caregiver as a channel of grace, will bring the healing presence of Christ to the places of pain and brokenness. That encounter with Jesus will be transforming. Light will come into darkness, Truth will set captives free, and sinful choices will give way to Spirit-filled living. People will find far more than a higher level of functioning. They will find Jesus Christ as the lover of their souls and the answer to their deepest fears. Inner healing prayer holds the promise of bringing deep and lasting change in peoples' lives. It is also an invitation for you to experience deeper intimacy with Christ, personal wholeness and a Spirit-empowered ministry of deep healing. Could it be that the Lord is calling you to be His appointed instrument of healing care?

If you or someone you know is interested in attending a seminar on Inner Healing Prayer with Dr. Terry Wardle, contact him at:

Healing Care Ministries
P.O. Box 216
Ashland, OH 44805

healingcare@earthlink.net

Bibliography

Spirituality

Bernard of Clairvaux. *The Love Of God*. Portland, OR: Multnomah, 1983.

Bounds, E. M. *Power Through Prayer*. Grand Rapids, MI: Baker, 1972.

Brother Lawrence. *The Practice of the Presence of God*. New York: Doubleday, 1977.

Christensen, Bernhard. *The Inward Passage: An Introduction to Christian Spiritual Classics*. Rev. Ed. Minneapolis, MN: Augsburg Fortress, 1996.

Crabb, Larry. *The Safest Place on Earth*. Nashville, TN: Word, 1999.

Curtis, Brent and John Eldredge. *The Sacred Romance*. Nashville, TN: Thomas Nelson, 1997.

de Caussade, Jean Pierre. *The Sacrament of the Present Moment*. New York: HarperCollins, 1989.

Edwards, Jonathan. *Religious Affections*. Portland, Oregon: Multnomah, 1990.

Fenelon, Francois. *The Seeking Heart*. Beaumont, Texas: Seed Sowers, 1992.

Foster, Richard. *Prayer: Finding the Heart's True Home*. San Francisco, CA: HarperCollins,1992

Foster, Richard, and James Bryan Smith. *Devotional Classics: Selected Readings for Individuals and Groups*. New York: HarperCollins, 1993.

Guyon, Jeanne. *Experiencing the Depths of Jesus Christ*. Beaumont, TX: Seed Sowers, 1975.

Hallesby, Ole. *Prayer*. Minneapolis, MN: Augsburg/Fortress, 1994.

Kelly, Thomas R. *A Testament of Devotion*. New York: HarperCollins, 1992.

Lawrence, Brother. *Practicing the Presence of God*. Wilmore, KY: Christian Outreach, 1979.

Lewis, C.S. *Mere Christianity*. New York: Macmillan, 1952

May, Gerald. *The Awakened Heart: Opening Your Heart to the Love You Need*. New York: Harper Collins, 1991.

Merton, Thomas. *No Man Is An Island*. Orlando, FL: Harcourt, Brace, Jovanovich, 1983.

Miller, Calvin. *Into the Depths of God*. Minneapolis, MN: Bethany House, 2000.

Mulholland, Robert. *Invitation to A Journey: A Road Map For Spiritual Formation*. Downers Grove, IL: Inter Varsity, 1992.

_____. *Shaped By The Word*. Nashville, TN: Upper Room, 1985.

Murray, Andrew. *The Prayer Life*. Springdale, PA: Whitaker House, 1981.

Nouwen, Henri J.M. *Lifesigns: Intimacy, Fecundity, and Ecstasy In Christian Perspective*. New York: Image, 1990.

_____. *Making All Things New*. New York: HarperCollins, 1981.

_____. *Reaching Out: Three Movements Of The Spiritual Life*. New York: Image, 1986.

Saint John of The Cross. *Dark Night of the Soul*. New York: Image, 1990.

Talbot, John Michael. *The Lessons of St. Francis: How to Bring Simplicity and Spirituality into Your Daily Life*. New York: Dutton, 1997.

Theresa of Avila. *The Interior Castle*. New York: Paulist, 1979.

Tozer, A. W. *The Pursuit of God*. Camp Hill, PA: Christian Publications, 1982.

Wardle, Terry. *Draw Close to the Fire*. Grand Rapids, MI: Chosen, 1998.

Watson, David. *Called and Committed*. Wheaton, IL: Harold Shaw, 1982.

Willard, Dallas. *The Divine Conspiracy: Rediscovering Our Hidden Life in God*. San Francisco, CA: HarperSanFrancisco, 1998.

_____. *The Spirit of the Disciplines: Understanding How God Changes Lives*. New York: Harper & Row, 1988.

General - Inner Healing

Allender, Dan B. *The Healing Path*. Colorado Springs, CO: Waterbrook, 1999.

Anderson, Neil T. *Breaking Through to Spiritual Maturity*. Ventura, CA: Regal, 1992.

_____. *The Bondage Breaker*. Eugene, OR: Harvest House, 1990.

_____. *Victory Over the Darkness: Realizing the Power of Your Identity in Christ*. Ventura, CA: Regal, 1990.

_____. *Walking Through the Darkness*. San Bernadino, CA: Here's Life, 1991.

_____. *Freedom From Fear*. Ventura, CA: Regal, 1999.

Attention Deficit Disorder: Rapha Booklet Series. Houston, TX: Rapha.

Backus, William. *Telling Each Other the Truth*. Minneapolis, MN: Bethany House, 1985.

Backus, William, and Marie Chapman. *Telling Yourself the Truth*. Minneapolis, MN: Bethany House, 1980.

Bitterness: Rapha Booklet Series. Houston, TX: Rapha.

Brand, Paul, and Philip Yancey. *Fearfully and Wonderfully Made*. Grand Rapids, MI: Zondervan, 1987.

_____. *In His Image*. Grand Rapids, MI: Zondervan.

Carter, Les. *Imperative People*. Nashville, TN: Thomas Nelson.

Cloud, Henry. *Changes that Heal: How to Understand Your Past to Ensure a Healthier Future*. Grand Rapids, MI: Zondervan, 1992.

Cloud, Henry and John Townsend. *Boundaries*. Grand Rapids, MI: Zondervan, 1992.

_____. *When Your World Makes No Sense*. Nashville, TN: Oliver Nelson, 1990.

Depression: Rapha Booklet Series. Houston, TX: Rapha.

Foster, Richard. *Prayer: Finding the Heart's True Home*. New York: HarperCollins, 1992.

Henslin, Earl. *The Way Out of the Wilderness*. Nashville, TN: Thomas Nelson, 1991.

Kraft, Charles. *Christianity with Power: Your Worldview and Your Experience of the Supernatural*. Ann Arbor, MI: Servant, 1989.

_____. *Deep Wounds, Deep Healing*. Ann Arbor, MI: Vine, 1993.

MacNutt, Francis. *Healing*. New York: Image Books/Doubleday, 1974.

McGee, Robert S. *The Search for Significance: Book and Workbook*. Houston, TX: Rapha, 1990.

McGee, Robert S., and Pat Springle. *Getting Unstuck: Help for People Bogged Down in Recovery*. Houston/Dallas, TX: Rapha/Word, 1992.

Minirth, F., P. Meier, and et al. *Happiness is a Choice*. Grand Rapids, MI: Baker, 1978.

_____. *The Path to Serenity*. Nashville, TN: Thomas Nelson, 1992.

_____. *The Thin Disguise*. Nashville, TN: Thomas Nelson, 1992.

Moon, Gary. *Homesick for Eden*. Ann Arbor, MI: Vine, 1997.

Price, Richard, Pat Springle, and Joe Kloba. *Rapha's Handbook for Group Leaders*. Houston/Dallas, TX: Rapha/Word.

Ritchie, Bill. *A Dad Who Loves You*. Sisters, OR: Multnomah, 1992.

Riter, Tim. *A Passionate Pursuit of God*. Downers Grove, IL: InterVarsity, 1999.

Sandford, Agnes. *The Healing Gifts of the Spirit*. New York: HarperCollins, 1966.

Seamands, David. *Freedom From the Performance Trap*. Wheaton, IL: Victor, 1991.

_____. *Healing for Damaged Emotions*. Wheaton, IL: Victor, 1981.

_____. *Healing of Memories*. Wheaton, IL: Victor, 1985.

_____. *Putting Away Childish Things*. Wheaton, IL: Victor, 1982.

Sell, Charles. *Unfinished Business*. Portland, OR: Multnomah, 1989.

Stoop, David. *The Intimacy Factor*. Nashville, TN: Thomas Nelson, 1991.

Sullivan, Barbara. *The Control Trap*. Minneapolis, MN: Bethany House, 1991.

Thurman, Chris. *The Lies We Believe*. Nashville, TN: Thomas Nelson, 1989.

_____. *The Truths We Must Believe*. Nashville, TN: Thomas Nelson, 1991.

Townsend, John. *Hiding From Love*. Colorado Springs, CO: NavPress, 1991.

Trent, John and Gary Smalley. *The Blessing*. Nashville, TN: Thomas Nelson, 1986.

Wagner, C. Peter. *The Prayer Shield*. Ventura, CA: Regal, 1992.

Wardle, Terry. *Wounded: How You Can find Inner Hope and Healing in Him*. Camp Hill, PA: Christian Publications, 1992.

_____. *How to Win the War*. Illinois: Harold Shaw, 1972.

Woititz, Janet. *Struggle for Intimacy*. Deerfield Beach, FL: Health Communications, 1985.

_____. *Guidelines for Support Groups*. Deerfield Beach, FL: Health Communications, 1992.

Wright, Alan. *Lover of My Soul: Delighting in God's Passionate Love*. Sisters, OR: Multnomah, 1998.

Anxiety/Fear

Anderson, Neil T. & Rich Miller. *Freedom From Fear: Overcoming Worry & Anxiety*. Eugene, OR: Harvest House, 1999.

Anxiety Attacks: Rapha Booklet Series. Houston, TX: Rapha.

Bassett, Lucinda. *From Panic to Power*. New York: HarperCollins, 1995.

Minirth, Frank, P. Meier, and et al. *Worry-Free Living*. Nashville, TN: Thomas Nelson, 1989.

Randau, Karen. *Conquering Fear*. Houston/Dallas, TX: Rapha/Word, 1991.

Wardle, Terry. *Whispers of Love in Seasons of Fear*. Grand Rapids, MI: Chosen, 1999.

Chemical Dependency

Black, Claudia. *Repeat After Me*. New York: Macmillan, 1991.

Chemical Dependency: Rapha Booklet Series. Houston, TX: Rapha.

Go Ask Alice. Avon Publishing. (for kids, on drug addiction)

Jesse, Rosalee. *Children in Recovery*. New York: Norton, 1989.

McGee, Robert S., P. Springle, and Joiner. *Rapha's Twelve Step Program for Overcoming Chemical Dependency*. Houston/Dallas, TX: Rapha/Word, 1990.

Rapha's Step Studies for Overcoming Chemical Dependency. Houston,TX: Rapha.

Woititz, Janet. *Adult Children of Alcoholics*. Deerfield Beach, FL: Health Community.

For Additional Books on Alcohol/Drug Abuse:

Hazelden Catalog, 15291 Pleasant Valley Road, Center City, MN 55012-0176

Codependency

Allender, Dan B., and Tremper Longman III. *Bold Love*. Colorado Springs, CO: NavPress, 1992.

_____. *Bold Love Discussion Guide*. Colorado Springs, CO: NavPress, 1992.

Beattie, Melody. *Beyond Codependency*. New York: Harper & Row, 1989.

_____. *Codependent No More*. New York: Harper & Row, 1987.

Buhler, Rich. *Pain and Pretending: Discovering the Causes of Your Codependency*. Nashville, TN: Thomas Nelson, 1988.

Codependency: Rapha Booklet Series. Houston, Texas: Rapha.

Hemfelt, R., F. Minirth, P. Meier, and D. & B. Newman. *Love is a Choice: Recovery for Codependent Relationships*. Nashville, TN: Thomas Nelson, 1989.

_____. *Love is a Choice Workbook*. Nashville, TN: Thomas Nelson, 1991.

Springle, Pat. *Close Enough to Care: How to Help a Friend or Relative Overcome Codependency*. Houston/Dallas, TX: Rapha/Word, 1991.

_____. *Codependency: Breaking Free From the Hurt and Manipulation of Dysfunctional Relationships*. Houston/Dallas, TX: Rapha/Word, 1990.

_____. *Rapha's Twelve Step Program for Overcoming Codependency*. Houston/Dallas, TX: Rapha/Word, 1990.

Compulsive Behaviors

Crabb, Larry. *Inside Out*. Colorado Springs, CO: NavPress, 1991.

_____. *Inside Out Study Guide*. Colorado Springs, CO: NavPress, 1992.

Hart, Archibald D. *Healing Life's Hidden Addictions*. Ann Arbor, MI: Servant, 1990.

Minirth, Frank, et. al. *We are Driven*. Nashville, TN: Thomas Nelson, 1991.

Eating Disorders

Banks, Bill. *Deliverance from Fat and Eating Disorders*. Kirkwood, MO: Impact, 1988.

Boone-O'Neill, Cherry. *Starving for Attention*. New York: Continuum, 1982.

Byrne, Katherine. *A Parent's Guide to Anorexia and Bulimia: Understanding and Helping Self-Starvers and Binge/Purgers*. New York: Henry Holt &

Company, 1987.

Eating Disorders: Rapha Booklet Series. Houston, Texas: Rapha Publishing.

Hall, Lindsey, and Leigh Cohn. *Bulimia: A Guide to Recovery*. Carlsbad, CA: Gurze Publications, 1989.

Hemfelt, R., F. Minirth, and P. Meier. *Love Hunger: Recovery from Food Addiction*. Nashville, TN: Thomas Nelson, 1991.

Jantz, Gregory L. *Hope, Help, & Healing for Eating Disorders*. Wheaton, IL: Harold Shaw, 1995.

McGee, Robert S., and Mountcastle. *Rapha's Twelve Step Program for Overcoming Eating Disorders*. Houston/Dallas, TX: Rapha/Word.

Messinger, Lisa. *Biting the Hand that Feeds Me: Days of Binging, Purging, and Recovery*. Novato, CA: Arena, 1986.

Family Issues

Berman, W.B., D.R. Doty, J.H. Graham. *Shaking the Family Tree: Use Your Family's Past to Strengthen Your Family's Future*. Wheaton, IL: Victor, 1991.

Carder D., E. Henslin, J. Townsend, H. Cloud, and A. Brawand. *Secrets of Your Family Tree*. Chicago, IL: Moody, 1991.

Carlson, Randy L. *Father Memories*. Chicago, IL: Moody, 1992.

Carter, William. *Kid Think: Understanding Your Child's Behavior*. Houston/Dallas, Texas: Rapha/Word.

Family Communication: Rapha Booklet Series. Houston, TX: Rapha.

Fish, Melinda. *Adult Children and the Almighty: Recovering from the Wounds of a Dysfunctional Home*. Tarrytown, NY: 1991.

Hemfelt, Warren. *Kids Who Carry Our Pain*. Nashville, TN: Thomas Nelson.

McGee, Robert S. *Discipline With Love*. Houston/Dallas, TX: Rapha/Word.

McGee, Robert S., Pat Springle, and Jim Craddock. *Your Parents And You*. Houston/Dallas, TX: Rapha/Word, 1990.

Stoop, David. *Making Peace With Your Father*. Nashville, TN: Thomas Nelson.

Stoop, David, and James Masteller. *Forgiving Our Parents, Forgiving Our Selves*. Ann Arbor, MI: Servant, 1991.

Van Vonderan, Jeff. *Families Where Grace is in Place*. Minneapolis, MN: Bethany House, 1992.

Homosexuality

Comisky, Andy. "Jesus: The Father's Justice for the Sexually Broken." *Equipping the Saints* (Fall, 1992).

_____. *Pursuing Sexual Wholeness: How Jesus Heals the Homosexual*. Creation House, 1989.

Payne, Leanne. *Crisis in Masculinity*. Wheaton, IL: Crossway, 1985.
_____. *The Healing Presence*. Wheaton, IL: Crossway, 1989.
_____. *The Broken Image*. Wheaton, IL: Crossway, 1981.
_____. *The Healing of the Homosexual*. Wheaton, IL: Crossway, 1984.
Saia, Michael. *Counseling for Homosexuals*. Minneapolis, MN: Bethany House, 1988.

Men's Issues

Dalbey, Gordon. *Father and Son*. Nashville, TN: Thomas Nelson, 1992.
_____. *Healing the Masculine Soul*. Nashville, TN: Thomas Nelson, 1988.
Jones, G. Brian, and Linda Phillips-Jones. *Men Have Feelings Too!* Wheaton, IL: Victor, 1988.

Sexual Abuse

Allender, Dan B. *The Wounded Heart: Hope for Adult Victims of Childhood Sexual Abuse*. Colorado Springs, CO: NavPress, 1990.
_____. *The Wounded Heart Workbook*. Colorado Springs, CO: NavPress, 1992.
Elliott, Lynda D. & Vicki L. Tanner. *My Father's Child: Help and Healing for the Victims of Emotional, Sexual, and Physical Abuse*. Brentwood, TN: Wolgemuth & Hyatt, 1988.
Frank, Jan. *A Door of Hope: Recognizing and Resolving the Pains of Your Past*. San Bernadino, CA: Here's Life, 1987.
Heitritter, Lynn, and Jeanette Vought. *Helping Victims of Sexual Abuse*. Minneapolis: Bethany House, 1989.
Kubetin, Cynthia A., and James Mallory. *Beyond the Darkness: Healing for Victims of Sexual Abuse*. Houston/Dallas, TX: Rapha/Word, 1992.
Rapha's Step Studies for Overcoming Sexual Addiction. Houston, TX: Rapha.
Sexual Abuse: Rapha's Booklet Series. Houston, Texas: Rapha.

Shame

Henslin, Earl. *The Way Out of the Wilderness*. Nashville, TN: Thomas Nelson.
Shame: Rapha Booklet Series. Houston, Texas: Rapha.
Smedes, Lewis B. *Shame and Grace*. New York: Harper & Row, 1992.
Wilson, Sandra. *Released From Shame*. Downer's Grove, IL: InterVarsity.
_____. *Shame-Free Parenting*. Downer's Grove, IL: InterVarsity.

Spiritual Abuse

Arterburn, Stephen, and Jack Felton. *Toxic Faith: Understanding and Overcoming Religious Addiction.* Nashville, TN: Oliver Nelson, 1991.
Blue, Ken. *Healing Spiriual Abuse.* Downers Grove, IL: InterVarsity, 1993.
Johnson, David, and Jeff VonVonderen. *The Subtle Power of Spiritual Abuse.* Minneapolis, MN: Bethany House, 1991.
Mains, David. *Healing the Dysfunctional Church Family.* Wheaton, IL: Victor Books, 1992.

Verbal Abuse

Ketterman, Grace. *Verbal Abuse: Healing the Hidden Wound.* Ann Arbor, MI: Servant, 1992.

Women's Issues

Sandford, Paula. *Healing Women's Emotions.* Tulsa, OK: Victory House, 1992.
Wright, Norman. *Always Daddy's Girl.* Ventura, CA: Regal, 1989.

For Those in Doubt

Collins, Gary R. *Can You Trust Psychology?* Downer's Grove, IL: InterVarsity, 1988.
Hurding, Roger F. *The Tree of Healing.* Grand Rapids, MI: Zondervan, 1985.
Kirwan, William T. *Biblical Concepts for Christian Counseling: A Case for Integrating Psychology and Theology.* Grand Rapids, MI: Baker, 1984.
Playfair, William L. *The Useful Lie.* Wheaton, IL: Crossway, 1991.
White, John. *Putting the Soul Back in Psychology.* Downer's Grove, IL: InterVarsity.

Spiritual Warfare

Anderson, Neil T. *The Bondage Breaker.* Eugene, OR: Harvest House, 1990.
_____. *Victory Over Darkness.* Ventura, CA: Regal, 1990.
_____. *Walking Through the Darkness.* San Bernardino, CA: Here's Life, 1991.
Blue, Ken. *Authority to Heal.* Downers Grove, IL: InterVarsity, 1987.
Bubeck, Mark. *The Adversary.* Chicago, IL: Moody, 1975.
_____. *Overcoming the Adversary.* Chicago, IL: Moody, 1984.
Bufford, Rodger K. *Counseling and the Demonic.* Dallas, Texas: Word, 1988.
Dickason, C. Fred. *Demon Possession and the Christian.* Westchester, IL: Crossway, 1987
Green, Michael. *I Believe in the Holy Spirit.* Grand Rapids, MI: Eerdmans, 1975.

_____. *I Believe in Satan's Downfall*. Grand Rapids, MI: Eerdmans, 1981.

_____. *Exposing the Prince of Darkness*. Ann Arbor, MI: Servant, 1991.

Kraft, Charles. *Defeating Dark Angels*. Ann Arbor, MI: Servant, 1992.

Murphy, Ed. *The Handbook For Spiritual Warfare*. Nashville: Thomas Nelson, 1992.

Lewis, C.S. *The Screwtape Letters*. New York: Touchstone, 1996.

Stedman, Ray C. *Spiritual Warfare*. Waco, TX: Word, 1978.

Warner, Timothy. *Spiritual Warfare*. Wheaton, IL: Crossways, 1991.

Wagner, Peter C. *The Third Wave of the Holy Spirit*. Ventura, CA: Regal, 1988.

_____. *Breaking Strongholds in Your City*. Ventura, CA: Regal, 1993.

_____. *Warfare Prayer*. Ventura, CA: Regal, 1992.

Appendix

Life Script/Autobiography

The following is a guideline for you to follow in developing your life script. The purpose of writing this is to get a clear picture of your life history, events and people which have had an impact on your development. It is understood that a separate medical history form will also be completed.

Please answer all items as fully and clearly as possible. Please print.

Name: _____

Age: _____   Sex: _____   Marital Status: _____

Address: _____

Occupation: _____

Spouse: Name _____

Age: _____   Occupation: _____

Name and address of person for emergency notification:

_____

Relationship: _____

WHAT IS YOUR BASIC PROBLEM as you see it? (Be concise). How long
have you had this difficulty _____

_____

_____

_____

(Continue on back).

Are there any other problems which seem to grow out of this one?

_____

(Continue on back)

.

WHAT FORMER HELP HAVE YOU SOUGHT for this?

Psychiatrist ( )   Prayer   ( )   Christian Science ( )
Chiropractor   ( )   Healing Evangelist ( )   Spiritistic Healer   ( )
Psychologist ( )   Social Worker   ( )   Counselor   ( )
Pastor   ( )   Medicine   ( )   Priest   ( )
Group Therapy ( )   Hypnosis by another   ( )
Self Hypnosis   ( )   Other   ( )

*The questions asked in the Life Script have been developed by Drs. Allison and Wardle or have been compiled from a variety of sources. The section on demonic involvement has been significantly impacted by the work of Neil T. Anderson.

VITAL STATISTICS

The last good book I read was:

Favorite heroes:

If I could do it all over again I would:

My fantasy is:

My most irrational act:

My friends like me because:

Behind my back people say:

My nickname is:

My nickname as a child was:

My major life accomplishments are:

I consider my greatest failure to be:

My biggest goal for the future is:

FAMILY

How many people were in your childhood family? Who did you live with? Who were you closest to and why?

What did you like to do with your family? How much time did you spend with them everyday?

Describe your parents briefly.

What did your mother say when she complimented you? Criticized you?

What did your father say when he complimented you? Criticized you?

What significant memories do you have regarding school?

Did anyone in your family drink too much? How did they act toward you if they had been drinking?

List four things you would like to change about your family and how you relate to one another.

How many people are in your current family?

Describe your relationship to your spouse, your children, your parents.

Describe the level of communication between family members.

What dysfunctions impede healthy relationships within your family?

IMPORTANT EVENTS

What is your earliest memory?

What is your happiest memory?

What is your saddest memory?

Describe any major losses in your life.

What other events have influenced your life in some way. Describe them and state how they influenced you.

Have you ever known anyone who attempted or committed suicide?

Have you ever thought of suicide? What happened?

SELF

Describe how you see yourself right now (physically, socially, emotionally and intellectually).

Do you like yourself right now? If you could change anything about yourself, what would it be?

List five strengths you have. List five weaknesses that you have.

How do you work on areas needing growth?

What is your biggest problem? Greatest joy?

FRIENDS

How much time everyday do you spend with your friends, including phone time?

How many friends do you have?

Who is your best friend and why?

How are you alike or different than your friends?

Have your social contacts changed recently? Why?

Do you have any enemies and if so why?

How do your peers influence your life?

What person do you admire most in your life?

What famous person would you like to be and why?

WORK

Describe work related experiences and their impact upon you.

Are you fulfilled in what you do?

What are your plans, dreams, and visions regarding your vocation?

To what degree is your identity linked to your vocation?

To what degree do finances drive you?

How do you view money? How important is it to you?

DIET/EXERCISE

Do you generally eat a healthy, well-balanced diet? Describe any imbalance.

Do you ever engage in consuming a large quantity of food even though you are not physically hungry? If yes, please describe (include frequency and type of food you are likely to overeat).

Do you ever greatly restrict your food intake for reasons other than spiritual fasting? If yes, please describe, including frequency.

How satisfied are you with your current body size, shape and physical condition?

Body size:

Extremely   Fairly   Somewhat   Neutral   Somewhat   Fairly   Extremely
Dissatisfied   Dissatisfied   Dissatsfied   Satisfied   Satisfied   Satisfied

Body shape:

Extremely   Fairly   Somewhat   Neutral   Somewhat   Fairly   Extremely
Dissatisfied   Dissatisfied   Dissatsfied   Satisfied   Satisfied   Satisfied

Physical condition:

Extremely   Fairly   Somewhat   Neutral   Somewhat   Fairly   Extremely
Dissatisfied   Dissatisfied   Dissatsfied   Satisfied   Satisfied   Satisfied

Do you, or others close to you, think you are overly concerned with your weight? If yes, describe.

Check which of the following you consume, indicating quantity and frequency:

Caffeine _____ Amount _____ per _____ (day, week, etc.)

High sugar snacks/desserts ____ Amount _____ per _____ (day, week)

High fat foods/desserts ____ Amount _____ per _____ (day, week)

Alcoholic beverages _____ Amount _____ per _____ (day, week, etc.)

Describe any physical symptoms or change in mood or behavior as a result of consuming or withdrawing from any of the above.

Do you ever experience a physical craving (beyond normal desire) for foods high in sugar? Salt? Carbohydrates?

Describe your current involvement in physical activity/exercise:

Type of exercise _____

Amount of exercise _____ per _____ (day, week)

Do you, or others close to you, think you are overly concerned with getting enough exercise? If yes, describe.

DRUG/ALCOHOL USE

Indicate which of the following substances you currently use or have used in the past:

Past	Present		Past	Present	
___	___	Heroin	___	___	LSD
___	___	Opiates	___	___	Inhalants
___	___	Alcohol	___	___	Benzodiazepine
___	___	Barbiturates	___	___	PCP
___	___	Amphetamines	___	___	Over-the-counter drugs
___	___	Methanphetamines	___	___	Other (specify) _____
___	___	Crack	___	___	Marijuana/ Hash/THC

Have you ever experienced negative consequences caused by your drinking or drug use? If yes, describe.

Have you ever received treatment for your own drug or alcohol use? If yes, please indicate type of treatment, dates and degree of success.

Do you ever experience blackouts, periods of time which you are unable to account for? If yes, describe.

SPIRITUAL INVENTORY

Describe your parents' Christian experience.

Were your parents married or divorced?

Was your father the head of the home or did your mother fill this role?

How did your father treat your mother?

How did your mother treat your father?

Was there ever an adulterous affair with your parents or grandparents?

Was there ever any incestuous relationship?

Were or are there addictive problems in your family history?

Was there any history or evidence of mental illness?

Which of the following has been an area of struggle for you personally?

Past	Present		Past	Present	
___	___	Day Dreaming	___	___	Pornography
___	___	Lustful thoughts	___	___	Overeating
___	___	Inferiority/low self-esteem	___	___	Fear
___	___	Inadequacy	___	___	Anxiety
___	___	Worry	___	___	Flashbacks
___	___	Doubts	___	___	Anger
___	___	Fantasy	___	___	Self-punishment
___	___	Obsessive thoughts	___	___	Insecurity
___	___	Blasphemous thoughts	___	___	Compulsive acts
___	___	Physical symptoms	___	___	Masturbation

Please elaborate on any of the above you have checked.

Do you have regular devotions in the Bible? When and to what extent?

Do you find prayer difficult? Explain.

When attending Church or other Christian ministries are you plagued with foul thoughts, jealousies, or other mental harassments? Explain.

Do you listen to music? What type do you enjoy?

How much TV and what types of programs do you watch?

If you were to die tonight and appeared before God in heaven, and He were to ask you, "By what right should I allow you into my presence," how would you answer Him?

I John 5:11-12 says: "God has given us eternal life, and this life is in His son. He who has the Son has the life; he who does not have the Son of God does not have the life."

Do you have the Son of God in you (2 Cor. 15:3)?

When did you receive Him (John 1:12)?
How do you know that you have received Him?

Are you plagued with doubts concerning your salvation?

Are you presently enjoying fellowship with other believers, and if so, where and when?

Has there been any involvement in the following? (please circle)

Hypnotism	Ouija Boards
Spiritualism	Levitation
Christian Science	Horoscopes
Mormonism	Blood Poets
Jehovah's Witness	Fetishism
Free Masonry	Eastern Religions
Eastern Star	Scientology
Rainbow Girls	Islam
Demolay	Hinduism
Pacts with Satan	Buddhism
Satanism	Seances
Witchcraft	Astral Projection
Fortune Telling	Spirit Guides

Dungeons & Dragons   Palm Reading
Tarot Cards   Astrology
Black Magic   White Magic
New Age Medicine

Do you ever experience any of the following symptoms?

___ Frequent or recurrent illness   ___ Addictions
___ Sleeplessness   ___ Bizarre behavior
___ Anger   ___ Depression
___ Fear   ___ Hearing voices
___ Seizures   ___ Mood swings
___ Supernatural power   ___ Nightmares

Please elaborate on any of the above you have checked: